TOWARD WORLD-WIDE
CHRISTIANITY

SUBJECTS OF THE COMMISSIONS

VOLUME I.   COMMISSION I-A
> *The Challenge of Our Culture*

What are the main features of the cultures of the world which challenge the Church and its gospel, and what is the nature of the challenge?   CLARENCE T. CRAIG: *Chairman*

VOLUME II.   COMMISSION I-B
> *The Church and Organized Movements*

What are the allied and opposed organized movements of our day with which the Church must deal?   RANDOLPH CRUMP MILLER: *Chairman*

VOLUME III.   COMMISSION II
> *The Gospel, the Church and the World*

What are the resources and limiting factors of the life and gospel of the Church as it faces the challenge of its world task?   KENNETH SCOTT LATOURETTE: *Chairman*

VOLUME IV.   COMMISSION III
> *Toward World-wide Christianity*

The Church and the churches.   What are the realities and possibilities of ecumenical Christianity?   O. FREDERICK NOLDE: *Chairman*

VOLUME V.
> *What Must the Church Do?*

An interpretive volume, presenting the challenge to the Church growing out of the preceding studies.   HENRY P. VAN DUSEN

The full membership of the Commissions is given at the end of the volume

Toward

WORLD-WIDE
CHRISTIANITY

O. FREDERICK NOLDE

Editor

The
INTERSEMINARY
Series

VOLUME FOUR

HARPER & BROTHERS · PUBLISHERS
New York and London

TOWARD WORLD-WIDE

CHRISTIANITY

FIRST EDITION

L-V

CONTENTS

7339

PREFACE

THE INTERSEMINARY SERIES

The five volumes which comprise "The Interseminary Series" have three main purposes: to outline the character of the contemporary world which challenges the Church; to proclaim afresh the nature of the Gospel and the Church which must meet that challenge; and to set forth the claims which ecumenical Christianity makes upon the various churches as they face their world task. Although the perspective of the volumes is American, it is nevertheless comprehensive in that it views the Church as the Body of Christ in the world, performing a mission to the whole world.

The immediate occasion for the publication of the series is a national conference of theological students scheduled for June, 1947, under the auspices and initiative of the Interseminary Movement in the United States. The volumes will serve as study material for the delegates to the conference.

From the outset, however, it has been the desire and aim of those sponsoring the project that the volumes have a wide appeal. They have been designed for the Christian public in general, in the hope that there may be in them help toward our common Christian task in the fateful postwar days.

To produce the volumes, the Interseminary Committee outlined the five major questions and organized the Commissions which are listed below. Each Commission met once, and in the course of a two-day meeting outlined, first, the chapters for its respective volume, and, second, the main elements to be contained in each chapter. Authors were assigned from within the Commission. A first draft of each paper was submitted to Commission members and the chairman of the Commission for criticism, returned and subsequently rewritten in final form. The fifth volume, which is a summary interpretation of the preceding statements, is written by a single author. It should be specially noted that the work of Commission I-B was graciously undertaken by the already organized Pacific Coast Theological Group to which were added a few guests for the purpose at hand.

The volumes thus represent a combination of group thinking and individual effort. They are not designed to be completely representative statements to which the Commissions, or the Interseminary Movement, would subscribe. They are intended, rather, to convey information and to stimulate thought, in the earnest hope that this may in turn contribute to a more faithful performance of our Christian mission in the world.

For the National Interseminary Committee:
ROBERT S. BILHEIMER
Executive Secretary

THE AUTHORS

JOHN C. BENNETT, whose A.B. is from Williams College, holds the B.A. from Oxford, the B.D. and S.T.M. from Union Theological Seminary in New York, and the D.D. from Church Divinity School of the Pacific. He is professor of Christian theology and ethics in Union Seminary. Among his publications are *Social Salvation, Christianity and Our World* and *Christian Realism.* Dr. Bennett is a member of the Congregational-Christian Church.

H. PAUL DOUGLASS holds the A.M. degree from Iowa College, the D.D. degree from Drury College, and is a graduate of Chicago and Andover-Newton Theological Seminaries. He is the editor of *Christendom.* Among his most recent publications are *Protestant Cooperation in American Cities, Church Unity Movements in the United States* and *A Decade of Objective Progress in Church Unity.* Dr. Douglass is a member of the Congregational-Christian Church.

CHARLES W. IGLEHART holds the A.B. degree from Columbia University, the B.D. degree from Union Theological Seminary, the Ph.D. degree from Drew University and the D.D. degree from Syracuse University. He is associate professor of missions at Union Theological Seminary. Dr. Iglehart is a member of the Methodist Church.

HENRY SMITH LEIPER, whose B.A. and D.D. degrees are from Amherst College, also holds the B.D. degree from Union Theological Seminary and the M.A. degree from Columbia University. He is the American secretary for the Provisional Committee of the World Council of Churches, and the executive secretary of the American Committee for the World Council of Churches. His most recent publications include *The Ghost of Caesar Walks* and *World Chaos or World Christianity*. Dr. Leiper is a member of the Congregational-Christian Church.

JOHN A. MACKAY holds the M.A. degree from the University of Aberdeen (Scotland), the B.D. from Princeton Theological Seminary, the D.Litt. degree from the University of Lima (Peru), the LL.D. degree from Ohio Wesleyan University and Albright College, the D.D. degree from Princeton University, the University of Aberdeen, Debrecan University (Hungary) and the Presbyterian College, Montreal, and the L.H.D. degree from Boston University and Lafayette College. He is president and professor of ecumenics at Princeton Theological Seminary. His publications include *The Other Spanish Christ, That Other America, A Preface to Christian Theology* and *Heritage and Destiny*. Dr. Mackay is a member of the Presbyterian Church in the United States of America.

ELMORE M. MCKEE, whose A.B. and B.D. degrees are from Yale University, also holds the D.D. degree from Union College. He is the rector of St. George's Church, New York City. His publications include *Communion with God, What Use Is Religion* and *Preaching in These Times* of which he is co-author. Dr. McKee is a member of the Protestant Episcopal Church.

O. FREDERICK NOLDE, whose A.B. and D.D. degrees are from Muhlenberg College, also holds the B.D. degree from the Lutheran Theological Seminary in Philadelphia and the Ph.D. degree from the University of Pennsylvania. He is professor of religious education at the Lutheran Theological Seminary (Philadelphia). His publications include *Yesterday, Today and Tomor-*

row, *The Church Worker* (with Paul J. Hoh), *Truth and Life, Christian World Action* and *Christian Messages to the Peoples of the World.* Dr. Nolde is a member of the United Lutheran Church.

W. STANLEY RYCROFT holds the B.Comm. degree from Liverpool University (England) and the A.B. and Ph.D. degrees from the University of San Marcos (Lima, Peru). He is the executive secretary of the Committee on Cooperation in Latin America. His publications include *On This Foundation* and *Indians of the High Andes* of which he is the editor. Dr. Rycroft is a member of the Presbyterian Church in the United States of America.

MATTHEW SPINKA holds the A.B. degree from Coe College, the B.D. degree from Chicago Theological Seminary, the A.M. and Ph.D. degrees from the University of Chicago. He is professor of medieval, reformation and modern church history at Hartford Theological Seminary. His recent publications include *The Church and the Russian Revolution, A History of Christianity in the Balkans, Christianity Confronts Communism* and *John Hus and Czech Reform.* Dr. Spinka is a member of the Congregational-Christian Church.

ABDEL R. WENTZ holds the A.B., D.D. and LL.D. degrees from Gettysburg College, the B.D. degree from the Lutheran Theological Seminary (Gettysburg) and the Ph.D. from George Washington University. He is president and professor of church history of the Lutheran Theological Seminary (Gettysburg). His publications include *A New Strategy for Theological Education, When Two Worlds Met* and *The Lutheran Church in American History.* Dr. Wentz is a member of the United Lutheran Church.

INTRODUCTION

O. Frederick Nolde

> . . . One world, waiting, surely, for who shall carry to
> it and place in its empty hands one Faith—the only thing
> that can ever truly and fundamentally unite it or deeply
> and truly satisfy it, bringing its one human race into one
> Catholic Church through the message of the "One Body
> and One Spirit, One Lord, One Faith, One Baptism, One
> God and Father of all, who is over all, and through all, and
> in all.[1]

The title of this book, *Toward World-wide Christianity*,
reaffirms a goal which roots in the tradition of the Gospel. It
carries an admission that, after these many centuries of Christian
activity, the goal has not yet been achieved. It recognizes our
responsibility, under the guidance of God's Spirit, effectively to
interpret the eternal truth of Jesus Christ to all men in the light
of the needs and opportunities of our generation. It bespeaks a
commitment to the demonstration of Christian fellowship in a
world community.

Thoughtful Christians are restive as they contemplate the
world scene on which the Church moves to fulfill its mission.
They are disturbed by the prevalence of selfishness and hatred,
by an indifference to spiritual and moral values, by social and
racial clashes, by the physical suffering and the mental anguish

[1] W. H. T. Gairdner, *Echoes from Edinburgh, 1910* (New York: Fleming H. Revell Company, 1910), pp. 6, 7.

of multitudes, by wars and rumors of wars. To this conflagration of evil they see applied a pitifully ineffective trickle from the full well of Christian resources. Their fear is not so much for themselves. In humility and trust, they commend themselves to God's goodness and mercy in this life and in the world to come. Their despair is not of the Gospel. They see in it "the power of God unto salvation to every one that believeth." Their concern stems rather from an apparent ineffectiveness of the power of God in individual and corporate life—a power which should be decisive to the ends of the earth. For this ineffectiveness they can account only in terms of man's weakness and ignorance. Within the family of accountable men, they sense that they themselves— the possessors of the heritage—have not adequately utilized the resources at their disposal. With disturbing insistence they ask themselves whether a substantial obstacle lies within the household of faith—in its competing claims, in its divided loyalties, in its unco-ordinated efforts.

Toward World-wide Christianity is an invitation to consider the manner in which the churches of our generation are seeking to fulfill their accepted mission. The distinguishing point of departure is within the structure of the churches and in the spirit which animates their relations in faith, life and work. The Commission charged with the preparation of this volume sought first of all to set forth a realistic picture of the present situation. There was need to weave into an integrated pattern the scattered threads of practices inherited from the past, of new visions captured under the exigencies of a chaotic world, of courageous experiments in co-operative Christian enterprise, of procedures demonstrated sound by the testing of Christian fellowship. The Commission thus interpreted its assignment. It selected authors who had demonstrated competence in their special fields and offered them valuable suggestions by a critical reading of manuscripts. The fact that a number of chapters had to blaze new trails made it necessary to omit specific references and to list general sources at the end of the book. In carrying its work to completion the Commission relied upon the discerning and never-failing help of Robert S. Bilheimer to an extent which baffles merited recognition.

In the first chapter Matthew Spinka portrays the situation as it now exists. He analyzes the current manifestation of Christianity in denominational groups and traces the divergent policies and interpretations in their development. Chapter II illuminates the ecumenical goal. In what direction ought the churches to move? John A. Mackay presents the Biblical and theological bases on which the objective rests. John C. Bennett describes and appraises the characteristics and the possible forms through which ecumenical Christianity may be expressed.

The state of the Church in our modern world cannot be accurately represented by a completely unbridged gulf between existing denominational groups and an emerging ecumenical goal. Encouragement is offered in four areas of development which mark a significant page in the history of evangelical Christianity. Henry Smith Leiper and Abdel Ross Wentz tell the story of the rise of ecumenical organizations. Here is more than a catalog of conferences and pronouncements. In the building of media for fellowship and action, there appears a divine "power essentially indivisible and yet capable of infinite expansion." This power became sufficiently decisive to enable the ecumenical movement to withstand the disrupting shock of the second World War. C. W. Iglehart, with the benefit of information secured by A. L. Warnshuis from personal observation of European conditions, continues the story of world Christian fellowship among the younger as well as the older churches under the trying conditions of total war. The chapter on the "Christian Community and World Order" emphasizes the broadened horizon and the sense of community with which the churches sought to lay foundations for a just and lasting peace. H. Paul Douglass focuses attention upon the American scene and sketches developments toward ecumenical Christianity in the churches of this country.

The optimism which may spring from a knowledge of achievement in first steps is tempered by a recognition of the long and tough road to be traveled. Encouragement is warranted. Complacency is unjustified and stultifying. W. Stanley Rycroft and Elmore M. McKee warn of obstacles to be encountered and mark out steps to be followed in achieving the ecumenical ideal.

The purpose of the foregoing brief analysis lies beyond such study and discussion as this volume may promote. The Commission in whose deliberations it originated sought more than a realistic picture of the present situation. Their eyes were fixed upon the Christian people through whose instrumentality God's work must be done in our day—pastors and leaders, seminary students, men and women in all walks of life. The restlessness of the thoughtful Christian must serve as a stimulus *Toward World-wide Christianity*. The progress implied in the successive chapters suggests possible steps in yielding to this stimulus:

A sympathetic understanding of the situation which exists in a divided Christianity.

An endorsement of the ecumenical goal and a recognition of acceptable forms in which it may find demonstration.

A sense of encouragement in organizations already established, in fellowship strengthened under the tensions of war, in the extended horizons of testimony to the world of nations, in the trend toward unity among our own churches.

Aided by lessons learned in the stream of Christian life, a commitment to purposeful effort in giving expression to the One Holy Catholic Church.

O. Frederick Nolde

TOWARD WORLD-WIDE
CHRISTIANITY

1

CHRISTIANITY AND
THE CHURCHES

Matthew Spinka

Introduction. 1. The non-Roman communions. (1) Protestant and Anglican bodies: (a) The American churches. Early theological differences, revivals and denominationalism, the effect of immigration, later theological diversity, sociological differences, American Christianity. (b) The European Churches: Lutheran, Reformed, Anabaptist, Anglican. (c) The "younger churches." (2) The Eastern Orthodox churches: Russian, Greek, and other Balkan churches, Orthodox theology. 2. The Roman Catholic Church: retrenchment and reform, papal ascendancy, Church and State, education and ideologies, Church and politics, doctrine.

INTRODUCTION

Christianity, as an organized movement, comprises a number of separate communions. The common fashion of grouping these bodies into two classes—the Church or churches, and sects—is, from the American point of view, lacking in clear meaning and justification. A Roman Catholic feels no embarrassment in the use of the terms. "To the Catholic the distinction of Church and sect presents no difficulty. For him, any Christian denomination which has set itself up independently of his own Church is a sect."[1] In a country where a state church exists it is possible to distinguish between it and the other communions by referring to the latter as "sects," although it is difficult not to use the term in at least slightly pejorative sense. But in the United States where there is no established church, even this excuse for discrimination is not possible.

If the Church is regarded as the communion of those who possess the spirit of Christ, as it has often been so defined throughout its history, and as the Russian Orthodox still do in their concept of *sobornost,* the use of the terms "church" and "sect" assumes a new and hitherto unusual meaning. For no existing ecclesiastical body can claim to be a Church. Only those members within all the communions who possess the spirit of Christ belong to the true—and invisible—Church. No external authority, ecclesiastical or secular, can separate them from Christ. But this view is obviously not applicable to corporate bodies as a whole.

Looking at the question from an institutional point of view, only such groups as have retained an ecumenical consciousness of belonging to the one catholic Church of which they are but a part may claim the name of churches. Those who set themselves up as the only true Church, and regard others as "false," have by their own action cut themselves off from the Church catholic, even though they claim that name in some exclusive sense. Thus, for instance, the churches of the Massachusetts Bay, gathered in the Cambridge Synod of 1648, declared that "a Congregational-Church, is by the institution of Christ a part of the Militant-visible-church. . . ."[2] These believers, therefore, were not sectarians. Only those who have repudiated or lost this ecumenical consciousness, whether they be Protestant or Catholic, constitute sects. No one can impose this classification on them. By their own action are they judged.

For lack of space, not all particular churches can be treated.

[1] "Sect and Sects," *The Catholic Encyclopedia.*

[2] *Platform of Church Discipline* (Cambridge, 1649), ch. II, par. 3, 6.

Only communions representative of a larger class or a particular group shall be given consideration as an illustration of the general characteristics of the whole group.

1. THE NON-ROMAN COMMUNIONS

(1) PROTESTANT AND ANGLICAN BODIES. Christian churches and sects, from the point of view of their present attitude toward the ecumenical movement, align themselves into two categories: the non-Roman communions, comprising most of the Protestant and Eastern Orthodox bodies, and the Roman Catholic Church.

(a) *The American Churches*

Early theological differences

In considering the American bodies of the former group, among the cause chiefly responsible for their difference of origin is the theological factor. During the seventeenth century, the American colonies were theologically surprisingly homogenous. Virginia, the Middle colonies, and the New England colonies were almost solidly Calvinistic. The first General Synod held in Cambridge in 1648 gave a "hearty assent and attestation to the whole confession of faith (for substance of doctrine) which the Reverend assembly presented to the Religious and Honorable Parliament of England," i.e., the Westminster Confession of Faith. Thus the American Congregational churches were theologically at one with the English Presbyterians. Let it be remembered that the Calvinism of the Westminster Confession had been ameliorated by the introduction of the "covenant theology," whereby the rigors of Calvin's view of God's arbitrary will were lessened. Perhaps Rhode Island and Pennsylvania, which granted freedom of religion, were the only exceptions to the prevailing religious homogeneity. But even there the Calvinistic groups were strong. Uniformity in the other New England colonies was secured by rigorous exclusion of all dissent. But the Puritans had emigrated chiefly for the purpose of establishing a church and state in which the will of God should be supreme. Accordingly, a fundamental disagreement as to the interpretation of the will of God threatened the very basis of both the church and the state. Hence, dissenters were forced to depart.

The Dutch of the Middle colonies belonged to the Dutch Reformed Church which adhered to the strictly Calvinistic Confession of Faith adopted by the Synod of Dort (1619). The Established Church of Virginia followed the theological lead of the mother church. The latter, since the days of Archbishop Laud, was increasingly turning to the Arminian interpretation of Calvinism. Yet, despite its differences, Arminianism still remained within the Calvinistic family of churches.

Although later in time, the Presbyterians and the Baptists increased the predominance of the Calvinistic bodies in America. The former owed their strength chiefly to the Scotch-Irish immigration which began at the turn of the eighteenth century. They settled mostly in western Pennsylvania, on the frontier, although in fewer numbers they were found in every other colony. The Reverend Francis Makemie, "the father of American Presbyterianism," organized the first American presbytery in Philadelphia in 1706.

The Baptists, who organized their first church in 1639 in Providence, Rhode Island (with the assistance of Roger Williams), experienced a period of rapid growth as the result of the Great Awakening in the second half of the eighteenth century. They particularly gained prominence in Virginia and North Carolina. Since the English Baptists were originally an offshoot of the Congregationalists, the differences which separated them from the latter were not great. They stressed believers' baptism and separation of church and state.

This predominantly homogeneous situation was changed with the establishment of the colony of Pennsylvania in 1681. William

Penn's "Holy Experiment" opened the colony to various persecuted groups, not only to his fellow Quakers. He had experimented with colonizing projects, which included religious freedom, when he had been part owner of West Jersey, even prior to his acquisition of Pennsylvania. The Quakers stressed the doctrine of the "inner light," the grace of God in the hearts of all men; consequently, they paid scant attention to the organizational and ritualistic aspects of Christianity. This differentiated them from those who regarded the Scriptures alone as the "rule of faith and life." During the latter part of the seventeenth and the first part of the eighteenth centuries, Quakers were the fastest growing religious body; but they later lost their lead to others.

Besides the Quakers, Penn's colony was soon filled with a motley of peoples from Europe who made Pennsylvania "the mother of churches." The chief among the immigrants were the Germans. They belonged to the Lutheran, Reformed, Moravian, Mennonite, Dunker, and many other religious bodies. Aside from their pronounced theological differences, their language separated them from their English-speaking neighbors. But even among themselves they remained disunited. Count Nikolaus Ludwig von Zinzendorf, the patron and bishop of the Moravians, strove, during his sojourn in America, to unite the three first-named groups into one body. But the old-world distrusts and rivalries prevented him from accomplishing the task. Thereupon, each group organized itself separately. The Lutherans found their principal leader in Henry M. Mühlenberg, who came to America in 1742. The Reformed owed their organization to the Reverend Michael Schlatter, who arrived in Pennsylvania in 1746 and welded the previously existing churches into a coetus under the general authority of the Dutch Classis of Amsterdam. The Moravians, after the failure of the unionistic scheme, likewise went their own way.

Another group which largely for linguistic reasons remained separated from the like-minded Quakers, was that of the Mennonites. In Germantown, founded by Francis Pastorius, they shared with the German and Dutch Quakers in a common meeting house. But later the groups separated. Mennonites represented the Anabaptist tradition of the Reformation: they stood for radical separation of church and state, since religion was a strictly personal matter. They held to the believers' baptism, and practiced nonresistance.

Revivals and denominationalism

Another fruitful cause of the rise and growth of denominationalism was the revivals. The Great Awakening of the middle of the eighteenth century has already been mentioned. A similar movement broke out toward the end of the century (1797), attaining its full strength during the first decades of the next century. It was particularly effective in the frontier communities, sweeping from Kentucky westward. Since the post-Revolutionary era was characterized by a tremendous westward expansion and consequently witnessed an unprecedented growth of frontier communities, revivalism and frontier missionary work went hand in hand. The denominations which adapted their methods and message to the frontier conditions, grew the strongest. The most successful were the Methodists, who organized themselves independently of the mother church in 1784. By adopting the circuit rider method and other measures admirably suited to frontier conditions, they were able, at a relatively small cost, to minister to a much larger number of local classes and churches than the Presbyterians or the Congregationalists, who insisted on an educated ministry and settled pastorates. Moreover, the free spirit prevailing on the frontier was congenial to the utmost freedom in religion: consequently, the opposition to "man-made" creeds and polity led to the rise of the Christian and Disciples denominations. Appealing to the Bible as the sole authority, repudiating all creeds, adopting an extremely "leftist" congregational polity, and developing to a large degree the "farmer-preacher" type of ministry, the Disciples gained large numbers on the frontier. The Baptists were equally successful, and for the same reasons.

The effect of immigration

Still another cause of the multiplication of religious communions in the United States was immigration. Although the vast majority of religious bodies were originally transplanted from their old-world origins, yet to a large extent they were religiously much more homogeneous than were the immigrants of the nineteenth and twentieth centuries. For during the colonial period Catholics, with the exception of those in Maryland, were not numerous in the colonies. But beginning with the Irish immigration in the forties of the nineteenth century, large numbers came from the Catholic countries in Europe—Poland, Italy and Ireland. Since 1880 over five million members have been added to the Catholic Church from immigration alone. With the Russian, Balkan and the Middle East immigrants, the Eastern Orthodox churches made their appearance. These newer groups of immigrants were differentiated from the older, predominantly Protestant bodies in doctrine, polity, ritual, as well as language and customs. For a long time, they were also socially and economically on a lower level. Immigration from the Scandinavian countries and Germany greatly strengthened the Lutheran element and led to the founding of several new Lutheran bodies.

The post-Civil War period added to the existing religious complexity by the organization of independent Negro churches among the Methodists and the Baptists. These groups at present number over five million communicants.

Later theological diversity

With the increase of denominational diversity sketched in the preceding pages, theological diversity naturally increased as well. The complexities of the European religious situation were transferred to the New World. Many groups, which in the country of their origin had been numerically insignificant and unimportant, gained influence as they increased in strength under the conditions of freedom afforded them in this country. Freedom, however, necessarily tends toward diversity of the forms of doctrinal formulation and organization.

If the theological pattern at first was predominantly Calvinistic, it did not remain so. Pennsylvania contributed greatly to the change. The Second Revival which followed close upon the lowest ebb of American religious life which was reached in the closing decades of the eighteenth century, was favorable to the Arminian type of theology. Although it would be inaccurate to imply that the Revival did not permeate the Calvinistic bodies as well, yet the evangelistic appeal, "whosoever will let him come," which is theologically Arminian, proved more consonant with the latter, rather than with the Calvinistic emphasis on predestination, which appeared to militate against such an appeal for a free decision.

The rising liberalism, which stemmed from the English latitudinarianism, also contributed to the weakening of New England Calvinism. Its early exponents—Charles Chauncy and Jonathan Mayhew—were vigorous and influential opponents of Jonathan Edwards and his school. In the end, this "left-wing" Congregationalism repudiated the Calvinistic view of man as derogatory of man's dignity and worth, and stood for a "humanistic" revision of that doctrine. When the traditional Trinitarian and Christological views were likewise repudiated, the situation reached the decisive stage of separation: in 1825, this led to the organization of the Unitarian denomination.

Although the Congregational churches were thus shorn of "left-wing" radicals, the liberalizing tendency continued. The "New Haven" theology of Nathaniel W. Taylor permeated large sections of Congregationalism. By 1865, when the "Burial Hill Confession" was adopted, the distinctive features of Calvinism were to a large extent omitted. Furthermore, through the home missionary comity arrangement which has existed since 1801 between the Congregationalists and the Presbyterians, this liberal tendency entered the ranks of the latter church as well. In the end, the Presbyterian General Assembly in 1837 "excinded" a number of Synods comprising some 100,000 members, on the basis of dogmatic and other charges. The Synods thus excluded organized themselves into the "New School" Presbyterian Church. Although in 1870 the two branches of the church were reunited, the liberal and conservative tendencies persist within that communion to the present.

It would be difficult to exaggerate the importance of the impact which the evolutionary theory has exerted upon religious thinking since the appearance of Darwin's *Origin of Species* in 1859. The divergent principles of the Renaissance and the Reformation now confronted each other in hostile and aggressive combat. Secularist or humanistic culture, traceable from the Renaissance through the rationalism of Descartes and the empiricism of Locke, as well as German idealism from Kant to Hegel, with the accession of strength derived from naturalistic evolutionism, now joined battle with the contemporary, largely conservative, theology. When to this impact was added Biblical criticism, the choice before the churches was plainly between resisting these forces which they regarded as predominantly subversive, or of accommodating themselves to them by absorbing such elements as were capable of being assimilated. Accordingly, some groups within the churches chose one, others the other alternative. The former became far more conservative than would otherwise have been the case, while the others became liberal or "modernist." In some extreme cases the former developed aggressive "fundamentalism," while the latter went to the far "left" by turning "humanist."

The most characteristic feature of this development is that it cut across the existing denominational lines, so that denominational differences as such became subordinated and sometimes quite secondary. Only a few denominations remained theologically homogeneous—either conservative or liberal. Most of the larger groups comprise both tendencies, occasionally with sharp cleavage between them. Some communions aim frankly at comprehension of such divergent tendencies within the bounds of their ecclesiastical framework. Such, for instance, is the Protestant Episcopal Church, which accommodates a wide variety of doctrinal and cultus divergences. But liberals and conservatives within such denominations feel spiritually closer to the likeminded contingent in other denominations than to their own fellow denominationalists who do not share their views. Accordingly, American Christianity is no longer truly differentiated by the traditional denominational differences so much as by the conservative-liberal types of theology.

But the situation remains fluid, and the familiar alignment just described is already undergoing radical changes. The two world wars through which humankind has recently passed have exerted their influence upon theological thinking. This is particularly true of the Continental theology, although it has affected American theological thinking as well. The most important of these influences are those of Barth and Brunner, although Kierkegaard and Berdyaev are not without a following. In this country, Barth has only a few out-and-out disciples, although Brunner is more influential. The chief form which the dissatisfaction with traditional liberalism has assumed is neo-orthodoxy, which has its most influential exponent in Reinhold Niebuhr.

Sociological differences

Sociologically, American Christianity has become stratified to a considerable extent. Such ecclesiastical form of class consciousness has been in evidence from the very beginning of the Protestant movement, as when the Anabaptists and the numerous sects in England during the Commonwealth period represented social cleavages between the "disinherited" and the socially more favored groups. Stratification historically established by reason of racial or national origins has already been mentioned. Some American denominations, such as the Roman

Catholic, which in their origin have been identified with the immigrant groups, still bear traces of this kind of social grouping. As a rule, the older Protestant communions represent to a large extent the middle and the upper social strata. Such social characteristics are exhibited by the Episcopalians, Presbyterians, Congregationalists, Methodists, and the Reformed, and to a lesser degree by the Baptists and the Disciples of Christ.

As a rule, the underprivileged groups, feeling estranged from the middle and upper classes by an unequal economic and cultural status, organize themselves separately on the basis of racial, emotional or traditional appeal. Thus the Negro churches to a very large degree still retain their separate denominational or local congregational organization. Even in the great merger of the Methodist bodies which in 1939 unified most of them into The Methodist Church, several Negro Methodist bodies remained outside the merger. Other emerging popular denominations, such as the Jehovah Witnesses and many so-called holiness sects, represent a resurgence of the emotional and traditional elements, along with emphases which no longer appeal to the classes on a higher cultural level. They bear witness to the continual vitality of such appeals to the nonintellectual groups to be found in society in all ages. In time, however, these movements approximate the cultural and religious levels of the larger, more established churches, only to make room for other emergent movements of the same order.

American Christianity

The character of American Christianity, as compared with the English or the Continental, manifests divergent features. The very fact that it is voluntaristic makes for greater variety and independence. The one decisive influence, apart from the great variety of such environmental forces as have been mentioned, was the American frontier. The most effective frontier methods were revivals, evangelistic, nontheological preaching, moral, often reformist, emphases, and a simple, democratic form of government and organization. Although many churches which grew out of this frontier environment—such as the Methodists and the Disciples—have gradually accommodated themselves to a type of worship no longer distinguishable from that of the other denominations which traditionally have served the middle and upper classes, the more primitive type is still discernible under conditions similar to those which gave these denominations their rise. But all denominations, even the Roman Catholic, were to some degree affected by the environmental conditions to which they all have been subjected. American Christianity has been affected particularly by the character of the religious forces of the colonial period; by the democratic spirit of our political institutions; by the predominant modes of thinking, such as regarding religious tolerance, liberty of conscience, and the separation of church and state; and by the frontier conditions prevailing during the period of its greatest expansion. Accordingly, it possesses a distinctly "American" character in comparison with European Christianity, for it is more "practical," activist, non-theological, than the more reflective and theologically-minded old-world Christianity.

As for the relative strength of the various denominations in America, according to the latest available statistics,[3] the 256 bodies report the total of 72,492,669 members inclusively; when only those over thirteen years of age are counted, their number is estimated at 59,717,107. This is the highest percentage of church members ever reported in this country. When one remembers that at the beginning of the nineteenth century, the church membership comprised only about 5 per cent of the population, this is a tenfold increase, even when the lower total is taken as the basis of computation. Thus church membership is steadily increasing, notwithstanding the popular impression to the contrary.

As for the relative proportion of the various denominations, the largest membership of any one denomination is that of the

[3] From *Year Book of American Churches*, 1945 edition.

Roman Catholic Church. This body reported 23,419,701 (of whom over six million are under the age of thirteen). Against this figure, the strength of all the Protestant denominations combined amounts to 42,734,661 (of whom over five million are under the age of thirteen). Accordingly, the ratio stands about two to one.

Among the Protestant bodies, the Baptists (nine bodies) report over fourteen million members; the Methodists (four bodies), close to ten million; Lutherans (seven bodies), almost five million; Presbyterians (four bodies), almost three million; the Protestant Episcopal Church, over two million; the Disciples, over one and a half million; and the Congregationalists-Christians, slightly over a million.

And yet, despite all this diversity, there is also a real and essential unity among the Protestants. A fuller treatment of this subject will be found in the article by Dr. Paul H. Douglass. Suffice it to say that the very genius of Protestantism—freedom of conscience, individual conviction and responsibility before God—necessarily implies a diversity of the resulting doctrinal interpretation and organizational and liturgical practices. This is the cost of liberty. But the overwhelming majority of American Christians are convinced that these precious benefits of freedom must be preserved even at the cost of denominational diversity. That does not justify, however, denominational rivalry or atomic disintegration of Protestantism as a whole. Mutual recognition of one another as members of the common household of faith, and as integral units of the Church universal, is relatively common and general among Protestants. In other words, the ecumenical consciousness is more pervasive among them than is sectarian exclusiveness. This spirit shows itself concretely in such organizations as the Federal Council of the Churches of Christ in America, the movements toward consolidation of separated groups of the same denomination—for example, the unification of the Methodist bodies in 1939—and mergers of denominations hitherto organically unrelated, as in the case of the Congregationalists and the Christians. There is a growing consciousness on the part of Protestants that in spirit they are one. In the World Council of Churches, this ecumenical spirit embraces the majority of the non-Roman communions.

(b) *The European Churches*

The European Protestant churches historically belong to four main families of churches: the Lutheran, the Reformed, the Anabaptist, and the Anglican.

Lutheran

Martin Luther did not originally intend to establish an independent communion. He desired to reform the existing church. When his well-meant endeavors met with resentment and reprisals, taking finally the radical form of excommunication by Pope Leo X, he then turned to the nobility of the German nation, exhorting them in an impassioned plea to do at least for Germany what the papacy had failed to do for the entire Church. Later, his ideal was reduced to that of a divided Germany. In the Religious Peace of Augsburg (1555), the division into Lutheran and the Catholic German states was legalized and made permanent. The establishment of Lutheran churches necessitated a virtual submission of the church to the state in external affairs, for the adoption of Lutheranism in a particular territory depended primarily on the decision of the prince. This was done in accordance with the long-recognized legal maxim: whose is the rule, his is the religion. In many of the Lutheran states, as for instance in Prussia, the ruler was given the title of *"summus episcopus."* The consequences of such an arrangement were not happy as a rule, and have vitally affected the German ecclesiastical life to the present.

Besides Germany, the Lutheran reform penetrated into, and was set up by, the state in the Scandinavian countries, and won numerous adherents in Poland, Bohemia and elsewhere.

Since the Lutheran reformation repudiated the medieval principle that the Church possessed supreme authority in spiritual matters, a new principle of authority was found in the Scriptures. They were now to be regarded as the sole rule of faith and practice. Nevertheless, Luther recognized as the core of the Scriptures, as the "Word of God," only such doctrine as was in accord with the Gospel. And he identified the gospel message with the Pauline teaching that salvation is by grace alone, without the works of the law, for "the just shall live by faith." Moreover, young Luther in his "Address to the German Nobility" (1520) boldly enunciated the radical doctrine of "the priesthood of all believers," which involved the right and duty of all Christians of studying and interpreting the Word of God for themselves. When he became responsible for the establishment and organization of territorial churches in states which adopted his reform ideas, he found it necessary to impose fairly uniform doctrinal and ritualistic systems. Henceforth, he opposed deviation both to the right (Roman Catholicism) and the left (Anabaptism and the teaching of the "spiritual" reformers). In fact, the most famous case of this kind is Luther's violent repudiation of Zwingli's interpretation of the doctrine of the eucharistic elements, despite the fact that Zwingli belonged to the "center" as did Luther himself. Luther vehemently affirmed that under the form of bread and wine there also was present in the sacrament the body and blood of the Lord (consubstantiation), while Zwingli interpreted the verb "is" in the words of institution, "this is my body," to mean "it signifies." This disagreement resulted in the separation of the Lutheran from the Zwinglian (and later Reformed) forces which persists to this day.

Under the impact of the Nazi regime, German Protestantism developed a small pro-Nazi "German Christians" group, and another small, but influential, "Confessional" group. The latter actively defended the autonomy of the Church in matters spiritual. The bulk of German Protestant membership, however, remained neutral. But even before the war Karl Barth found many disciples among the theologians, clergy and laity, so that the liberal group lost its leadership.

Reformed

The Reformed family of churches owe their origin partly to the Swiss reformer, Ulrich Zwingli, and partly to the Genevan reformer, John Calvin. With the aid of numerous influential local reformers, the views of these outstanding leaders, particularly Calvin, became officially dominant in many Swiss cantons, in Scotland, Holland, and to a lesser degree were disseminated in Hungary, Bohemia (which, however, possessed its own native church, The Unity of Brethren, which antedated the German Reformation by some three quarters of a century), France and Poland. In the reign of Queen Elizabeth, the Anglican Church interpreted its XXXIX Articles in the Calvinistic sense.

Calvin, who belonged to the second generation of reformers, became the theological systematizer of the Reformed movement. He leaned heavily on the Pauline-Augustinian traditions as well as on Luther and Bucer. His most influential work, *Institutes of the Christian Religion*, became the classic exposition of Reformed theology, and exerted tremendous influence upon the subsequent times. Calvin's central principle is that the sovereign will of God shall ultimately prevail over all men may do to the contrary. Thus God shall reign, His will shall be done on earth as it is in heaven. It is this sublime confidence in the power of God which gives his system strength and calm trust in the face of all that may happen. Furthermore, he stressed the doctrine of salvation by grace in an extreme form: man was chosen by an act of God, before all ages, either to salvation or damnation; the predestined were then given the necessary prevenient grace which enabled them to accept the proffered salvation; this grace was irresistible; moreover, they likewise were secured against falling away from their divine calling by the grace of perseverance. Calvin also placed far greater emphasis upon church discipline, a life of sanctification, than did Luther. It was this feature of his system which eventuated in Puritan morality.

The ruthless rigidity of Calvin's view of the seeming arbitrariness of the Divine will, as well as other doctrines, soon caused dissatisfaction. In the beginning of the seventeenth century, these protests found an expression in Arminianism, which asserted the freedom of man either to choose or reject salvation offered in Christ to all men. It was this form of Calvinism which found increasing acceptance in the succeeding centuries.

Anabaptist

The Anabaptist groups, savagely persecuted during the age of the Reformation, held views which have become, in time, very influential, particularly in the United States. Many of these views were accepted by other bodies, which did not originally belong to the Anabaptists. Fundamentally, they held that religion is a private affair, and in the nature of the case is not subject to the external authority of the magistrate. John Locke arrived at the same views, although on very different grounds, and much later. Accordingly, the Anabaptists demanded the separation of church and state. A Christian, therefore, could not hold public office or serve in the army. They granted the right of private interpretation of the Scriptures, although the latter were to them the only rule of faith and life. They accepted the tenet of believers' baptism. Some held extreme views which led small groups among the Anabaptists to commit acts which brought discredit upon them all. The remnants of these persecuted groups were organized in the Netherlands by a converted Roman Catholic priest, Menno Simons. They were named after him Mennonites. Besides, other small bodies of Anabaptists, bearing various designations, still exist.

Anglican

The Anglican Church was established as a Protestant body in the reign of King Edward VI, although the papal jurisdiction over England had been abolished by Henry VIII (1534). Under

Queen Elizabeth, the position of the Church assumed the character of a "*via media*." For reasons of state, the Queen could not continue the Roman Catholic regime of her sister, Mary, who preceded her; for Elizabeth was the daughter of Anne Boleyn, whose marriage with Henry had been declared invalid by the pope. Accordingly, in the eyes of Catholics she was held to be illegitimate, and as such not entitled to rule England. On the other hand, she was opposed to the policy of the thoroughgoing Calvinistic theologians who had flocked back to England after Mary's death, and who would have desired to change the English church in conformity with the Genevan model. Hence, she chose the middle course. But on that account she not only antagonized the Roman Catholic element in the nation, but also the Puritans, as the radical reformist party came to be called. She proscribed the Separatists, who repudiated the Established Church altogether.

When Archbishop Laud was appointed to the See of Canterbury (1633), he instigated measures intended to crush the Puritan party. Some of the Separatists had removed from the country even earlier. Now the Puritans emigrated in large numbers, particularly to the Massachusetts Bay colony. Laud likewise influenced the interpretation of the official doctrine in the direction of Arminianism, as a further measure of opposition to the Puritans.

In 1831, after Parliament passed the Catholic Emancipation Act, some earnest Anglicans protested against the Church's subjugation to the state. The movement which resulted stressed the spiritual autonomy of the Church by a revival of the patristic doctrines of the Church. It came to be known as the Tractarian Movement. But in time it developed Roman Catholic tendencies, and a considerable number of prominent Anglicans went over to Roman Catholicism. The most eminent among these converts was John Henry Newman (1845), who later was raised to the cardinalate. Under the leadership of Pusey, the movement was then directed into the Anglo-Catholic channels. This "high-church" group within the Anglican communion repudiated the Protestant character of the English Reformation, and regarded itself as Anglo-Catholic, although not Roman Catholic.

(c) *The "Younger Churches"*

Since Christianity by its very nature is a universal, rather than an ethnic or racial religion, i. e., since it holds that its truths are of universal application and validity, and therefore not the exclusive possession of any particular nation or group of people, it follows that it must be a missionary religion. Accordingly, it is not by any means some "religious imperialism" which motivates its missionary policies, but an impulse to share with all what is properly intended for all.

It has been the glorious achievement of the late nineteenth and the first decades of the twentieth centuries to have at last realized the extension of the Christian Church throughout the world. The so-called "younger churches," mostly the product of missionary efforts of the American and European Christian bodies, naturally at first partook of the characteristics—both doctrinal and ecclesiastical—of their parent bodies. But as these churches grew in numbers, they came increasingly under the influence of native cultures. Moreover, the peculiarities of the parent churches, never grounded in their own indigenous tradition, grew glaringly incongruous and meaningless. Under pressure to present a common front against the non-Christian native culture of their people, Christians of the "younger churches" increasingly sought to divest their understanding of Christianity of forms of thought and modes of expression from foreign cultures, and to express the essence of Christianity in their own cultural terms and practices. Also, they sought to secure an increasingly prominent share in the administration of their own churches. This pattern of nationalizing the modes of thought and practice on the part of the newer Christian communions has been the same throughout the ages. It may be looked upon as a sign of the "coming of age" of the modern missionary churches.

On the other hand, these same forces likewise produced a movement toward unity among the "younger churches." Since the causes which had resulted in denominational disunity at home were not indigenous to the churches abroad, they were not felt to any great extent. Accordingly, the unifying tendencies operated much more freely among the latter than among the former bodies. It is not surprising, therefore, in the light of these considerations, to find many forces tending toward church unity abroad, such as have taken place in South India or even in Japan (where the initial steps were forced on the churches as a war measure, but may be voluntarily continued). It is devoutly to be hoped that the "younger churches" may render the whole of Christendom a service by providing an example and a pattern of a basis of church union which may be followed even by the mother churches. At any rate, the World Conference held in the Madras Presidency in India (1938), which consisted predominantly of representatives of the "younger churches," affords ample proof that Christendom has already entered upon the "ecumenical" stage, and that all alike, older and younger members of the world-wide household of faith, stand in reciprocal relation to one another. The West can no longer ignore the East or indulge in a provincial sense of superiority. All parts of the World Church are mutually interdependent.

(2) THE EASTERN ORTHODOX CHURCHES. As the Roman Catholic Church survived the downfall of the Roman Empire, so did the Byzantine Church outlive the ruin of the Byzantine Empire. When Sultan Mohammed II conquered Constantinople in 1453, he not only preserved the institution of the patriarchate, but even extended the patriarchal functions. Since the Koran was regarded as embodying both civil and religious laws, the non-Muslim could not be subjected to its requirements. Accordingly, the Christian subjects had to be formed into separate communities, called *milets*, and allowed to be governed in their own

traditional manner. In this way, the ecumenical patriarch became the ethnic, as well as religious, head of all the Orthodox Christians within the Turkish Empire.

Thus the patriarch of Constantinople ultimately gained power over the formerly independent historic patriarchates—Alexandria, Antioch, and Jerusalem—as well as over the Balkan patriarchates of Serbia (Pech), Bulgaria (Ohrid), the metropolitanates of Greece (Athens), and of Moldavia-Wallachia (the present Rumania). This situation lasted until the nineteenth century. With the breakup of the Turkish Empire, there also came the liberation of the ethnic churches from the authority of the ecumenical patriarch. Because of the long domination of the latter over the racially heterogeneous subject churches, the whole group is still popularly referred to as "Greek." In reality, only a minority of these peoples are racially Greek; accordingly, the designation of them as "the Eastern Orthodox" is far more accurate. Moreover, the relatively short span of time during which they have enjoyed independence goes far to explain the cultural lag which many of them exhibit.

Russian

Besides the Christian churches within the Turkish Empire, the only independent Orthodox churches were those of Russia and Georgia. Because of its growing political might, its numbers, and its wealth, Russia became the most influential as well as the most powerful member of Orthodox Christendom. Originally a mere metropolitanate of the Constantinopolitan patriarchate, the Russian Church was governed for the most part by Greek hierarchs. But in 1448, after repudiating the union with Rome to which the Byzantine Church had willy-nilly consented at the Council of Florence, the Russian Church proclaimed itself independent and set up a native metropolitan at its head. In 1589 the Church was raised to the rank of patriarchate. Soon after breaking away from Constantinople, the Russian Church came to regard itself as the head of Eastern Orthodoxy, on the ground that the hegemony had passed from Constantinople—now in the hands of the "infidel" Turks—to Moscow. This sense of leadership and pre-eminence, by reason of the fact that Russia had preserved Orthodoxy in its purity, while Constantinople had not, led in the end to a schism which has not been healed to the present day. The Russian Patriarch Nikon wished to harmonize the liturgical services of his church with those in use among the Greeks, for a considerable discrepancy had developed since the two churches had gone their separate ways. But such an opposition was raised against the measure by the "traditionalists" that in 1666 the Schismatics (*Raskolniki*) or Old Believers repudiated the state church which had accepted the Nikonian reforms. Another consequence of this significant event was the subjugation of the church to the state. This was consummated in the reign of Peter the Great, who abolished the patriarchate altogether by the simple expedient of not appointing a successor to Patriarch Adrian, who had died in 1700. In 1721 Peter reorganized the entire ecclesiastical administration by creating the Holy Governing Synod, which was in effect one of the government bureaus for the administration of the Church.

During the nineteenth century the Russian educated classes became almost altogether estranged from the common people. This was particularly true of the Westernists, who believed that the cultural salvation of Russia depended upon a wholesale acceptance of Western civilization. This party in its own way continued the work of Peter the Great. On the whole, they were politically revolutionary, repudiating tsarist absolutism. Their culture was materialistic and positivist. Religiously, they professed atheism. It is the Marxian contingent of this party which, in 1917, gained ascendancy in Russia. Their opponents, the Slavophiles, believed that the native culture contained valuable cultural elements not present in the decaying Western civilization. The religious Slavophiles made a particularly great contribution in restating the principles of Orthodoxy in contemporaneous cultural terms. The most influential among them were

Khomyakov and Dostoevski. A related school of Russian religious philosophy comprises in more recent times men like Vladimir Solovev and Nicolas Berdyaev.

World War I produced radical changes in Orthodox lands, and consequently in the status of Orthodox churches. Perhaps the most disastrous religious upheaval occurred in Russia. The Soviet regime, as early as January, 1918, published the fundamental legislation separating the church from the state and the school. Although theoretically liberty of conscience was granted (but even this provision was vitiated by forbidding all under eighteen years of age to receive group religious instruction), the intention of the government was plainly directed toward the liquidation of all religion altogether. This hidden motive became explicit in 1929, when the Constitution of the R.S.F.S.R. was amended. In the words of Article IV, "liberty of religious confession and of anti-religious propaganda is granted to all citizens." Thus only the forces opposed to religion were granted the right to propagate their views openly, by numerous state-supported publications, by the organization of atheistic centers and societies, by the teaching of atheism in the schools, and by every other means available. The churches, in the meantime, were restricted to bare religious services. Church members suffered innumerable forms of discrimination. The clergy were particularly subjected to fierce and fanatical persecution. A five-day week was adopted which made it immeasurably harder for the churches to hold Sunday services. Religious holidays were abolished.

In December, 1936, the new Constitution was issued. The provisions regarding religion were not changed. But the disfranchisement of the clergy was rescinded. The next year, however, the fiercest of the recurrent purges broke out. During this time religious persecution was resorted to again.

At last, in January, 1939, the New Religious Policy was adopted. Although the laws regarding religion were not greatly modified even to the present day, Soviet official agencies were directed to stop all attempts at liquidating religion. The seven-day week was restored. The chief antireligious publications were discontinued. Gradually, closed churches were reopened. Most significantly, in 1943 the government at last permitted the calling of a national Council for the election of patriarch. The acting-patriarch, Metropolitan Sergius, was then elected to the vacant patriarchal see, and in turn gave his blessing to the government. After his death, in 1944, a new Council was convened in January, 1945, and elected Metropolitan Alexei. The state once more exercises direct influence upon the churches by setting up, since 1943, two Councils: one for the Orthodox Church, the other for Religious Affairs in general. This setting apart of the Russian Orthodox Church from the other communions gives it a kind of preferred status. In the recent past, training of priesthood was permitted, and the teaching of religion to children was likewise allowed. The church is also given an opportunity to publish literature.

Greek

To return now to the other Orthodox churches: as has already been mentioned, the rise of Orthodox churches independent of the direct authority of the ecumenical patriarch was conditional upon the political independence of the people involved. Thus, to begin with the Church of Greece, its establishment in modern times goes back to the year 1833, three years after the Greeks succeeded in gaining freedom from the Turks. But it was not until 1850 that the ecumenical patriarch acknowledged the Church as independent of his authority. Nevertheless, even though it gained freedom from the patriarch, it was still not free from the sway of the state. This condition has been particularly evident since the outbreak of the first World War. When, in 1917, Venizelos established a provisional pro-Allied government, he was anathematized by the Archbishop of Athens, Theocletos. When King Constantine was exiled and Venizelos became the head of the government, he promptly expelled the Archbishop, the King's tool, and secured the election of his friend, Metropolitan Meletios. But when the elections of 1920 went against Venizelos and King Constantine was restored, Archbishop Theocletos regained his see, while Meletios was expelled.

The close relationship existing between the church and the government was apparent even during the second World War. When in 1941 the Nazis ordered Archbishop Chrysanthos to induct into office the puppet government set up under their auspices, he refused. Thereupon he was promptly removed from office. Metropolitan Damaskinos succeeded him, despite his liberal record (which was not discovered by the Germans). And although he, on several occasions, defied the German masters, he escaped deposition. After the liberation of Greece, he was the only person sufficiently trusted by all parties to become the regent of Greece. No other Greek hierach had risen to such high political office before.

There are other Greek churches in the Near East, the most important of which are three ancient patriarchates—Constantinople, Alexandria and Jerusalem. The fourth, Antioch, is no longer a Greek see, the native Syriac element having secured control of it since 1899.

As for the patriarchate of Constantinople, the aftermath of the first World War inflicted upon it catastrophic calamities such as it had never suffered before. Mustapha Kemal Pasha, the leader of the nationalist Turks, having revolted against the supine policy of the Sultan, defeated King Constantine of Greece, who had invaded Asia Minor. Thereupon, he turned upon the ecumenical patriarch, Meletios, who had supported Constantine. He resolved upon the total destruction of the patriarchate, regarding it as the source of perpetual anti-Turkish intrigues. The British, at the Lausanne Conference in 1923, scarcely restrained Kemal from carrying out his bold resolve. In the end, the Turkish leader was persuaded to allow the patriarchate to exist, but stripped it of all functions except those of a strictly ecclesiastical character. Patriarch Meletios, however, had to go.

Moreover, the Lausanne Conference allowed Mustapha Kemal to expel forcibly all Greek population from Turkey, with the exception of the old Greek settlers in Constantinople and its environs. Asia Minor, that cradle of primitive Gentile Christianity, was now emptied, for the first time in nineteen centuries, of its Christian population. The once powerful ecumenical patriarchate was now reduced to almost insignificant proportions. The ecumenical patriarch still enjoys pre-eminence of honor, but his actual power is exceedingly limited.

Of the other two Greek patriarchates, Alexandria and Jerusalem, the latter is engaged in a fierce struggle for survival. Its power is menaced by the native Arabic element. The Brotherhood of the Holy Sepulchre, comprising some one hundred Greek monks, is trying to retain control over the overwhelmingly native membership of the church. The Alexandrian situation is not quite so acute, for the Greeks there possess a two-thirds majority.

Balkan

The other Balkan Orthodox churches have also experienced radical changes, particularly since the first World War. The largest of them is the Rumanian Orthodox Church. The Kingdom of Rumania, after the War, more than doubled its territory. The consolidated church, composed of the formerly separated units, was then raised to the rank of patriarchate—a dignity it had never before possessed. The first patriarch elevated to the new see was Metropolitan Miron Cristea. Since Rumania lost, in the second World War, some of the territories it had acquired in the first, its ecclesiastical structure will have to be adjusted accordingly. What conditions it will encounter under the dominant Soviet influence remains to be seen.

The Serbian Church has also expanded greatly as the result of the first World War. With the unification of the Serbians in the new Kingdom, the six formerly separated Serbian ecclesiastical bodies were unified in one Serbian Church. As befitting the new status, the ancient patriarchate of Pech was restored.

True to the tradition of a close co-operation between the church and the state, the Serbian patriarch, Gabriel (Gavrilo), a Montenegrin Serb elected to his office in 1937, was one of the leaders in the *coup d'état* which placed young King Peter II on the throne in order that he might repudiate the pact with Germany which had been negotiated, soon after the second World War broke out, by the regent, Prince Paul. When the Germans overran Yugoslavia in 1941, the patriarch was imprisoned and later compelled to go on foot and clad only in his shirt, all the way across the country from Montenegro to a monastery near Belgrade. Upon their evacuation of the country, the Germans transferred the brave patriarch to a concentration camp somewhere in Germany. But hitherto, no trace of him has been found.

The Bulgarian Orthodox Church has the distinction of being the only Orthodox communion the liberation of which from the authority of the ecumenical patriarch preceded the liberation of the country from the yoke of the Turks. But the struggle for religious independence, which succeeded in 1872 when the Turkish government granted it autonomy, over the vigorous opposition of the ecumenical patriarch, led to a schism with the Greek churches. The patriarch of Constantinople refused to recognize the newly created Bulgarian exarchate, and pronounced it schismatic. This strained relation has lasted until recently. But in 1945 it was at last terminated. Moreover, the metropolitan of Sophia, Stephan, was elected exarch of the Church (formerly the exarch had his official residence in Constantinople). There are indications that soon the Bulgarian Church will restore to life the ancient patriarchate of Ohrid.

There are a number of smaller Orthodox bodies in existence. Moreover, there exist in the East separated churches, many of which are very ancient. The most important among them are the Armenian and the Syrian churches.

The Eastern Orthodox churches form a loose federation. They are bound together by their common acceptance of the doctrinal pronouncements of the seven ecumenical councils, and of the conciliar regulations regarding polity (canons). But otherwise they are organized independently, and are free to govern themselves within the framework of the canons. The ecumenical patriarch enjoys the honors of a *primus inter pares*, but otherwise has no jurisdiction over the other independent communions. Accordingly, he is in no sense an Eastern "pope."

Orthodox theology

As for the doctrinal norms of the Eastern Orthodox churches, there exists no comprehensive, binding creed in the Western sense of that term. Only the creedal definitions of the seven ecumenical Councils held at periods ranging from A. D. 325 to 787 are regarded as dogmas, i.e., as essential to the Christian faith. The most authoritative of these dogmatic formularies is the Niceno-Constantinopolitan Creed, which Alexei Khomyakov, "the father of modern Russian theology," characterized as "a full and complete expression of the Orthodox faith." They consist of the doctrine of Incarnation—that God revealed Himself in a true human body, soul and spirit—the Trinitarian doctrine, asserting that the one divine substance is known to the human mind under three hypostases or aspects; and the doctrine of the two natures, divine and human, comprising the one person of Jesus Christ. Beyond this, the Eastern churches acknowledge as testimonies, defining the theological views of Orthodoxy as against the Roman Catholic and Protestant formulations, the decrees of the two synods of Jerusalem (1643 and 1672). Besides, certain catechisms are regarded by some national churches as authoritative doctrinal summaries, although none of them is equal in authority to the dogmas. It is in the catechisms that such doctrines as that of the Virgin Mary, the veneration of saints, and the transmutation of the eucharistic elements (but not transubstantiation) are taught.

There has arisen in Orthodoxy—particularly in the Russian Church—a progressive theological movement of great significance and promise. Beginning with Khomyakov in the middle of the last century, these theologians—mostly lay—formulated a modern interpretation of the traditional Eastern Orthodoxy which takes into account the entire philosophical and theological development of the West. Among the most distinguished figures in this movement are Feodor M. Dostoevski, the novelist, Vladimir S. Solovev, the philosopher, and Nicholas Berdyaev, also an outstanding figure among the present-day philosophers. The insight of these theologians is essential for a full appreciation of ecumenical Christianity, for their interpretation of the faith is a valuable corrective to the rationalism and Aristotelianism of much of Western theological thinking. At least, it cannot be asserted that Orthodoxy is "theologically stagnant."

Besides the theological reconstruction which is going on, there is likewise a demand for reform of canons. As early as 1918, an essay written by a hierarch of the Patriarchate of Constantinople, Gennadios, urged that the church adapt herself to modern conditions, and advocated the remarriage of the parochial priesthood (at present only one marriage, prior to ordination, is allowed), married episcopate (which would put an end to the monopoly which monks hold at present in respect to the episcopal office), amelioration of divorce regulations, popularization of the liturgy and modification of fasts. Patriarch Meletios in 1923 invited all Orthodox communions (the Bulgarian excepted) to a pan-Orthodox Congress, which would prepare the way for the Eighth Ecumenical Council (the Seventh was held in 787). But the other patriarchs refused to join in the call. As a result, the Congress turned out to be only inter-Orthodox. Nevertheless, several reforms were adopted, and actually put in practice, without waiting for their formal adoption by the projected Council. Thus a reformed calendar was adopted, which differs from the Gregorian so slightly that no discrepancy will occur until the year 2800. The synodical party within the Russian Church went so far as to introduce the married episcopate, although this measure was repudiated by the

Patriarchal party. The Council was to be called in 1925, but the hostile attitude of the Turkish government prevented the project from being carried out; the matter has been held in abeyance ever since.

The polity of the Orthodox churches comprises a large element of democratic procedure. Laymen are given a prominent place in the administration of the church, from the local congregations to the highest administrative councils. It is not surprising, in view of these various features which characterize the Eastern Orthodox churches, that these bodies should have found it possible to play an increasing part in the setting up of the organization of the World Council of Churches.

2. THE ROMAN CATHOLIC CHURCH

The Middle Ages have achieved a considerable degree of cultural unity, thanks largely to the unifying spiritual influence of the Church. The first breach of this unity was caused by the rise of the humanistic spirit which took the form of an interest in classical antiquity. This Renaissance movement was the true beginning of our modern secularism, which regards man, instead of God, as the measure of all things. Although at first its essential character was not always apparent, nevertheless, the Renaissance was at bottom secularistic, and thus fundamentally opposed to the God-centered consciousness of the Middle Ages. Rabelais wrote over the door of his Abbey of Theleme the significantly modern motto: "Do as you please!" St. Augustine's dictum is vastly different: "Love God and do as you please." These mottoes characterize the real difference between the Christian and the humanistic outlooks upon life. It was the former which became dominant in the modern period.

The Reformation certainly did not side with the Renaissance humanistic world view. It aimed mainly at correcting the abuses of the Church, rather than at subverting its essentially theocentric view of life. As has already been mentioned, Martin

Luther wished originally to purge the Church of its undoubted corruptions, to remove the abuses which for several centuries had been an offense to the spiritually-minded within the Church. But the Church judged otherwise, and cast him out. Nevertheless, the time was to come when it itself was to admit tacitly—never explicitly—that Luther was right in his criticism of the existing abuses; for it proceeded to put its own house in order.

Retrenchment and reform

Although the Catholic Church, at the Council of Trent, resolutely and explicitly repudiated the Protestant attempt at reform, and thus closed the doors upon any possibility of reconciliation entertained until then by Emperor Charles V, yet it undertook to reform itself in its own way. The action of the Council made the Protestant-Catholic schism permanent. For the aim of the papal policy was to define the Catholic dogma in such a way as to exclude the Protestant interpretation. Thus the Scriptures and tradition, both interpreted by the Church, not subject to private judgment, were declared to be the sources of religious authority, contrary to the Protestant principle of *sola Scriptura*. This decision affects the formulation of many doctrines. This is clearly seen in such a dogma as the Immaculate Conception of the Virgin Mary (1854), the bases of which are entirely extra-Scriptural, derived from tradition. Nor can it be said of this tradition that it had been held "from the beginning, everywhere, and by all." Moreover, the Vulgate version of the Bible was declared the authoritative text. The doctrine of justification by faith alone, in a sense not held by the Protestants, was solemnly anathematized, although quite a respectable minority in the Council defended the doctrine in a modified sense. With good will, an agreement with the Protestants on this doctrine was not impossible. The sacramental teaching of the Church, including the dogma of transubstantiation, adopted in 1215, was reaffirmed.

Besides, strict reform measures were adopted. Simony was

ordered eradicated; episcopal absenteeism forbidden: the lucrative dispensations curtailed. The Inquisition was greatly strengthened. The militant spirit of Ignatius Loyola now took possession of the Church. In its moral and spiritual earnestness, the post-Tridentine Church is vastly different from that of the age of Alexander III, Julius II and Leo X.

The reform of the Church was characterized by the zeal of Cardinal Carlo Borromeo, the Archbishop of Milan, as well as by the persuasive, gentle and thoroughly sane and wise piety of St. Francis de Sales, the Bishop of Geneva. The latter's *Introduction to a Devout Life* is a beautiful example of the best type of spiritual life which has always found expression in the lives of devout Catholics. The deep mystical insight of St. John of the Cross, or the practical goodness of St. Theresa of Avila, are likewise examples of the virility of the spiritual life produced by the Church.

But aside from this emphasis on the life of the spirit, another dominant interest of the Church was reasserted, particularly in such organizations as that of the Jesuit Order. The Catholic Church had long been committed to the view that in order to secure conditions favorable to religious life, it must dominate society. It is the old ideal of Pope Gregory VII which was most successfully realized by Pope Innocent III. In the period under consideration, the Jesuit Order was the most efficient embodiment of that policy. The Jesuits, first of all, took the lead in the efforts to stop the growth of Protestantism and to regain some of the lost territory. In this they were quite successful. Not only was the further expansion of the dreaded "heresy" arrested (except in the English colonies of North America), but much of the territory lost to the Protestants was regained. Notable examples of the former are to be found in France and Poland, and of the latter in Bohemia, where the population formerly over 90 per cent Protestant was, in the course of centuries, to a very large extent won back. The Jesuit policy was greatly aided by their effective educational system, which technically excelled the antiquated systems then prevailing. Also by securing the posts as father-confessors of many princes and other influential members of society was the Order able to exert a considerable degree of control in the political sphere.

Papal ascendancy

Through these and similar means, the ascendancy of the papacy was assured. The ultramontane policy of the centralization of all power in the hands of the papacy ultimately triumphed. This tendency has existed since the early centuries, but in the conciliar period (the fourteenth century onward) it received its most effective check. Since then the two theories—the ultramontane, asserting the supremacy of the papacy over the Church, and the conciliar, claiming that the General Councils are superior even to the popes—struggled for victory. In France, the conciliar theory became a part of the law of the land as early as the beginning of the sixteenth century, in the reign of Francis I. Louis XIV attempted to realize it, and thus to set up practically a national French Church, in his Gallican Liberties of 1684. Although he failed, the essential feature of his program, namely, the right of national sovereignty over ecclesiastical matters, was reaffirmed in the Civil Constitution of the Clergy passed by the Constituent Assembly in 1781. Similarly in Austria, under Emperor Joseph II, the principles of national sovereignty, known as Josephinism, were asserted.

Despite these attempts to oppose the ultramontane tendencies, in the end the victory lay with the papal policy. During the first half of the nineteenth century, when the principles of the French Revolution were everywhere combatted as dangerous, and when the Holy Alliance was imbued with the spirit of conservation and reaction, ultramontanism benefited thereby as the mainstay of stable order. The change of intellectual climate which expressed itself in the Romantic reaction to the aridities of the preceding period of Rationalism and Enlightenment, likewise proved favorable to Catholicism. No wonder that the long reign of Pope Pius IX (1846-78) witnessed the final victory of ultramontanism.

Papal victory culminated in the formal proclamation of the dogma of papal infallibility by the Vatican Council in 1870. But a practical assertion of this dogma had been successfully made by Pius IX as early as 1854, when he, on his own authority, had defined the dogma of the Immaculate Conception of the Virgin Mary. In fact, this act can hardly be understood on any other basis but as a test case in which the Pope had sought to ascertain the temper of the Church in regard to his assumption of the conciliar power of defining dogmas. Since the Church had accepted this definition without any effective demur, the decision made fourteen years later by the Vatican Council was a foregone conclusion. That act only ratified a *fait accompli*.

Accordingly in a certain true sense the papacy since 1870 has acted in a new role, hitherto implicitly and passively accepted by a considerable section of the Church, but never acknowledged as *de fide* until 1870. In spite of the loss of temporal sovereignty, the papacy of the new era never faltered in the prosecution of the agelong aims of its entire history. Its spirit is well character- ized in the Grand Inquisitor of Dostoevski's *The Brothers Kara- mazov*: sinful and weak humanity must be saved by force, even against its will! The goal of the modern papacy is still the domi- nation of society in the interests of religion—i.e., Roman Cathol- icism. For there is only one true religion. Pius IX in his *Syllabus of Errors* (1864) stated in clear language that Protestantism cannot be regarded as a different form of true Christianity. "Prot- estantism is not merely a different form of the same Christian faith in which God can be pleased as well as in the Catholic Church." The pontiffs since his time have repeatedly affirmed this stand in their official pronouncements. In his encyclical "*Immortale Dei*," Pope Leo XIII positively affirms, "It is not lawful for the state . . . to hold in equal favor different kinds of religion." Such views are "the same thing as atheism." As

Father Hughes summarizes this point in his work, *The Popes' New Order*:

> Religion is not . . . the mere individual sentiment in a particular citizen's mind. It is the *true* religion, i.e., that religion organized by Christ Our Lord in the Catholic Church, organized by God's will as a public society, therefore, with its hierarchy of officials, one of them "the head of all, the chief and unerring teacher of truth."

Church and State

Accordingly, in its relation to the state, the Church has supreme authority in matters spiritual, while the state is equally endowed by God with power over matters temporal. As Leo XIII has formulated the view, Christ gave the Church "unrestrained authority in regard to things sacred . . . with the power of making laws, as also with the twofold right of judging and of punishing, which flows from that power." It is the duty of the state not only to acknowledge the Church as possessing the exclusive authority and jurisdiction in the spiritual realm, but also to protect it in the exercise of these rights. Consequently, the principles of modern democratic government such as the granting of liberty of conscience, the separation of church and state, freedom of speech and press, are necessarily denied. Therefore, Pius X rejected on principle the French law of 1905, separating the Church and state, and his successors have similarly repudiated like legislation, wherever it was passed. Soviet Russia, Mexico and Spain are examples of this practice.

Not only has the Church claimed the right to exercise jurisdiction in matters spiritual, but the papacy tenaciously insisted that the performance of its spiritual functions necessitates the possession of temporal sovereignty. Although much evidence could be presented in support of the thesis that the loss of the temporal possessions was beneficial to the papacy, which had regained much prestige and influence during its self-imposed "imprisonment" in the Vatican, yet the papacy relentlessly pursued a policy of demanding the restoration of its temporal sovereignty. Leo XIII terminated the *"Kulturkampf"* in Germany, hoping thus to secure the support of the Kaiser in behalf of the restorationist policy. When disappointed in that hope, he turned toward France. But finally Pius XI became convinced that the restoration of the *status ante* was impossible. Thereupon he decided to accept Premier Mussolini's offer of the recognition of the principle of sovereignty, even though he had to be satisfied with a mere token of territorial restitution. The Lateran Pact of 1929 recognized the Vatican City as a sovereign state, with the right of political representation, an army, telegraph and telephone services, and other appurtenances of sovereignty. The Pope himself stressed these gains as essential:

> A true and proper and real territorial sovereignty
> . . . [is] a status which is self-evidently necessary and due
> to One who, in virtue of His divine mandate and divine
> representation with which he is invested, is unable to be
> subject to any sovereignty on Earth.

Education and ideologies

Another of the persistent claims which the Catholic Church makes under all conditions and circumstances is to the education of Catholic children in Catholic schools. All concordats negotiated by the Vatican stress this feature. Any infringement of this very important right leads to conflict. It was because of such an infringement by Nazi Germany and Fascist Italy— despite the Concordats—that Pius XI denounced these measures as constituting flagrant violations of the rights of the Church. And they did.

Furthermore, since modern political, economic and cultural philosophies are in conflict with the Catholic views on these matters, the Church found itself in opposition to them. This is the reason why as early as in the pontificate of Pius IX, that pontiff found it necessary to denounce both the positivist trends of the reigning philosophies, and socialism, communism and the

liberal movements in general. The *Syllabus of Errors* declares
that "the pontiff neither can be, nor ought to be, reconciled
with progress, liberalism, and modern civilization." Feeling the
need for a more positive directive as to the official teachings of
the Church, Pope Leo XIII elevated the system of Thomas
Aquinas to the position of normative theology. It was the same
fear of the "acids of modernity" which inspired Leo's successor,
Pope Pius X, to expel all traces of modernism from the Church.
This he accomplished, although in doing so he had to excom-
municate such devout and loyal Catholics as Alfred Loisy and
Father George Tyrrell. That modern saint, Baron Friedrich von
Hügel, escaped a like condemnation only because of his discreet-
ness and his lay status. The same spirit animates the Church in
the present-day opposition to the wholly secularized and often
atheistic theories of communism.

Church and politics

Since Roman Catholicism is committed to the theory of the
necessity of dominating society in the interests of religion, the
Church finds it necessary to participate in the political sphere.
Obviously, since the secularized democratic forces have been
combatting the conservative, and even reactionary, forces for
power in modern states, the Church, which judges the respective
programs solely as to what benefits are offered it by the con-
testants, often sides with the latter. This accounts for what
appears to the outside observer as at best political opportunism.
As an illustration, one may cite the divergent policies of the
Church in America and England, as compared with Spain and
Slovakia. But the ultimate criterion for the Church is not some
abstract loyalty to one or another form of government or political
theory, but only the best advantage of the Church.

Doctrine

A doctrinal summary of Roman Catholicism, particularly of
the points of disagreement between it and Protestantism, may

prove useful for a clearer understanding of the two communions. The concept of the church is central. The Roman Catholic Church is not one among many other true Christian churches, but the only true Church. She is the body of Christ on earth. Christ himself endowed her, through Peter and his successors, the popes, with authority to rule all the faithful the world over; to dispense the sacraments which are channels of supernatural grace; and to guard the purity of truth which is contained not only in the Scriptures, but also in the tradition in her keeping. Accordingly, outside the Church there is no salvation, because there is no fullness of truth, or of sacramental grace, or of divine authorization to govern. The Church has for its mission the salvation of fallen humanity and the restoration in God of the "reconciled world." For this task it is necessary that men accept the true doctrine. This, according to Thomas Aquinas, consists not only of "revealed" truths, but first of all of "natural" truths which may be attained by all intelligent human beings. These latter consist of religious knowledge derived from sense-perceptions and reason. Such, for instance, are the existence of God, His attributes, His work of creation, man, ethics and political and social organizations of human society. The "revealed theology," resting not on knowledge but on faith, since it is based on truths which are above reason but not contrary to reason, consists of such doctrines as the Trinity, the Incarnation, original sin, the sacramental grace and eschatology.

The sacraments are particularly stressed, since they are the visible symbols, or rather channels, of invisible grace. They do not depend for their efficacy either upon the character of the officiating priest, or upon the spiritual preparation of the recipient, but "sanctify through themselves," or in technical language, "*ex opere operato*." Therefore they are infallibly efficacious, provided they are properly administered. Thus it is obvious that the Roman Catholic Church must claim exclusiveness for herself, particularly when one considers in this connection the dogma of papal infallibility and supreme authority.

Because of the exceedingly unsettled political situation of the world, and the consequent uncertainty as to the future church and state relationships, it would be hazardous to venture an opinion regarding the future of the various component parts of Christendom. It may, however, be affirmed without any fear of successful contradiction that Christianity has proved itself a stable and essential force in the world. It has been subjected to persecutions such as it had not experienced since the pre-Constantinian or Moslem periods, and withstood the test. In fact, it has often been the only force which dared to challenge the otherwise victorious antireligious governments in such countries as the Soviet Union and Germany. Nor can a better future world be built except on the principles, and by the transforming power, of Christianity. For there can be no better world without better men and women.

2

THE ECUMENICAL GOAL

Part I. *The Biblical and Theological Bases for the Ecumenical Goal*

John A. Mackay

1. What is the ecumenical goal? The meaning of "ecumenical"; false concepts of ecumenical unity; the true concept of the ecumenical goal.   2. The theological basis of the ecumenical goal: the Church is the New Israel; the Church is the Body of Christ. 3. Theological guidance for the ecumenical movement.

1. WHAT IS THE ECUMENICAL GOAL?

What do some Christians in our time mean when they speak about ecumenical unity and the pursuit of an ecumenical goal? It is important that we have a clear understanding as to what they mean and do not mean. The whole concept of ecumenicity, so-called, calls for clarification.

The ecumenical goal means something much more specific than the influence of Christian principles throughout the world. It is to be clearly distinguished from anything which might be called Christian civilization. It is nothing less than the fulfillment by the Christian Church of its total task, on a world front, in the spirit of Christian unity. Ecumenical unity means church unity within a world context. As there is but one Church of Jesus Christ, that Church cannot undertake its full task nor fulfill its true destiny unless unity marks the relations between its members. Ecumenical Christians of today take up afresh the aspiration of the Protestant Reformers at the famous Diet of Spires who affirmed that they looked forward to the next "free General Council of Holy Christendom."

The meaning of "ecumenical"

But what is meant by "ecumenical," by "ecumenical" movement, "ecumenical" Church? The term "ecumenical" is not new, but in recent years it has taken on a new significance both in the language of secular culture and in the language of religion. At the first dawning of the era of global unity, when the airplane and the radio were beginning to unite the world, making all men neighbors by transcending space, and all men contemporaries by transcending time, the German philosopher Keyserling began to speak of an "ecumenical era" and an "ecumenical organism." We have entered, he said, a time when any major happening in the world affects the whole world, when any major stimulus applied to the body of mankind in any representative part affects the entire body.

In the sphere of religion the term "ecumenical" had hitherto been confined almost exclusively to the early Ecumenical Councils of the Christian Church, that is to say, to the councils that were held when the Church was still undivided. It would seem that the usage which has recently become current in the religious language of non-Roman Christianity dates from the Oxford Conference of 1937 on Church, Community, and State. In the Report of the Commission on the Universal Church and the World of Nations, the term "ecumenical" was used as a synonym of the term "universal." Its etymology is both stimulating and instructive. The term comes from the Greek word for "dwelling," *oikos*. In classical Greek *he oikoumene* meant "the inhabited earth"; but the Greeks, having the greatest disdain for all people who dwelt outside the bounds of Greek culture, confined the designation to the Greek world, as the only part of the world that was *really* inhabited. For the Romans *he oikoumene* was co-extensive with the bounds of the Roman Empire, so that the Emperor was called *ho oikoumenikos*, "the ruler of the inhabited world." It is interesting to find that in the Gospel of Luke (2:1) the term *he oikoumene* is used. The Evangelist remarks that orders had been given by Caesar Augustus that "the whole world," literally the "whole inhabited earth," should be taxed.

When the term "ecumenical" is studied in its classical and Biblical context the aspirations of non-Roman Christianity in our time become vivid and meaningful. The ecumenical movement is a movement towards Christian solidarity in life and work throughout the inhabited globe, that is to say, wherever Christians live and move and have their being upon this earth. The pursuit of the ecumenical goal has, in recent years, given birth to a new science, the science of Ecumenics. This science might be defined as the study of the Church Universal, its nature, its functions, its relations, and its strategy.

False concepts of ecumenical unity

It is very necessary to distinguish the concept of ecumenical unity from certain related concepts with which it is sometimes confused.

(1) Ecumenical unity does not mean the achievement of world community. World community is a secular concept which connotes harmonious human relations across the boundaries of nation, race and clan. In the secular order there is no higher goal to be pursued than world community. It must ever constitute the ultimate objective of statesmanship. Ecumenical unity or community, on the other hand, is something totally different. It means harmonious relations between Christian churches, denominations and groups. While it is true that nothing will make a greater contribution to world community than a world Church,

the possibility must also be contemplated that a world Church, a Church united in Jesus Christ with a membership in every part of the inhabited globe, might find itself in a very hostile world. In fact, there is something everlastingly hostile in the secular world order to the spirit that informs the Christian Church. It is equally a fact of history that there is no way in which Christians can make a greater contribution to world order than by promoting church order, that is to say, in seeing to it that the Christian churches form a unity in the truth and a worthy instrument in the hands of God for the blessing of the nations.

(2) It is no less important to remember that ecumenical unity does not mean the prudential reunion of unreconciled churches. While Christian unity is a most desirable goal, and while it is true that the Christian Church can never be what God intended it to be until the relations between all Christian groups are harmonious, Christians must resolutely set themselves against the union, or reunion, of ecclesiastical groups for purposes of pure expediency. Christian unity must be unity in the truth or it is not true unity. Those who unite must share the same basic outlook upon God and life. They must be moved by a common aspiration to give a united expression to their corporate life, in loyalty to their Saviour and Lord. It is, of course, true, that providential pressures which Christians encounter in special political situations and in challenging frontier conditions in urban or rural life tend and should tend to produce church unity. Unity becomes real and ecumenical only when such external pressures or challenges lead Christians to consider afresh their common faith and their obligation to be one.

Nothing is more painful to witness, nor can anything be more dishonoring to the true concept of ecumenical unity, than church unions which are consummated because the parties concerned have ceased to believe that there are any ultimate values in religious thought or practice. That being so, they find no valid reason why they should not merge their mutual vacuity. In no scheme for church unity should the basic differences between Christian groups be ignored. It would be much better that union be postponed until their differences have been frankly faced. The projected union would then be consummated, not by compromising things that are true, but by transcending things that are minor.

(3) Equally antagonistic to the true spirit of ecumenical unity is the tendency which has appeared in some ecclesiastical circles to elevate questions of order, that is to say, questions relating to church organization or to hierarchical distinctions between Christian ministers, into questions of faith. This is what is done by the distinguished poet, T. S. Eliot, in his recent article, "Reunion by Destruction," in which he violently attacks the famous South India scheme of church union. Speaking as a High Churchman, Eliot proclaims that were this particular project of church reunion to become a reality, it would mean the destruction of the Church of England. With sardonic sarcasm he describes the proposed union of Christian churches in South India, which many Christians have come to regard as the harbinger of a new day in ecumenical relations, as an "elaborate artifice," a "pantomime horse," an "amiable masquerade." While no true Christian should be interested in the slightest degree in any kind of church union which does not take the Christian religion seriously, and while he should repudiate with all his heart any trend toward a watery undenominationalism, the attitude represented by Mr. Eliot must be indicted as an assault upon the spiritual inwardness of the Body of Christ.

(4) Still more false is that concept of ecumenical unity which would regard the ecumenical goal as the submission of Christians throughout the world to a supreme hierarch. What the Roman Catholic Church means by ecumenical unity is the submission of all non-Roman Christians to the church which claims to be, in institutional terms, the one true and only Christian Church. For the great Roman communion the essence of the Church is organization. To all intents and purposes, the organization is

the vicegerent of God upon earth. All relations, therefore, between men and Deity must be mediated through the hierarchically constituted organization.

It ought to be stated with all frankness and clarity that there never should be and never can be an expression of ecumenical unity whose consummation would involve the acceptance of the Roman pretension. For this pretension involves three major aberrations from the Christian religion. It involves a gulf between priests and people; a gulf between the episcopate and the Pope; a gulf between a church which claims to be the whole Church, thus making itself schismatic, and churches which have striven to be faithful to Jesus Christ and have experienced his grace while not presuming, any one of them, to represent the one and only Church. It is not inappropriate, at this point, to express the personal conviction that as a result of the position formulated by the Roman Catholic Church at the famous Council of Trent, that Church became something different in its inmost nature from the historic Christian Church.

The true concept of the ecumenical goal

If the supreme aspiration of Christians should be ecumenical unity in faith, in life, in work; if false concepts of unity should be assiduously avoided, what is it that constitutes the true ecumenical goal? The goal of true Christian aspiration within history must ever be: concrete corporate allegiance to Jesus Christ.

What does it mean for Christian churches to give unqualified corporate allegiance to Jesus Christ? It means, to begin with, to take seriously the Utrecht formula of 1938 which laid the foundation of the World Council of Churches soon to be constituted, namely, to accept Jesus Christ as "God and Savior." It means to commit themselves to Him who by His historical life showed us what God is and what man through Him can become; who as the crucified Redeemer died for human sin; who as the risen and living Lord is Head of the Church and supreme Lord of history. It means to dedicate themselves to the cause for which Christ died and lives, namely, to "make disciples of all nations." It means to manifest "the mind of Christ" in every expression, personal and social, of Christian thought and life.

Such allegiance can be expressed only in corporate terms. At no time was the Christian movement in the world a collection of spiritual atoms. Christianity broke upon the world as a fellowship. The Church is inherent in the Christian religion and is an integral part of the Gospel. For the Church, therefore, "to be the Church" means that it must express itself in every aspect of its witness in a way worthy of what it is essentially in Christ. It is the contemporary task of the Church of the world to express in universal or ecumenical terms two supreme objectives: Christ's redemptive passion for all men, and His concern formulated in the commandment which He added to the Decalogue, that His followers should "love one another."

2. THE THEOLOGICAL BASIS OF THE ECUMENICAL TASK

An important question now arises. What is our ground for believing that this whole concept of ecumenical unity is not a romantic ideal, a fond aspiration projected into the future, an unrealizable dream not grounded in the realities of human nature or in the central trends of human history? What is there which can give Christians the intelligent certainty that the Church and its world mission belong to the very nature of spiritual reality? How shall Christians be led to take the Church and the ecumenical movement as seriously as Marxist communists take the party and its program, firmly believing that the cosmic hour has struck for the manifestation of the world's proletariat? Here we raise a theological question, a question concerning the nature and status of the Christian Church in relation to God and His purpose. The prevailing intellectual confusion in our time, both in the Church and in the secular order, coupled with the deep craving for authority and the desire to understand the meaning of faith, are producing a return to Christian theology. This circumstance is one of the most encouraging features of our intellectual climate today.

There is but one source where an authoritative understanding of the meaning and future of the Christian Church can be obtained. That source is the Bible, which is the record of God's self-disclosure for the redemption of mankind. It is vain and fruitless to approach the study of the Church in merely sociological terms, as if the Church were no more than an institution of society like all other institutions. It is true that the Church as an institution is subject to the relativities and contingencies of history, but it is not merely a social institution. It is equally futile to find the presuppositions for a theology of the Church in philosophy. While the Church expresses the highest reason, and is, when properly understood, the most reasonable of all institutions, its reality is not grounded in the purely rational. Too often the Church has submitted to the patronage of reason, which has fitted it into some rational scheme of the universe, and made it subordinate, as in the great Hegelian system of philosophy, to a world view in which the State, not the Church, was the supreme spiritual reality. In the words of Hegel, "While the gates of Hell have not prevailed against the Christian Church, the gates of reason have." At a time when the Christian Church faces a world in which a unifying world view is lacking and deeper rifts exist than at any previous time in history, nothing is more important than that the Church should become fully self-conscious of her true nature and destiny within the context of God's redemptive scheme of things. This means that all who would understand the Church and shape her future must become Biblically minded and seek in the Biblical records the clew to the Church's meaning and the goal of the Church's destiny.

Creative study of the Bible in quest of the meaning of the Church and its ecumenical goal must conform to a basic principle. The Bible must be studied in terms of the categories that are native to itself. It must be studied, that is to say, in terms of the very structure of Biblical thought and not in terms of concepts projected into the study of the Bible from philosophical systems or world views which involve an outlook upon God and human life totally different from the outlook of the Biblical world view. The categories of a naturalistic world view, for example, which has no place for a transcendent God and the supernatural, and which does not take seriously the great fact of sin and man's consequent need of redemption, cannot supply principles of interpretation for a true theology of the Church.

When we approach the Bible in terms of its own native concepts and principles we discover that the Gospel, the "good news" of God's approach to man in the interests of man's salvation, constitutes the core of the Bible and the clew to its understanding. We discover, moreover, that the supreme permanent expression of the Gospel in history is the Church. The Christian Church is a witness to the Gospel in a double sense. It is a creation of the Gospel and it exists in the world to bear witness to the full implications of the Gospel. Viewing the Church in this light, two things can be said regarding it which have a profound bearing upon the ecumenical goal: The Church is the New Israel; the Church is the Body of Christ. Examining the meaning of these two affirmations we shall discover how a true ecumenicity is inherent in the very nature of the Christian Church.

The Church is the New Israel

The Hebrew people were, in a unique sense, the people of God. This small and insignificant race, living at the crossroads of empire, in a small territory on the eastern seaboard of the Mediterranean Sea, was used by God for His redemptive self-disclosure to mankind. When the history of Israel is studied in the light of the Hebrew prophets, who were its great and inspired interpreters, three great moments in the national history of this people take on special significance. There was first the Redemption from Egypt whereby God manifested His power to deliver the children of Abraham from thralldom to the Pharaohs and to constitute them a separate people. Then came Israel's consecration whereby the people entered into covenant with God. The concept of the Covenant between God and Israel, by which God became the God of Israel and Israel became the people of God, is the central category in Old Testament history and the key to understanding Israel's religion. There is also the inheritance, the promised land of Canaan in which, after its conquest, the Hebrews were to enjoy peace and prosperity, provided they remained loyal to God's Covenant and eschewed all idolatry. But, alas, Israel's native tendency toward idol worship brought doom to the nation. A rift ensued in national unity. This was followed by the separation of a large section of the people from the soil. First, ten tribes were dispersed among the nations, and then Judah and Benjamin became exiles in Babylon.

Israel's great prophets found two things that were deeply significant in the history of their people: the national unity of Israel and the world mission of Israel.

The unity of Israel was a religious unity, a unity in God. The people of God's election were required to manifest that kind of unity in life and purpose which was in keeping with the Divine mandate that the chosen people should follow a prescribed course of behavior, both in their relations to God and in their relations to one another. The interesting and important thing is, however, that Israel was never allowed to believe, either that its election was based upon special racial virtue or goodness, or that its unity and prosperity would be contingent upon its own wisdom or might. National unity had its source in God. It could only be maintained through loyalty to God, whose ultimate purpose it was that the unity of Israel should become a rallying point for the spiritual unity of mankind. There is no deeper thought in the Old Testament than this: it was God's purpose that Israel, united in loyalty to Him, should become a means of blessing to the whole world. In this way the nations of mankind would become one through their devotion to the God of Israel, who was also the God of the whole earth.

Among the many glowing visions in the Hebrew Scriptures which set forth Israel's mission to the world, none combines purer poetry and truer prophecy than the 87th Psalm. In this matchless poem God's purpose of creating a world community upon the basis of Israel is set forth in glowing and moving imagery. Interpreting the affirmation, "Glorious things are spoken of thee, O City of God," the God of Israel is represented as standing upon the rock of Zion with a census roll in His hand. He begins to enfranchise the nations. He first writes in his roll the names of citizens of Egypt and Babylon; citizens of the nation where Israel in bondage made bricks without clay by the banks of the Nile, and citizens of the land in which Hebrew exiles hung their harps upon the willows of the Euphrates. God next looks toward the plains of rural Philistia. In His census book He inscribes the representatives of a sturdy warrior race which had lived in constant conflict with the sons of Jacob. Then follow children of Tyre, the seat of a great commercial and industrial civilization. Last of all are enfranchised the dark children of Ethiopia, members of a primitive race living in the high uplands of Africa. The prophetic meaning is clear. Jerusalem, the Holy City, will yet have spiritual significance for all mankind. Representatives of all races will belong to the spiritual kingdom whose seat is Zion. The new world community will be formed by the representatives of earth's mighty empires, the representatives of a simple rural culture, the representatives of commercial and industrial civilizations, and the representatives of the colored peoples of the world. Then would be fulfilled the promise to Abraham, "In thee and in thy seed shall all the families of the earth be blessed."

In the thought of the New Testament, the Christian Church takes over the role of Israel in the basic and key aspects of Israel's historical existence. The Church is the community of the redeemed. It is the community of those whom God has consecrated by a "new covenant," according to which the Divine law is written in the heart of the redeemed person, while allegiance to God is no longer an allegiance to an external law, but the expression of a spiritual inwardness, the manifestation of a redeemed nature. The Church's inheritance is the whole world of the spirit, a new world of reality which the Holy Spirit creates in personal life and corporate relations. The Holy Spirit Himself is the supreme inheritance of the individual Christian, and especially of the redeemed community. The Spirit leads the community into the increasing conquest of new areas of truth and to the domination of the forces of evil which prevent the full Lordship of Jesus Christ in communal life.

It is the function of the Church, as the New Israel, to be a blessing to the nations and to be the rallying center for a new kind of unity among mankind. The Church is charged with the task of "making disciples of all nations." The new community shall become coextensive with the inhabited earth. Everything that is most truly human in individual and corporate living reaches its highest fulfillment in the world community of the redeemed, whose supreme function it is to see to it that all things are summed up in Jesus Christ, who is both the source and the goal of the Church's unity.

The Christian Church is the Body of Christ

The Church as the new Israel expresses the continuity of the Divine purpose in history, which unfolds in the "fullness of time" and gives birth to a community with a world mission. The Church, as the Body of Christ, expresses the continuity of this community with the historical life and witness of Jesus Christ and its permanent relationship to Him as the Risen Lord. The Figure of the Church as a *body* is the third of three great New Testament figures, each one of which sets forth an important aspect of the Church's reality and role in history. By the figure of a *temple*, built upon the foundation of the Apostles and Prophets, in which Jesus Christ Himself is the chief cornerstone, the truth is set forth that the Christian Church is continuous with the two most important groups of people in human history, the Prophets of Israel, and the Apostles of Christ, while the structure owes its strength and unity to its relationship to Jesus Christ Himself who is history's center and history's Lord. By the figure of a *bride*, who prepares herself for spiritual nuptials at the coming of her Divine lover, the truth is affirmed that the historical existence of the Church will have a glorious consummation. Its full meaning will be unveiled at history's close, in the eventual fulfillment of God's purpose through the Church. This figure directs the gaze of Christians to the future and to the eschatological meaning of the Divine society. The figure of the *body*, on the other hand, is the appropriate figure to express the reality of the Church militant between the times, between its founding in the apostolic era and its consummation in a mystical marriage at history's close. The *body* is the figure which sets forth the reality of the Church as the corporate continuation in history of the incarnation of Jesus Christ, who continues in a very real sense in "the Church which is His body." We must beware, of course, of taking the metaphor of the body and turning it into an allegory. At the same time, the New Testament makes clear that we are justified in regarding the Christian Church as the visible, corporate expression of the living Christ, to whom it owes its reality, whose it is and whom it serves, and whose redemptive purpose must continue to be manifested in the unity of the Church. If the figure of the "body" has any meaning at all, it means that the Church's supreme task is to be in very truth the Body of Christ, in its conscious, active life, responding utterly to the will of Christ, drawing its strength from Him, and in all its relations fulfilling the new commandment of Christ to "love one another."

Being the Body of Christ, the Christian Church is an organism and not merely a society. It came to the birth as a fellowship, made up of people who were born into the community because of a common experience of renewal. Unlike the membership of a lodge or fraternal organization, the Church is not merely a group of people who have decided to band together. As a living organism, the Christian Church owes its very being to the quality of its response to Jesus Christ who is its head. To Him the Church must respond with all its soul, its strength, and its mind. This response must be absolute and totalitarian, if the organism is to be truly unified and function as an effective instrument of the will of Christ.

The response of the heart to Jesus Christ is supremely expressed in worship. The Church as the Body of Christ is bereft of true meaning unless professing Christians are willing to worship God together in praise and prayer, through the Word and the Sacraments. The Body of Christ is tragically wounded when those who profess to love Him refuse to worship Him together, especially when they refuse to express their love and faith and oneness in their Lord in the holy communion.

The response of the mind to Jesus Christ finds its highest expression in Christian theology. An ecumenical theology, that is to say, a theology in which the whole Church of Christ shall express its insight into Him, its experiences of Him, and the implications of its devotion to Him, is the theology to which the Christian Church as the Body of Christ must look forward, and for which it must work incessantly.

The response of the will to Jesus Christ involves an instrumental view of the Church's reality. The Church exists to serve Christ, to be the organ of His will in history, the chief agent for the coming of God's kingdom among men. If this is so, the closest solidarity is required among all Christians in order that they may make a common approach to the problems that confront the Church in the world. Unity is thus an attribute of the whole Church of Christ. Unity in worship, unity in doctrine, unity in life and action are necessary if the Christian Church is to be truly Christ's Body in history, carrying forward, to a glorious consummation, all the implications of God's purpose in Israel and in Jesus Christ.

In closing this section upon the theological basis of ecumenical unity two observations are appropriate. The first is this: Christian unity is, above all else, a unity in the Spirit. Instead of being a unity of order, it is a unity of faith and love and work. Questions of order and organization in the Christian Church must always be secondary to questions of faith and love and work. Biblical theology, and particularly the New Testament view of the Church, do not sanction, in any way, the ideal of a single world organization as being the most expressive visible unity of the Christian Church. A true and effective world Christian community does not necessarily involve a single organizational form.

The second observation is this: The book of the Bible which contains above all others the charter of the ecumenical Church is Paul's Letter to the Ephesians. This great document of Holy Scripture is the most relevant of all the Biblical records to the present situation of the Christian Church in the world. The Epistle to the Ephesians is not only the supreme compendium of Christian truth, it is theology set to music. It is also the Church's first great liturgy, in which heart and mind combine to praise God whose eternal purpose brought together Jesus Christ and the Church. This letter likewise sets forth the kind of life and activity which ought to mark Christian unity in action. The ecumenical goal will be advanced and ecumenical unity will become real in the measure in which the Epistle to the Ephesians inspires the thinking and the living of the Christian Church in our time.

3. THEOLOGICAL GUIDANCE FOR THE ECUMENICAL MOVEMENT

The greatest and most significant movement in contemporary life, that is, the movement toward Christian unity, must be saved from everything which in the remotest degree approaches sentimentality or expediency. If this is to be the case, its life and policies must be carried forward increasingly under the guidance of sound theological insights. We venture to formulate four principles which it is important for the ecumenical movement to observe as it moves towards its goal.

(1) *Let the ecumenical movement become more Biblically minded.* The Church must listen more and more to the Word of God as He speaks to her through the personalities, the episodes, the words of Holy Scripture. The Bible is the supreme medium through which God addresses Himself to men. The more it is studied after the Spirit, and not merely after the letter, the more unity will be manifested in the Church of Christ. The significance of the Bible as a document of the Church Universal has elsewhere been expressed by the writer:

> The Bible is more than a repository of great literature and of high religion; more than the source book of revealed truth; it is above all else *the supreme medium of divine-human intercourse.* This view of the Bible stands closest to the pristine Christian tradition, and is that which is representative of Protestant Christianity at its best. In the Bible we have more than an account of God's self-disclosure in word and deed. Here God speaks directly to men today in all the complexity of their need, in all the phases and aberrations of their human situation.[1]

(2) *Let the ecumenical movement in the United States recognize that the "sect" type, rather than the "church" type, has been predominant in American religious history.* In a recent article entitled "The Ecumenical Issue in the United States,"[2] Professor Reinhold Niebuhr analyzes the conditions of church life in our country at the present time. He observes that "many of the debates of the great world conferences, dealing with the problem of the reunion of the Churches on a world scale, seem quite irrelevant to the American scene." The reason for this lack of vital interest in the ecumenical issue, he writes, is "the fact that

[1] *Theology Today,* October, 1944, p. 291.
[2] *Theology Today,* January, 1946, pp. 525-536.

American Churches are historically and predominately under the influence of the 'sect' idea of the Church or the 'sect' protest against the order, the liturgy, and the theology of the Church." This means that, in general, "sectarian Christianity is . . . more conscious of the corruptions of the order of the Church, of its theology and its liturgy than it is appreciative of them as means of grace." What are the implications of these words in terms of effective Christian statesmanship?

The Protestant Reformation must be taken seriously in every effort to achieve Christian unity. Certain truths were given classical formulation by the great Reformers and constitute a permanent part of the Church's heritage of faith. Forms of Christian living and ranges of Christian piety have been expressed in the post-Reformation era which are also permanent aspects of the Christian heritage. While we rejoice that the centrifugal movement in organized Christianity which began to manifest itself at the Reformation is, in God's good providence, being transformed in our time into a centripetal movement towards unity in faith and practice and devotion, it cannot be affirmed that the denominational history of Protestant Christianity has fulfilled no Divine purpose. In the promotion of the ecumenical movement, should any attempt be made to make that particular conception of order which is associated with the catholic view of the Church the ecclesiastical norm for all Christians, the ecumenical movement can easily be wrecked. Any attempt, moreover, on the part of those members of the Body of Christ who feel that they belong more truly to classical Protestantism to rule out from membership in the projected World Council of Churches certain "sectarian" groups which are evangelically loyal could lead to equally disastrous results. All Christian denominations which acknowledge Christ as God and Saviour and which manifest institutional validity and historical continuity have the right, however small their numbers may be, to fellowship within the ecumenical unity of the Christian Church.

(3) *Let each Christian tradition and denomination rediscover its soul and its mission.* It is a sobering fact that the Christian religion should be represented today by three major traditions: the Protestant, the Roman Catholic and the Eastern Orthodox, and by a great variety of denominations of which there are two hundred and fifty-six in the United States alone. The moment has now come, however, when the three great Christian traditions and the many denominations by which Christianity is expressed in our time, should each one face itself. While it is a tragic fact, from the viewpoint of Christian unity and the mind of Christ regarding His Church, that His Body should be thus broken, so rifled by schism and so lacking in co-ordination, it is not necessary to suppose that all this diversification has been a complete evil and has contributed nothing to the understanding and progress of the Christian religion. There is rather ground for affirming that in the sovereign, overruling purpose of God, the very diversified expression of the Christian Church has contributed something, both to our understanding of Christ and to the vigorous propagation of the Christian religion. It should always be borne in mind that wherever Christianity has been represented by a single ecclesiastical expression, that expression has tended to become a very static and eventually unspiritual form of Christianity. Let each Christian tradition and denomination become concerned to know itself. Let there be no evasion or flight from self scrutiny. Let each one examine itself and its record in the light of God's self-disclosure of Himself, in the light of the Biblical concept of the Church of Christ, in the light of Christian history in general, and also in the light of the needs of the Church and the world at the present hour. Let it then, in deep penitence, seek grace to repudiate and slough off whatever in its heritage has been unworthy. Let it, on the other hand, bring into the ecumenical unity of the Church of Christ that which it has been or done which is clearly of divine origin and designed by God

to constitute the special witness of that group to Christian faith or Christian living.

(4) *Let us strive after evangelical catholicity.* By the evangelical catholicity of the Christian Church we mean that form of universality which has the Gospel and the spirit of the Gospel at the heart of it. The kind of Christian unity which we should strive after is a unity which shall take seriously the sovereign Lordship of Jesus Christ and the sovereign working of the Holy Spirit. Wherever Christ is, there is the Church (*Ubi Christus, ibi ecclesia*). Wherever the graces of the Spirit are made manifest in the individual or corporate life of Christian believers, the Spirit of God is present as a token that such people are within the bounds of the Christian Church. Christ alone, through the workings of the Spirit, can set the bounds of His Church, just as He alone can rear and inform its true structure. The important thing, therefore, is that Christians should become united in that allegiance of faith and that purity of life which constitute the evangelical form of the Christian religion. The Gospel as the chief category in Holy Scripture must become also the chief reality in the Christian Church. The great bond of unity among Christians must ever be their experience of, and their corporate witness to, the love of God in Christ Jesus our Lord.

Part II. *The Forms of Ecumenical Christianity*

John C. Bennett

1. The rediscovery of the Church: reasons for new interest in the Church, the nature of the Church, developing conception of the Church. 2. Forms of unity, ecumenical goals: unofficial organizations and fellowships that have a special purpose; mutual recognition; federation for co-operative witness; federal union; full corporate union. 3. The responsibility of the Church for society.

~~~~~~

During the past generation Protestants have come to see clearly three related truths. They have been led to an understanding of the importance of the Church for Christian faith and life, and in the light of that understanding they have begun to think through the meaning of the Church for theology. They have come to see that the present divided condition of the Church is intolerable both because it is in itself a denial of Christian love and because it is a grievous handicap to the witness and work of the Church in the world. They have also learned the full extent of the responsibility of the Church for every aspect of the world's life. These three truths have become real during the same period to the same people. They are not inevitably related to one another logically, for it would be possible to have a united Church that took no interest in the problems of civilization; but it happens that all three of them are closely related in our minds. There are many differences in the way in which they are understood by contemporary Christians

59

—differences of application, some of which this chapter will attempt to review and appraise; but those three convictions can guide us a long way.

1. THE REDISCOVERY OF THE CHURCH

Reasons for new interest in the Church

The Church has come to be essential to many Protestants, who had neglected it, for several reasons. Those who have been converted to some form of Catholicism would have their own distinctive testimony; but I am thinking here only of those whose experience remains within the framework of Protestantism.

Perhaps the most common reason is that we now must accept the fact that as far ahead as we can see there will be a contrast between the Church and secular society. The hopes that the world at large would soon be Christianized have proved to be illusory, and now it is evident that we shall have to live in a world that is in varying degrees hostile to Christian faith and unable to build its common life according to the Christian ethic. I do not think that we should be fatalists and say that we know just how far it is possible for society to be leavened by Christianity. Many doors remain open to us, and there are at least indefinite possibilities of progress toward a civilization that is consistent with Christian purposes. But it is a fact which our hopes cannot hide and that our fears need not exaggerate that Christians are at this moment of world history facing a society that is in its goals and assumptions alien. In such a world the Christian Church becomes necessary for the individual in a way in which it may not be necessary if he thinks of himself as part of a society that is gradually becoming Christian. He needs desperately a community, within the larger community, where he is trained in the Christian tradition, where he is supported by a Christian fellowship, where he can join in corporate worship, where he can find those with whom he may co-operate in the world, where it is possible to embody Christian love in the actual forms of community life, where his judgment can be corrected in making difficult decisions as a citizen and in his own vocation.

A second reason for this new emphasis upon the Church is that it is seen as the necessary bearer of the Christian tradition. The individual Christian knows now how much he needs to be reinforced and guided by the experience and the thought of the centuries. The new emphasis upon the Church has been accompanied by a return to the Bible as the medium of revelation. The Biblical revelation will always remain normative for the Protestant churchman, but the Bible cannot be separated from the Church, for the Church was called into existence by the revelation to which the Bible bears witness. Also it is true that the Bible as a canonical book was the production of the Church. Christianity is the religion of a distinctive community, the Christian Church. If there were no such community, what we now refer to as revelation would be something half-forgotten, belonging only to the past. It is within the Church that the response to the revelation has been concentrated. Any Christian who has discovered in a fresh way the Church of history has a resource that is incalculably great.

A third reason for the new emphasis upon the Church in Protestantism is the appearance of unexpected vitality and strength in sections of the contemporary Church. The revival of theology has given new power to the Church's message. The resistance of the Church to totalitarian tyranny in many nations, not least in Germany, has revealed toughness of fiber in its life. The reality of the world Church and of the bonds between Christians on both sides of the recent war has made it evident that the Church is not just a reflection of the secular order. One can observe now, in the early postwar period, a very marked difference between the way in which the people of Ger-

many and Japan are regarded in the nation at large and the
attitudes toward them that are characteristic of the Church.
In the former case we find both callous thoughtlessness and
vindictiveness, but in the latter case there is evidence of a desire for reconciliation and of belief in its possibility. The Church
is far too often a reflection of the world, but here in our relation to former enemies this is definitely not the case.

A fourth reason for this new emphasis on the Church is the
ecumenical experience of many Christians in the past two or
three decades. This experience on the international level has
been limited to a few thousand persons but these have been the
leaders and thinkers of the churches in every nation. This ecumenical experience has revealed to many the Church at its best,
its universality, the unity that can be found in spite of differences, its self-criticism, its capacity to speak a prophetic word
to the world. Here the pettiness and parochialism of churches
as institutions were transcended and it was possible to have a
vision of what the Church should be. This vision has guided
most of the thinking about the Church to which I refer in this
chapter.

The nature of the Church. Developing conception of the Church.

This new interest in the Church has resulted in fresh thinking about the nature of the Church. This thinking has long been
called for because there is no area of Christian thought that
has been more neglected. Canon Theodore Wedel, following
Frederick Denison Maurice, claims that the Roman Catholics
have no doctrine of the Church as a community.[3] They have
much to say about the hierarchy, about the authority of the pope
and about the sacraments, but about the Church as a congregation of Christians they have little to say. Is it possible to say that
there is a coherent doctrine of the Church emerging in Protestantism? One would have to admit that no such doctrine can

[3] Theodore Wedel, *The Coming Great Church* (New York: The Macmillan Company, 1945), p. 95.

be discovered that would unite the left-wing Baptist or the Quaker and the high-church Anglican. But there are several ideas which are becoming widely accepted that may prove to be materials for a doctrine of the Church acceptable to the great central body of Protestants.

The first affirmation that can be made about the Church quite generally is that the continuing community of Christians is one of the "given" aspects of Christianity which each generation inherits. It is absurd to suggest, as Schleiermacher did, that it is normal in Protestantism for the child to come first to Christ and then to the Church. The Church is the environment within which the child first knows Christ, at least the Church as the community which includes within itself not only individuals but families. The question of baptism is relevant here, but it can easily be made into a false issue. The children who grow up in homes where infant baptism is rejected belong to this community even though it is important, not only for them but for all Christians, to decide for Christ and to acknowledge their faith at a later time. Since Baptists do not usually believe in baptismal regeneration, the absence of baptism in infancy is not the important thing, but rather the emphasis upon the later decision which all Protestants regard as important. This continuous community, and not any institutional structure, is the essential given factor. This emphasis upon the community rather than the institution is, of course, one point of difference between Protestantism and Catholicism, but it is conceivable that this might become less important than it is if it were clear that Protestants are not primarily individualists but that they do both in life and thought start with the continuous community.

This community has a divine aspect in the sense that in it is concentrated the redemptive activity of God. Within it the grace that was in Christ is mediated directly to countless souls. Its presence in human history is an essential part of the divine strategy.

This community is also very human. Its members and the

corporate bodies which it includes are fallible and sinful. It is subject to the special temptation that comes when men emphasize its divine aspect and cover its failures and its sins with a false sanctity. It is of the utmost importance that the Church be kept under the criticism of the Biblical revelation. It is dangerous to claim that the Church is the kingdom of God in history, because that so easily leads to false confidence on the part of the Church; and it involves the failure to recognize that outside the boundaries of the Church the rule of God is present, under which, from time to time, there emerge forces that are used to purge the Church itself of pride, superstition, injustice and cruel intolerance.

The boundaries of this community are not known with precision. That it includes the churches both Catholic and Protestant is usually clear enough; but there may be institutions that call themselves Christian churches that are really outside the true Church. Fortunately, it is not often our responsibility to rule on this and to say of any group of people who call themselves a Christian church that they are no such thing. One gain of immeasurable importance is that most Protestant denominations are willing to admit that they are partial, that they are not indispensable, that they belong to a larger body. Roman Catholicism does not reciprocate, and there is some ambiguity about the position of the Eastern Orthodox.

This community is the whole people and not even primarily the clergy. One of the chief emphases in Canon Wedel's book on *The Coming Great Church* is what he calls "the people's Church." This is in sharpest contrast to the Roman position for which the active church is the hierarchy, with the laity playing a passive role. The Eastern Orthodox with their doctrine of *sobornost* could find much common ground with Protestants at this point. There is the possibility of considerable variation here in the place given to the clergy. Without accepting a sacerdotal estimate of the clergy, we can see the immense importance of the function of ministers in mediating the past to the present and in representing the larger Church to the local church. The clergy are in a special way tempted to take to themselves the sacredness that belongs to the things that they represent.

These are the convictions about the Church that can be seen to be taking shape in contemporary Protestantism. They become most real within the ecumenical experience of Christians. They imply Christian unity and some form of Church unity. What forms of Church unity should be sought ?

2. FORMS OF UNITY: ECUMENICAL GOALS

It would be well to begin a discussion of the forms of unity that should be sought with some recognition of the actual spiritual unity that exists. If it were not for the fact that Christians are already aware of a measure of unity in spite of differences, in spite of both ecclesiastical and cultural barriers, we should not now feel bound to strive for more complete unity. In other chapters this existing unity will be fully discussed. At present unity is already real over a very large area of the Church in two ways. There is, in the first place, a genuine sense of belonging together. This is especially vivid on those occasions when Christians of different traditions meet together for worship. Those who attended the great world conferences of Christians report consistently that it was at the services of worship that they felt closest together. In the second place, there is a surprising overlapping of mind already in the churches. One can see the fruit of this in the reports of the ecumenical conferences, reports that cover a very wide range of Christian thought and yet which display few differences of the type that form any basis for ecclesiastical separation. Allowance must be made for the fact that in such conferences churchmen are disposed to emphasize their agreements, and that they often settle in controversies for words and symbols that are somewhat ambiguous. But the differences that are really important theologically, except for those that concern the doctrines of the Church, the ministry and the sacraments, represent permanent contrasts that can be found within most denominations. For example, the theological issues that are discussed in the arguments between those who are influenced strongly by Karl Barth and those who remain in the liberal tradition cut across most Protestant ecclesiastical divisions. This common mind that already exists can be observed if one compares several of the most influential theologians. Take as examples William Temple, Reinhold Niebuhr, Emil Brunner and Berdyaev. Those four men represent quite different backgrounds and theological traditions. They have contacts with both Protestant and Catholic forms of Christianity, though no one of them is strongly Catholic. They link together both the Anglo-Saxon and the continental worlds of thought. Among them there are contrasting types of mind and temper. They differ from one another on many questions. Yet, they have shown the capacity to appreciate profoundly one another's thought, and the reader could go from one to the other and feel that there is among them real continuity of faith and insight.

The current literature on church unity makes use of the distinction between Christian unity and church union. There is already a far greater amount of Christian unity than an outside observer of the Church would think to be possible. Comparatively little progress has been made toward church union. Dr. Henry P. Van Dusen rightly says that "Christian Unity which does not imply and make possible whatever degree of Church Union may be held to be the ultimate desideratum is something less than genuine and true Christian Unity."[4] In fact, unless we can at least achieve the form of church unity that will be called "mutual recognition," all that we may regard as Christian unity is distorted by the refusal to treat fellow Christians as

[4] Henry P. Van Dusen, "The Issues of Christian Unity," *Christendom*, Spring, 1946.

equals in the Church, and it may soon be destroyed by pride answered by resentment.

In outlining the forms of church unity toward which we may move, the writer has drawn heavily upon both Bishop Angus Dun's pamphlet written in preparation for the Edinburgh Conference, *The Meanings of Unity*, and the aforementioned article by Dr. Van Dusen.

The forms of church unity may be classified in the following way:

(1) Unofficial organizations and fellowships that have a specific purpose.
(2) Mutual recognition involving:
    (a) Interchange of membership.
    (b) Interchange of ministries.
    (c) Intercommunion.
    (d) Comity arrangements in missions and church extension.
(3) Federation for co-operative witness, teaching and action.
(4) Federal union which presupposes mutual recognition and adds to it a federation to which is committed responsibility for missions and other selected activities of the churches.
(5) Full corporate union that involves a single church government as well as the forms of unity previously mentioned.

(1) *Unofficial organizations and fellowships that have a specific purpose*. This kind of co-operative activity is really closer to what we mean by Christian unity than it is to church union. On the other hand, it does involve organization, and may help to prepare the way for ecclesiastical unity. Examples of this kind of Christian organization are: the Student Christian Movements federated as they are in the World's Student Christian Federation, and the World Alliance for International Friendship Through the Churches (this was a major factor in the de-

velopment of the Universal Christian Council for Life and Work which became an official organ of the churches and which is one of the bodies forming the World Council of Churches). There are many organizations that are not federations of churches but that do combine officially agencies of churches, namely, church boards. The International Council of Religious Education, the Home Missions Council, the Foreign Missions Conference, and, in part, the International Missionary Council are examples of this type of organization. It is expected that six of these agencies in America will become absorbed into a more inclusive federation, and hence give real substance to a form of church union. It would be impossible to overestimate the importance of this kind of organization for co-operative action that cuts across denominational lines. Dr. Van Dusen in a recent address said that at the Oxford Conference he looked over the leaders on the platform and observed that those men, official representatives of churches from all parts of the world, were personal friends of long standing, and he attributed their friendship to their long association in the Student Christian Movement. It is safe to say that if it had not been for the years of comradeship on the part of those leaders there would now be no such ecumenical movement on the ecclesiastical level. It is also important to say that movements of this sort will be necessary even if a rather close type of church union is realized. When co-operation is left to official channels alone, there is a loss of spontaneity and of pioneering.

(2) *Mutual recognition.* Church union in the form of mutual recognition involves all of the theological difficulties that now impede efforts to achieve church union in the more complete sense, but at the same time it does not bring with it the dangers that do attend the development of a unified ecclesiastical organization. Moreover it would remove the real sting of disunity, the denial of full Christian fellowship across denominational lines, particularly the denial of fellowship at the Lord's Table. This is not the place to discuss the difficulties that stand in the

way of mutual recognition. They are amply discussed in the literature of the ecumenical movement. There has developed almost a pamphlet war on the subject within the Church of England in relation to the scheme for church union in South India. My purpose is to show how very far mutual recognition would take us if it could be achieved.

It should be realized that mutual recognition in the four forms mentioned—interchange of membership, interchange of ministries, intercommunion, comity in missions, etc.—is a reality as between many Protestant denominations already. Denominations that would find many practical difficulties in the way of full corporate union are already one here. In the United States this mutual recognition has become a necessity of church life because denominations are so close to one another in most communities. The tendency to change from one denomination to another without feeling a serious conflict about it is a common characteristic of American church life. It should be admitted that this mutual recognition takes place only within the great central core of American Protestantism. There are churches on the ecclesiastical right and on the ecclesiastical left that have no part in it. The basic presupposition of such mutual recognition is that no denomination has a monopoly on Christian truth or is in any way necessary for salvation. Each is partial, and each recognizes the Christian character of the other. As a matter of fact, in the interplay of American life, each has become much like the other.

Mutual recognition would, as I have suggested, take the sting out of disunity. It would remove the temptation of any group of Christians to patronize another group—a tendency that is now rampant in spite of many protestations of fellowship. An illustration of the results of full mutual recognition may be seen in the case of the churches that belong to the Anglican Communion, the various Episcopal churches that are in communion with the Church of England. Here there is mutual recognition, but no closer forms of institutional unity. Each branch of the Anglican Communion is administratively independent. The Archbishop of Canterbury has no power whatever over the bishops of the Protestant Episcopal Church in America, for example. The Lambeth Conference which meets every ten years and brings together bishops from the whole Anglican Communion has enormous prestige but no legislative authority. The polity of the various churches, polity in the sense of government, shows great contrasts, such as the contrast between the state-related government of the Church of England and the free, representative polity of the Episcopal Church in the United States. I have used this illustration to indicate that mutual recognition is a form of church union, usually included under "organic union," which does not necessarily raise any of the problems that accompany the concentration of ecclesiastical power. It is true that these branches of the Anglican Communion do not overlap geographically, and there is, therefore, no competition between them. Any plan for church union in America would necessarily involve some organs of federation that would at least have the power to restrain, not necessarily to end, ecclesiastical competition. But it is important that it is at least possible to overcome the greatest bars to Christian fellowship that inhere in disunity without setting up a vast united Church with a single government. There are good reasons for being hesitant about church union in this last sense, but they need not deter any Christian from working for the widest and deepest possible mutual recognition.

When we consider the next three forms of unity, (3), (4), and (5), we cannot find any absolute lines separating them; but it remains true that the differences between (3) and an extreme form of (5) would be momentous. Also, it should be said that the range and also the quality of the federal activities under (3) would depend to a large extent upon mutual recognition. Where that exists, co-operative planning for mission work can be effective. Where it is lacking, competitive mission work becomes logically necessary, though fortunately the logic of this is not always carried out.

(3) *Federation for co-operative witness.* We already have federation for co-operative witness, teaching and action in such agencies as the Federal Council of Churches, the International Missionary Council, the World Council of Churches and the International Council of Religious Education. There are many degrees of effectiveness here, and the range of such co-operation often depends upon the range of mutual recognition. This dependence is not as serious in the case of either teaching or action on ethical issues as it is in the case of religious witness. Nor is occasional or sporadic co-operative religious witness necessarily prevented by the absence of mutual recognition. What is blocked by the lack of mutual recognition is the building of local co-operative churches, and this is in many situations an enormous obstacle to the Church's effectiveness. Our existing federal agencies have great importance, because on many public questions there is a sufficient consensus for common action. Usually the differences have nothing at all to do with ecclesiastical divisions. A recent book on the Federal Council of Churches[5] makes much of the fact that the Federal Council has become an important teacher of the American churches and even of the American community. Its commissions, such as the Commission on a Just and Durable Peace, the conferences that are called under its auspices, the work of its Department of Research and Education and many projects of its other departments have done a great deal to inform and guide the thought of American Protestants. The Federal Council has made good use of the method of appointing officially a committee or commission to make a report that is unofficial so far as the Council is concerned. The reports of the Commission on the Church and the War in the light of the Christian Faith had this status, and they illustrate the extent to which it is possible to get a body of common teaching

[5] John A. Hutchison, *We Are Not Divided* (New York: Round Table Press, 1941), ch. VIII.

on a highly controversial issue. The Preaching Missions in American cities held under the auspices of the Federal Council of Churches show that a type of co-operative witness is possible. If these missions are sometimes criticized for giving too much prominence to a few individuals, that is a fault that can be easily corrected. Careful thought is now being given to the best way in which the World Council of Churches can speak a word to give guidance to the Christians of the world, a word that will not be official but which will carry great weight because of its truth and relevance.

The limitations of this first form of federation are the familiar ones that we meet in discussing the problems of world organization. The federation has no power at all over the churches. It can only do that to which all consent. The chief weakness is that it cannot at any point prevent competitive activity by the churches except in the case of those denominations which do enter specific agreements for that purpose. We have here the ecclesiastical equivalent of as limited a federation as the League of Nations (more limited than the U.N.) supplemented by treaties between specific states.

(4) *Federal union.* Federal union would presuppose mutual recognition as in the case of the branches of the Anglican Communion, but it would also involve the delegation to the central authority of real powers over existing churches. It would be greatly aided by many full unions between specific denominations so that much existing competition could be undercut at the source. It should be remembered that the problem of local competition among churches that belong to one united denomination is not easily solved! These powers would have to do chiefly with the missionary or extension work of the churches in the federation. One may observe an analogy for what such a federation might be like in the present constitution of the Congregational-Christian Churches. (This may be an example of the universal ecclesiastical pretension that makes everyone find the best clew to the united Church in his own denomination's

polity!) The local church in Congregationalism is still independent so far as its internal affairs are concerned. That might
still be true of the denomination in a federal union. The missionary and extension work of the Congregational Churches is
done by boards that have authority over it, though that
authority comes through the consent that is repeated each bien-
nium by the representatives of the local churches now chosen
indirectly. At least we have here congregational independence
in combination (not in all respects logically integrated) with
the delegation of real power to boards that actually do the work
for the churches in their own fields. This is no argument for
independency, because I am using the local church here as an
analogy for the denomination within a federal union. Also, I
should hope that the process of uniting particular denominations
with one another more fully would proceed as at present. One
could imagine its proceeding more rapidly! This is of greatest
significance when the denominations belong to different ecclesiastical families and have different cultural backgrounds.

(5) *Full corporate union.* The most complete form of church
union, that which involves a single church government, is a
good pattern for the union of several existing denominations,
but it is an undesirable pattern for the ecumenical Church in the
United States or in the world. In the minds of many who fear
"organic union" what is really feared is the development of an
immense ecclesiastical machine that will impose uniformity.
It is important to emphasize the fact that it is possible to have
organic union in terms of mutual recognition, in terms of a federal structure that is tighter than any that now exists in the
Church without running the risk of the development of a great
monolithic Church.

*Church union in this final form might actually become a
threat to Christian unity.* When an ecclesiastical organization
gives the opportunity for one group to exercise power over another group, fears, resentments and defensiveness destroy Christian unity. Obviously it is impossible to avoid such use of power

in any form of church union that is to be effective, but at all times it is important to protect minorities from being swamped by majorities as far as this is humanly possible. It is important to preserve variety of expression and to guard spiritual and intellectual freedom. The larger Church must include communities that preserve such a distinctive tradition as that of the Quakers. This will be a good test of any united Church. Will it have a place for the Quakers, and not drown out the Quaker silence?

If our plans for church unity *on the governmental level* are too ambitious they may become self-defeating. We have emphasized freedom too much up till now, but if now we emphasize unity too much the unity will be broken by a new reformation. We need to stop speaking of our divisions as though they were to be traced only to sinfulness. Many of them were the result of a necessary protest against the dominant church. The sectarian tradition in the history of the Church has represented criticism and correction of the Church in the light of a purer understanding of the Gospel that has often been needed. "The coming great Church" must make room within itself for the freedom to pioneer and to criticize that characterized the sects at their best. If it fails to do this, the radical ferment in the Christian gospel will break through the carefully wrought, unified structures of the Church, and a new sectarian protest will have to find its home outside the united Church.

3. THE RESPONSIBILITY OF THE CHURCH FOR SOCIETY

The third major insight that has usually accompanied Christian striving after unity has been the recognition of responsibility for the institutions of society. Interest in church union has often developed among those who were co-operating to make the social order more consistent with Christian purposes. A generation ago it was widely assumed that this co-operation could take place without any consideration of problems of faith and theology. The Stockholm Conference proceeded on this basis, but even then it was discovered that there are differences of theological conviction that impede practical co-operation. The preparation for the Oxford Conference sought to correct this neglect of theology, and much was done to help the churches face those differences in theology that affect Christian understanding of the function of the Church in society. There was an important truth in the older emphasis on the separation of practical co-operation from doctrine. It has proved to be the case that differences on the very questions that create the greatest obstacles to church union do not prevent this practical collaboration. So, it will still remain sound strategy to emphasize this collaboration and to hope that in the course of it Christians will discover deeper levels of unity. The Oxford Conference was the high point in the history of the modern church's attempt to relate its faith more significantly to the problems of the world, and it was also the source of a good deal of the spiritual momentum behind the development of the World Council of Churches. Only a Church that is united can speak a convincing word to a world that is in conflict. Only a Church that is united can act effectively as an instrument of God's love for the distressed and shaken peoples.

It was said earlier in this chapter that we can no longer expect that in any period that can be foreseen there will be a "Christian civilization" in the sense that institutions and collective behavior will be fully Christian. We can expect varying degrees of Christianization with the very real possibility of the extension of the authority of the Christian conscience and of Christian faith. It is something to be thankful for when we do find great communities still able to recognize that Christian ethics has a claim upon them and still wistfully and with faith or half-believingly keeping their children under the influence of the Church. To bring the minds and consciences of men under the authority of Christ is the task of the Church, and it is wrong to begin with the fatalistic notion that no great results are possible, just as it is wrong to take the nominal Christianity of the majority in any nation as a sign that it is a Christian nation. The unity of the Church is a condition of effectiveness in winning the nations.

The Church can influence civilization indirectly in many ways if it is true to itself. It can raise the moral tone of the community. It can help to unify those who belong to opposing social groups though this will depend upon the correction of the Church so that it ceases to reflect the divisions of the world in its own life. Already we see some real gains here in the way in which the Church has been able to bring together in a spirit of reconciliation its members who have been enemies in the recent war. The Church can also make indirectly a contribution to freedom by being true to itself and demanding its own right to speak the truth. There is abundant evidence that in Nazi-controlled Europe the Church did keep the door ajar for spiritual freedom.

This indirect influence of the Church can be greatly increased if the Church teaches and disciplines its own members so that they come to understand what the Christian faith means in relation to economic justice and human unity. What I am suggesting is that teaching within the Church on these questions can correct and enhance the indirect influence of the Church at the points already mentioned, and that it can contribute more directly to the solution of the problems that are now so fateful. At this stage I am concerned to stress merely the teaching by the Church that results in action, not by the Church itself, but by its members in their respective vocations and as citizens. Such teaching would have to begin with a very elementary correction of the false individualism so common in modern Protestantism and show the relevance of the Christian faith to the problems of the social order. It would include the defining of Christian standards by which existing institutions and all programs for their alteration should be criticized. It would have to make such criticisms very concrete in terms of our actual behavior now. It would, from time to time, set forth major objectives, so-called "middle axioms," that have a strong Christian sanction—such an objective as full employment or the achievement of world order or the overcoming of racial segregation. It would attempt to bring Christian people to a better self-knowledge, so that they would be able to see how their own opinions are often distorted by group pride or economic interest, and hence make them more open to the need of changes that they have resisted. This teaching would finally lay stress upon the responsibility of the individual Christian to find the best way of relating Christian purposes to his own vocation.[6]

If the Church really carried out this kind of program, so that its own members were brought to a new understanding of their Christian responsibility, it would make its greatest contribution to the solution of the problems that harass us. But it is probably true that if this job is done well Christian people will call for more direct action by the Church in the world. We cannot lay down in advance hard and fast rules as to what the Church should or should not do in this way. It is easier to say what should be done when there is some obvious evil to be resisted than it is when there is some rather ambiguous good to be supported. Still, it will be necessary for the Church to find ways in which at times of decision its word can be spoken to the world and it can be counted on one side or the other. This will be demanded when Christians have been moved in their minds and consciences by the imperatives of their faith; but it is actually of less importance than the Church's indirect witness and action, day by day, through its members in the world after they have been made sensitive to the conflicts between their present collective life and the purposes of God.

[6] For an elaboration see J. H. Oldham, ed., "The Church and the Economic Order," *The Oxford Conference, Official Report* (Chicago: Willett, Clark & Company, 1938).

3

ECUMENICAL HISTORY

Part I. *The Rise of Ecumenical Organizations*

Henry Smith Leiper
and
Abdel R. Wentz

1. The scope of the inquiry. 2. The means employed: person-alities, conferences, study, Continuation Committees, organiza-tions, responsibility. 3. Unity resulting from the missionary enterprise: the Edinburgh Conference, the International Mission-ary Council. 4. Unity resulting from common ethical endeavor: the movement toward world peace, the concern for the life and work of the Church. 5. Unity resulting from a consideration of theo-logical differences. 6. Special agencies. 7. The World Council of Churches.

---

1. THE SCOPE OF THE INQUIRY

The ecumenical movement is first of all a *movement*. It is not a distinct entity of which one can say "Lo, here," or "Lo, there." It is a vast impulse, appearing in some degree in virtually every land in which there is a Christian church. It is made concrete, not in one, but in a thousand different organizations. Its power arises from the deep rooted conviction and the high hopes of multitudes of people. It is a movement.

It is, however, a movement with a definite direction. This has not come about by conscious, previous planning. The ecumenical movement is not the result of the projection of a future scheme and strategy for the Church by a few or by many people. The direction which it is unmistakably taking is, as it were, spun out in the history of the Church, and that by a Power and a Wisdom greater than man's. We discover the nature of the ecumenical movement, not so much through a definition of the term ecumenical, as by an examination of the reality in the life of the Church to which it refers. Such an examination shows the clear direction of the whole. It is, on the one hand, a movement towards the achievement of a Church which is universal in its scope. The ecumenical movement, in its varied manifestations and methods, is committed to the full pursuit of the *world* mission of the Church. Because of this commitment, it has become increasingly clear that there must be a greater unity in the Church. Again, specific plans, actual organizations and the ideals and motives behind them, have varied from church to church and from country to country. But that there is an obviously apparent and profound spiritual urge among Christians for unity among the churches is clear.

This is the other pole in a bi-polar concept. Ecumenicity means an intrinsic propulsiveness that will not rest until it embraces the whole world. It proceeds from within outwards, and that by inherent compulsion. It is neither centripetal nor centrifugal. It is vital, organic, inherent propulsiveness that, without abandoning its heart and center, yet because of its essential nature, thrusts itself outward infinitely. Only the grace of God in Jesus Christ is ecumenical. God's love, from the very nature of it, goes out unceasingly from the divine heart to every human soul and will not rest until it has touched every person in the universe and permeated his entire being. Jesus illustrated ecumenicity with a live mustard seed planted under proper conditions. It is a power capable of infinite expansion and it is essentially indivisible. The ecumenical movement is dedicated to the world mission and the unity of the Church of Christ.

A full history of the ecumenical movement would trace the origin and development, as well as the diverse forms, of both elements. It would show the way in which the Church has attempted, from age to age, to fulfill its world-wide mission. This cannot be our task here, partly because of the limitations of space, and partly because such a summary exists elsewhere in this series.[1] It must be constantly borne in mind, however, that a basic, if not the most important, aspect of the ecumenical movement is its vision of a universal Church.

Our present subject must, therefore, be that part of the ecumenical movement which refers to the unity of the churches. Even here, however, so widespread is the development and so many and varied its different elements, that we cannot be exhaustive. Those efforts, for instance, which have not directly resulted in the creation of the present ecumenical organizations we must omit. Yet they are of crucial importance, for they are evidence of the spiritual basis and they have provided the experimental ground out of which the present world organizations have arisen. Moreover, it would be but to repeat material given elsewhere in this volume, to which the reader is referred.[2] Nor can we here show the progress which has been made in different countries, again a matter of direct relevance to the emergence of the world bodies.[3] We must limit ourselves to a treatment of the rise of the main ecumenical organizations, as they exist on a world level.

In one sense, these are the fruit of all that has gone before, and, as in the case of their origin, depend for their future upon

[1] Kenneth Scott Latourette, "The Church and Christian Society Today in the Perspective of History," *The Gospel, The Church, and the World,* Kenneth Scott Latourette, ed., Vol. III of "The Interseminary Series" (New York: Harper & Brothers, 1946).

[2] See ch. 2, pt. II.

[3] See, for America, ch. 5.

the interplay of forces not directly related to them. As the result of a spiritual movement, they will in large part be determined in the future by the growth or, conceivably, the decay of that movement. Yet they have an importance in themselves. Although in no sense are the ecumenical organizations designed to control, they are nevertheless intended to provide leadership for Christians throughout the world. As such they have a significance in themselves, which makes the understanding of their origin and development of first importance.

2. THE MEANS EMPLOYED

It is important at the outset to note the means which have been generally employed in the development of the ecumenical organizations. These have been evolved, hammered out in the year by year work as the need has arisen. There has, by and large, been little precedent, since the ecumenical movement is in itself a new thing. Yet, just as the direction of the ecumenical movement has become apparent in the life of the churches, so the means used have also become clear and widely accepted.

Personalities

Again and again in our account of the history, we shall be obliged to refer to individuals and their influence. No less than in other great movements within the Church, God has used great men in the ecumenical movement. The monastic movement, the Protestant and Catholic Reformations, the Evangelical Awakening, to suggest but a few, have each had their great figures. This has been conspicuously true also of the modern ecumenical movement. They have been men of vision, of commitment, of energy, of wisdom and of prayer. One cannot tell the whole story in terms of the influence of individuals, but one must recognize that in many instances it has been the imagination of a single man, or at most a small group of men, which has conceived a venture of far reaching importance, and that it has been the courage and dedication of others that have carried it on.

Conferences

The succession of conferences of world-wide significance, beginning in 1910, to which we shall have reference, have been the inspiration of Christians across the globe. Here has been revealed a method of prime importance for all ecumenical advance. At bottom it rests upon a faith in God and in the working of His Holy Spirit. Faced with a problem, be it the evangelization of the world or the unity of the churches, men have come together in representative meetings seeking a wisdom which separately they did not possess. There has been a recognition that only by a face to face gathering of those duly qualified to do so could honest differences of conviction be understood and surmounted. Common testimony has been that the wisdom and power resulting from the conferences was more than the sum total of added human energies. The ecumenical conferences have been occasions when men have sought collectively to wait the coming of the Holy Spirit.

Though great inspiration has always come to those in attendance at the conferences, they have not been held primarily for this purpose. They have been called in order to face a given problem. They have been consultative in nature, work during them being carried on for the purpose of achieving findings which are in turn submitted to the constituting bodies for such action as may seem desirable. Delegates have not gathered for the purpose of hearing solutions already thought out; they have rather come together in order that a common mind may emerge.

These meetings have not been binding upon the churches represented in them. As we shall note presently, it has been one of the strengths of the ecumenical movement that it has not sought to set up a controlling agency at any point. The conferences have been advisory, relying for their influence upon the

prestige which has invariably been attached to them, upon the
increased efforts of the delegates returning from them, and
upon the organizations set up to continue the interests of the
conferences themselves. In essence, this is again the expression
of confidence in the spiritual factor. Far from seeking to determine the life of the churches by any kind of legal action,
they have vigorously pursued their work, leaving the results
ultimately in the hand of God.

Study

A third method has been that of ecumenical study. First begun
in connection with the Edinburgh Conference of 1910, this has
become a necessary means of advance. In part, it is a collective
research; in part it is a consultation by means of written articles
for the purpose of mutual understanding and discovery of truth.
Whether it is carried on for purposes of research or for purposes of consultation, the usual method is through the organization of commissions of scholars, the members of which are generally located in different countries and are members of different churches. Topics are assigned, papers are written, circulated
to critics in still other countries and from other churches, returned to the writer and finally published. The best-known
series of volumes which have resulted from this type of interchange are those produced in connection with the Edinburgh,
Jerusalem, Oxford and Madras Conferences. This type of study,
however, has not been confined to the work of the conferences.
The continuing organizations set up by them and lately the
Provisional Committee of the World Council of Churches have
carried on a constant process of cross-consultation and research.

Continuation Committees

As the world conferences have met, there has inevitably arisen
the desire to continue the work started in each, and to extend
the influence of the decisions reached to an even wider circle.
A permanent organization of some type was needed. This has

generally been found in the "Continuation Committee," a group authorized by the conference, and composed of representatives from various countries and churches. These committees have generally carried a budget, employed a staff and followed through with a specific program entrusted to them. They have been the groups which have called further conferences after a due period. The usual evolution has seen the "Continuation Committee" develop into a permanent organization, as the Continuation Committee of the Edinburgh Conference in 1910 was superseded by the International Missionary Council. As an interim device, however, sufficiently organized to carry forward a program, yet tentative enough so as to allow for its disbanding at any advisable moment, the "Continuation Committee" has proved an effective method.

Organizations

We need here only note the fact that permanent organizations, albeit of different types, have soon become necessary. This is testimony in large part to the strength of the fundamental ecumenical spirit; it is also evidence of the need for a duly constituted body of sufficient stability and power to represent the churches in the tasks which it has been desired to do in common. Four types of organization have emerged. There is, first, that which has been created by the action of co-operative groups in different countries to do a specific task on the world level. The major example is the International Missionary Council.[4] Second, is the organization which is created by the individual churches for the purpose of performing a specific task. Two examples would be the Universal Christian Council for Life and Work and the World Conference on Faith and Order. The third type, represented by the World Council of Churches (in process of formation), is constituted by the individual churches for more generalized purposes than indicated by the two foregoing organi-

[4] The constitution of the International Missionary Council appears on p. 251 ff.

zations.[5] The fourth type is that which is organically unrelated to
the churches, but which exists for the purpose of contributing to
the general work and life of the Church. A well-known example
is the World's Student Christian Federation. It must again be
stressed that the emergence of these types of organization has been
by no conscious design. They have been developed to meet the
needs, and in accordance with the wisdom of, the given situation.
They are thus rooted, not in preconceptions of the nature of
church unity, but rather in the common consent of men and
churches desiring to meet difficult problems in the most fruitful
way. Such a basis of present organization indicates the open possibility of continued change and growth.

Responsibility

In its leaders, conferences, study, committees and organizations
the ecumenical movement has shown a consistent sense of responsibility. This is hardly a "means" in the sense of the foregoing;
yet it is of paramount importance. Throughout the history of the
growth of the ecumenical organizations there is exhibited a
careful and on the whole successful attempt to keep all developments in accord with the desires of the churches themselves.
Tangential organizations, or agencies desiring to wield their
own power irrespective of their constituting groups, have been
conspicuously absent in work on a world level. The Life and
Work, Faith and Order, and missionary movements have all proceeded according to the authorization of the churches or related
agencies which have participated in them. One would not maintain that these movements have not exercised leadership in their
respective spheres; yet with rare wisdom they have been careful
to proceed in their objectives only on such a basis as would be
in general welcomed by the churches. The ecumenical movement has, in other words, kept its aims and programs indigenous
to the churches which it has sought to influence, and therein has

[5] The proposed Constitution of the World Council of Churches appears
on p. 245 ff.

been one of its great strengths. In so doing, it has shown a sense of keen responsibility.

3. UNITY RESULTING FROM THE MISSIONARY ENTERPRISE

It will be convenient to divide our account of the growth of the ecumenical agencies into five sections: unity resulting from the missionary enterprise; unity resulting from a consideration of the ethical task of the Church; unity resulting from the facing of theological differences; unity resulting from more specialized interests; and the World Council of Churches.

From the missionary movement has come perhaps the earliest and most insistent demand for closer Christian unity. There the need for co-operation was felt even when there was no corresponding sense of need for it among the constituents of the "sending" churches. Accordingly, the agencies responsible for sending missionaries began the practice of assembling their representatives both internationally and interdenominationally, and from this came an increasing awareness of the fundamental one-ness of their task. A series of seven international interdenominational missionary conferences was begun with a gathering in New York in 1854. It would be confusing to refer to each of them, but that held in London in 1888 was particularly notable, since it marked the end of the first century of modern missions. The seventh was held in New York in 1900, where for the first time the word "ecumenical" was held to describe such a meeting. In this, as in the others of this series, however, only the churches of the Western World were represented. Members of the "younger churches" of Asia and Africa and the Islands were yet to be invited.

The Edinburgh Conference

Nothing that happened, however, from 1854 to 1910 could be compared in importance to the World Missionary Conference

held at Edinburgh in that year, although the culminative effect
of previous councils, conferences, assemblies and alliances were
registered in that meeting. Without the earlier efforts at unity
it could not have achieved what it did. These had clearly been
used by Providence to nurture in the hearts of increasing numbers of Christians the disposition to co-operate and to seek unity
in ever widening areas of church life. It is plain to the student
of history that something uniquely dynamic took place there on
the historic heights of "the Rock" in the Assembly Hall of the
Church of Scotland in the summer of 1910. The sense of need
for greater unity came to Christians from all over the world as
they planned for the extension of the Church.

Three factors must be singled out. First, it was in connection
with the Edinburgh Conference that the idea and methods of
ecumenical study were developed on any comprehensive scale.
Nine volumes were prepared, on the evangelization of the world,
the state of the Church in the mission field, Christian education,
problems in connection with the missionary message, the preparation of missionaries, the home base, missions and government,
co-operation and unity and on the records and addresses of the
Conference. Each volume was the result of research carried on
by persons of different churches and in different countries. It
was the most comprehensive, indeed the initial, effort at ecumenical study attempted to that time, and it set the pattern for
similar successive efforts. The second special factor in the Conference was the appearance as delegates of a few members from
the "younger churches." They were, to be sure, a tiny minority,
but they were there, and their presence began a trend which in
the missionary conferences which were to follow was to be
greatly expanded.

The third factor was the influence of the Conference on certain
individuals. It was there that John R. Mott emerged as the foremost leader in the movement toward unity in the missionary
enterprise. Already experienced both in his work in the Young
Men's Christian Association and in the World's Student Chris-

tian Federation, as chairman of the Edinburgh Conference and of its Commission I on the Evangelization of the World, he assumed a place of leadership which was to be of first importance in the development of the International Missionary Council and its other world gatherings. It was at the Edinburgh Conference also that Archbishop Nathan Soderblom of Sweden began to catch a vision of another approach to the problem of unity among the churches, the approach, namely, of work undertaken in common as the churches seek to face their ethical task in the world. Similarly, Bishop Charles H. Brent, of the United States, also a delegate, began during the conference to glimpse the significance of a frank facing of the theological differences among the churches, and to devise ways and means of bringing this about. We shall return to these figures and their influence later; here we must note that the Edinburgh Conference was important not only in itself, but for its influence on certain persons upon whose leadership future developments were heavily to depend.

Although the Conference was a gathering of individuals in the interest of more unity in world missions, and not a meeting of an organization, it had large continuing influence. It adjourned leaving behind it a Continuation Committee, to which was committed the study of ways to develop the trends towards co-operation which had been so manifest during the Conference. The Continuation Committee met in the same year, 1910, and in three successive years. Though World War I seriously interrupted its work, plans were made for the holding of a series of twenty-one conferences throughout Asia to which missionaries and the leaders of the "younger churches" were invited. Branches of the Continuation Committee were set up in strategic areas, and these in turn became in due time National Christian Councils— co-operative bodies representing the churches and other agencies of their respective territories. They were at first, and inevitably, rather under the influence of the mission agencies, but they have progressed steadily toward their goal of being genuine instruments of the "younger churches" in each of the given areas.

The International Missionary Council

When it was clear that such bases of united action had been assured in the lands to which missionaries were sent, it became apparent that the way was open to link these new bodies with the older co-operative bodies of the mission societies in the sending countries, as for instance the Conference of Missionary Societies in Britain and the Foreign Missions Conference of North America. The result was the formation of the International Missionary Council, representing twenty-eight such co-operative agencies throughout the world.

The International Missionary Council has held two particularly notable world gatherings since that in 1910. The first was at Jerusalem in 1928, on the Mount of Olives, and it produced among many other fruits a great affirmation of common agreement about the Christian mission: "Our message is Jesus Christ. . . . We must give nothing less, we can give nothing more."[6] The second was at Madras-Tambaram, India, in 1938. This "enlarged meeting of the International Missionary Council" as it was called, brought together more representatives of the "younger churches" than had ever before participated in an ecumenical conference. Among many other notable products of that meeting was a poignant appeal from the "younger churches" for unity among the "older churches" of the West. "For you unity may be a luxury. For us it is a life and death necessity" was the burden of their appeal.[7]

Particular note must be made of the importance of these meetings. First, they were of unmeasurable significance for the Chris-

[6] The Jerusalem Meeting of the International Missionary Council, Vol. I, *The Christian Message* (New York: The International Missionary Council, 1928), pp. 402-407.

[7] For an account of the major activities of the International Missionary Council throughout World War II, see ch. 3, pt. II.

tian world mission. To attempt to trace this in any detail would take us outside the scope of our subject. It is clear, however, that each provided a greatly augmented impetus, both to the sending churches in the West and to the missionaries and the "younger churches" in the Orient and Africa, for the aggressive continuation of their task. Moreover, the increasing prestige attached to the conferences has meant that the influence of their decisions has been widespread. More and more, they are viewed as the occasions on which the broad strategy of the world mission of the Church is developed. Second, as we have mentioned but must stress again, the Jerusalem and Madras meetings carried further the trend started at the Edinburgh Conference of representation from the "younger churches." This is of incalculable significance, for it meant the end of the hitherto almost exclusive leadership of the churches of the West, and the emergence of a true community of joint planning and thinking in the councils of the Church. Third, both meetings followed the example of ecumenical study set by the Conference in 1910, each of the later meetings producing a series of volumes, to the end that this technique of such far-reaching importance was by the conclusion of the Jerusalem Conference virtually established procedure for ecumenical gatherings of all types. Fourth, we must mention again the influence of the meetings upon individuals, noting especially the emergence into prominent leadership of William Paton of England at the Jerusalem meeting. His work was of importance not only for the International Missionary Council, but also at a later date for the newly formed World Council of Churches as well.

Through the holding of world conferences, the development of ecumenical study, the creation of the International Missionary Council and its constituent co-operative bodies, its gift of Christian statesmen, and its increasingly insistent demand for unity both on the mission field and among the "older churches," the missionary movement has been of major importance in the world movement towards unity. In part, the impulse within the missionary movement has been the result of the heavy pressure of an avowedly non-Christian environment upon a Christian minority; in part it has been the clear vision of that minority of the demands of the Gospel. One may venture the forecast that a chief, if not the main, urge to unity in the future will also come from the "younger churches."

4. UNITY RESULTING FROM COMMON ETHICAL ENDEAVOR

The two main world organizations concerned with the ethical task of the Church arose in conjunction with the spirit of unity developed in the missionary enterprise. In two ways the movements were directly related. On the one hand, leading personalities were the same in many cases. Those who were active in the stream of events which led to the organization of the International Missionary Council were also active in the two bodies we have now to consider. On the other hand, and at a more profound level, the fundamental desire for unity which originated and found its first organized expression in the missionary enterprise, provided the basis for unity in different areas. While missionary co-operation antedated in origin by a few years world co-operation in other spheres of interest, both efforts were so young as to be for all practical purposes contemporaneous.

The movement toward world peace

In the summer of 1914—actually only a few hours before the outbreak of World War I—there came into existence the World Alliance for International Friendship Through the Churches, conceived as a co-operative organization for the promotion of peace. Its major leadership was American and British. Although during the war years from 1914 to 1918 it began to function, full activity was not possible until peace came. Following the war, however, the Alliance grew until it included thirty-one national units throughout most of the Western world. A few of these were composed of churches, most were associations of individuals, and some were a combination. A number of them included Roman Catholics and Jews, but the majority of the participants were non-Roman Christians. All groups were functionally centered on the one great problem of attacking the war system.

For our present purposes it is important to note that the Alliance held a number of sectional and some widely representative international meetings in the years between the two world wars. Through this means it was able to provide additional experience in international co-operative effort and to give further impetus to the desire of Christians to work together on pressing ethical issues. Through the Alliance a most significant contact was established with the Eastern Orthodox Churches, particularly in the Balkans, resulting in a broadening base of ecumenical activity. The Alliance suffered as well as gained from the fact that it was almost entirely financed from America through the grants of the Church Peace Union, liberally endowed by Andrew Carnegie. The power of the purse tended to lessen the reality of international collaboration. Nevertheless these generous grants made largely possible the travel of delegates from different countries to the conferences which were held, and thus contributed in no small measure to this aspect of ecumenical development. It is perhaps at this point that the Alliance has its greatest significance for our present account, for it was in the meetings of the Alliance that there came together those leaders who were later to be of such large influence in the broader "Life and Work Movement." Here, again, the function of the ecumenical organization in producing individual statesmen is marked.

The concern for the life and work of the Church

The leaders of the World Alliance together with the leaders of the Federal Council of the Churches of Christ in America were instrumental in bringing into being that which was popularly called the "Life and Work Movement." In the summer of 1920, a meeting known as "the preliminary meeting to consider a Universal Conference of the Church of Christ on Life and Work" was held in Geneva on call of the Federal Council. There representatives of the leading non-Roman communions of the Western world planned a conference to be held in Stockholm in 1925, which addressed itself to the task of creating a better social, political, economic and international order in the world.

The Stockholm Conference was noteworthy for three reasons. First, it directed the attention of the churches co-operatively upon the full sweep of the function of the Church in society. Hitherto the preoccupation had been only with one aspect of this total work, but now the entire problem came into focus. Second, it was the most representative modern ecumenical conference to be held; to it delegates came from more than one hundred communions, including—for the first time in a large world gathering —representatives from the Eastern Orthodox churches. Third, two organizations, which were finally merged, came into existence in order to carry on further the work started at the conference. A Continuation Committee of the Conference itself was authorized; and a permanent body, the Universal Christian Council for Life and Work, was established with its headquarters at Geneva.

In this brief account, only two achievements of the Universal Christian Council can be mentioned. Under it was organized a study department, which carried on a process of international collaboration among the leading scholars of the various churches. This gained increased respect, and issued in the plans and the publication of the seven volumes preparatory to the Oxford Conference of 1937. Hardly a spectacular endeavor, the results of this ecumenical study have nevertheless been far-reaching in bringing to mutual understanding and a more common mind the leading thinkers of Christendom. It was, secondly, under the Universal Christian Council that the great world conference on Church, Community and State was held at Oxford in 1937.

No account of the rise of the ecumenical organizations would be complete without particular reference to this highly important conference in itself, even apart from its action in helping to inaugurate a World Council of Churches. It was clear from 1933 on that the full-fledged deification of the fascist-type state was in process, with dire consequences for Christianity. The research department of the Universal Christian Council at Geneva was particularly effective in dealing with the evidences of a rising tide of intolerance, with violence as its method and world domination as its aim. Because the ghost of Caesar was walking on the highways of Europe and beckoning to the ghosts of Hirohito's ancestors in Japan, it was highly important that the churches of the world should study the relation of Christ's Lordship, his teachings, and his Church to the secularism of the day; particularly when it was clear that that secularism was turning demonic and threatening to destroy the fairest fruits of Christian civilization. It was also increasingly clear that Bishop Brent had been well within the truth when he exclaimed at Stockholm in 1925: "The world is too strong for a divided Church!"

When the delegates from 119 churches in 45 nations met at Oxford in the summer of 1937, the atmosphere was tense. There was a fairly widespread expectation that war was imminent. Persecution was already in evidence, proof that fascism feared the power of a united Christianity. The delegates of the German Evangelical Church were denied the privilege of leaving Germany to attend. The credentials committee was told by the delegates of at least ten nations that they feared what would happen if word of the actions of the Conference got back to their respective governments—which were already feeling the force of the movement to deify the state and deny all real freedom to religious bodies, particularly the churches.

But the very atmosphere of apprehension tended to create a new sense of urgency with respect to co-operation and unity. And vast areas of agreement were discovered with respect to the problems of the Church in the modern world. The record of them is set down in the volumes which record the proceedings or the documentation of the Conference.[8] We cannot here analyze these findings, but we may note that the timing of the Conference, the comprehensiveness of the preparation for it, the incisiveness of its findings and its widely representative character were of extensive and profound influence on the total ecumenical development.

5. UNITY RESULTING FROM CONSIDERATION OF THEOLOGICAL DIFFERENCES

The beginnings of the Faith and Order Movement illustrate dramatically the influence of a single man. It will be remembered that at the Missionary Conference at Edinburgh in 1910, Bishop Charles H. Brent of the Protestant Episcopal Church in the United States first began to consider the possibility of achieving unity through a discussion of the theological differences between the churches. First through his own church, and then through other churches, he worked almost singlehanded until sufficient impetus was gathered to hold a world conference on the problem.

Bishop Brent's conception involved the idea that a restudy of the elements in the faith and order of the churches would be fruitful, because of the fact that the reasons often given for the divisions of Christendom have to do with the faith or the polity of the churches. His main objective was to secure support for a plan to hold an inclusive conference, which would use for its basis proposals for the reunion of the churches set forth by the Lambeth Conference of the Anglican churches. These held that there was a fourfold practicable basis for the discussion of actual differences, namely, the Bible, the Apostles' and Nicene Creeds, the two Sacraments and the historic Episcopate. Under the vigorous encouragement of the Protestant Episcopal Church

[8] The official Oxford Conference Books (Chicago: Willett, Clark and Company, 1938).

in the United States and with the dynamic leadership of Bishop Brent himself, the plans developed for a World Conference on Faith and Order.

The Conference met in Lausanne, Switzerland, in 1927, just two years after the Conference on the practical application of Christianity had met in Stockholm. Like the latter, it brought together representatives of not only the Western non-Roman churches, but leaders from Eastern Orthodoxy as well. Thus to the idea of co-operation in missions, the effort to establish international peace and the practical application of Christian ideals to the problems of social relations, there came to be added an orderly study of theological approaches to Christian unity.

Two facts attest the importance of this study at the Lausanne Conference. The first is the progress made, full record of which has been preserved, in the discovery of wide areas of theological agreement among churches of diverse traditions. The scope of this agreement is indicated in the message of the Conference[9] to the world, now generally recognized as a classic statement of the Christian gospel. The second is that this Conference, like its predecessors, in the confidence that further progress could be made, authorized a Continuation Committee for the purpose of carrying on additional discussions, largely through the processes of ecumenical study and consultation which we have already described. These discussions have had concrete results. During the last thirty years there have been more than thirty major mergers of churches in all parts of the world involving many different types of communions. Of these, many can be traced, directly or indirectly, to the influence of the Faith and Order Movement.

It became clear that a second world conference was needed, and after a series of negotiations—to which we shall allude

[9] See p. 231. For the record of the findings of the Conference, see H. N. Bate, ed., *Faith and Order* (New York: Doubleday, Doran & Company, Inc., 1928).

presently—it was decided to hold the meeting at Edinburgh in
1937 immediately following the Oxford Conference on Life and
Work. As the Conference assembled, Hitler was arresting Nie-
moeller in Berlin and Hirohito was unleashing his armies upon
Shanghai. The mutterings of the gathering world storm were to
be heard by sensitive ears in both East and West.

The agreements reached at Edinburgh were amazing. The
most cynical critic could not but discern the signs of a spirit
which made for increasing unity across wide areas of the life of
the Church. An Affirmation of Unity demonstrated this spirit to
the world. Definite theological agreements were reached on
virtually every important issue save the authority of the ministry
and the nature of the sacraments. Recognition was given to non-
theological factors which contribute to disunity. Meeting under
the pressure of impending war and at the crest of a growing tide
of unity among the churches, the delegates from the one hundred
and twenty-three bodies represented provided a significant un-
folding of the degree of unity already attained.[10]

6. SPECIAL AGENCIES

The account of the emergence of the main ecumenical organizations would not be complete without reference to several agencies, Christian and world-wide in scope, which have existed for
specialized purposes, but have not had an organic relation to
the developments we have been sketching. Of these we would
note particularly the World Sunday School Association, the
World's Alliance of Young Men's Christian Associations, the
World's Young Women's Christian Associations, the World's
Student Christian Federation, and the Amsterdam Conference.

It is not possible here to enter into a discussion of their respective histories and particular purposes. As their names indicate,

[10] For a full record of the findings of the Conference, see Leonard
Hodgson, ed., *Faith and Order* (New York: The Macmillan Company,
1938).

they are nonecclesiastical agencies, which, however, in their purposes and in the main thrusts of their program are contributory to the Church. The World Sunday School Association relates directly to church programs; the other agencies find their work largely outside of the institutional church, viewing themselves as arms of the total work of Christ in the world.

Particular mention must be made of the World Conference of Christian Youth, held in Amsterdam in the summer of 1939. In an age of representative meetings, it was the most representative of the nations and the churches that has ever been held. It was sponsored equally by the World's Alliance of Y. M. C. A.'s, the World's Y. W. C. A., the World's Student Christian Federation and an Ecumenical Youth Commission. This Youth Commission had been set up jointly by the Universal Christian Council for Life and Work and the World Alliance for International Friendship Through the Churches, and had sent youth delegations to both the Oxford and Edinburgh Conferences. Under the leadership of its secretary, R. H. Edwin Espy, and together with the other sponsoring agencies, it planned the youth conference in 1939. Three factors give it special importance. First, its entire program centered on the Bible, providing an ecumenical setting for the study of the Bible which was a revelation to those in attendance. Second, it brought forcefully home to the representatives of the youth of seventy-five nations a vision of the ecumenical movement. Third, there grew out of it the desire for permanent youth work on a world level. This has now crystallized in the formation of a Youth Department of the proposed World Council of Churches, and in the formation of a joint Youth Commission composed of the World's Alliance of Y. M. C. A.'s, the World's Y. W. C. A., the World's Student Christian Federation and the World Council Youth Department. As an instrument for awakening the youth of the world to the realities and possibilities of ecumenical Christianity, the Amsterdam Conference is unsurpassed.

Our chief interest in these agencies is in regard to the contri-

bution which they have made—and are still making—to the
ecumenical movement in terms of the basic spirit of unity among
Christians and in terms of individual leaders. Each of the
agencies is interconfessional, and thus in all of the daily work
which they carry on serve to bring Christians together on the basis
of mutual recognition of one another as Christians. In their
councils and in their larger conferences, therefore, they have
served to make real that fundamental spirit of unity upon which
the whole ecumenical movement rests.

Particularly significant is their contribution of individual
leaders. It would be impossible to list all of those who, catching
their first vision, and finding their first experience in one or
more of these agencies have then devoted their energies to the
unity of the churches directly. Archbishop Temple was one. W.
A. Visser 't Hooft is another. William Paton was a third.

We have purposely left till now extensive reference to another
such person, he who is properly considered the elder statesman
of the ecumenical movement. Dr. John R. Mott has been associated with all of the main ecumenical organizations. As general
secretary and later chairman of the World's Student Christian
Federation, in which his first ecumenical experience was developed, as chairman of the Edinburgh, Jerusalem and Madras
Conferences of the International Missionary Council and of
the International Missionary Council itself, as chairman of the
World's Committee of the Young Men's Christian Association,
as chairman of the Business Committee of the Oxford Conference,
and as a vice-chairman of the Provisional Committee of the
World Council of Churches, his influence has been felt in every
major development of the ecumenical movement of the past half
century. Of some of these developments he was the originator;
of others he has been a central force in their promotion and
expansion. There is no other living figure in whom the varied
aspects of the modern ecumenical movement is so well summed
up.

7. THE WORLD COUNCIL OF CHURCHES

The background for the World Council of Churches is all of
the foregoing. In literal truth, had there not been the varied
approaches—through the missionary enterprise, through the Life
and Work Movement and through the Faith and Order Movement—together with the solid achievements attained through
these different areas of work, the proposal for a world council
of churches would have fallen on deaf ears. Proof of the fact
is that as far back as 1845 an American Lutheran, Dr. Samuel
Schmucker, made a proposal for a union of the churches on a
federated basis, upon which, incidentally, the proposal for the
World Council of Churches drew heavily, but which in 1845 was
premature. Though for a brief time, beginning in 1846, an
organization known as the Evangelical Alliance, based in part
upon Dr. Schmucker's proposal, had an influence, the full plan
was not adopted, and the Evangelical Alliance itself finally died
out. The time was not ripe; the full succession of events, and
all that they implied, were necessary before such a proposal
could be countenanced.

It was, moreover, necessary to develop experience and leadership in order to launch such a venture as the World Council of
Churches. It would be impossible to single out any one or any
dozen leaders as primarily responsible. Into the total effort the
combined leadership of all the movements we have been describing was poured. Yet one person stands out. William Temple
was the dominating figure of the early days of the World Council. His interest in the ecumenical movement was of long dura-
tion. Noticed by John R. Mott as a student of unusual capabili-
ties, he was sent by the World's Student Christian Federation
to the Student Movements in the Australasian areas. He attended
the missionary conference at Edinburgh in 1910 as an usher in
the gallery on the left of the speaker's dais. There he stood with
bowed head toward the close of the Conference and promised

God that he would devote his life to working for the unity of Christendom. It was a vow well lived out. Associated particularly with the Faith and Order Movement he devoted his keen mind, large vision and immense influence as a churchman to this cause. It is to him that the World Council of Churches owes its greatest single debt.

The first concrete step toward the establishment of the World Council of Churches involved the drawing together of the Life and Work and the Faith and Order Movements. In the initial stages this was largely a matter of consultation among the leaders of the two movements, always under the inspiration and guidance of Archbishop Temple. The most important concrete result of these contacts was the decision to hold the Oxford and Edinburgh Conferences in near-by cities on consecutive dates so as to emphasize their complementary character. This was symbolic of a growing recognition that theological discussion could not fruitfully take place without reference to the life of the Church; and that the ethical tasks could not be discerned properly without reference to theological considerations. But it was more than symbolic. It was a means of insuring considerable contact between the participants in both meetings.

The decision to place before both the Oxford and Edinburgh Conferences a proposal for a world council of churches was reached in 1935 at a meeting held in Princeton, New Jersey. The response in America, Britain and on the Continent was immediate and enthusiastic, and led to the creation of a Committee of Thirty-five, entrusted with the task of working out the actual proposal for a method of procedure to be placed before both Conferences.

The record would be incomplete without mention of the ecumenical service of worship held in St. Paul's Cathedral in London between the two Conferences of 1937. Though technically it was unrelated to the Conferences or the proposal for a world council, it was an occasion of great spiritual power. As such it was directly contributary to the spirit with which the proposal was received.

With the adoption of the proposal unanimously by the delegates in both the Oxford and Edinburgh Conferences the way was open for the actual construction of a world council. Each Conference had appointed seven persons, making a Committee of Fourteen, to draw up a constitution; but it was soon discovered by that Committee that a larger and more representative body was needed. Accordingly, in 1938 a "constitutional convention" was held in Utrecht. A constitution was drawn up and adopted with complete unanimity. Moreover, it was decided, in order that work could immediately begin, to establish a Provisional Committee, with authority to make plans and to operate until the first Assembly of the World Council of Churches could officially establish the body. To this Provisional Committee was given the staff and offices of the Universal Christian Council for life and work, already well established. It was intended that the first Assembly should be held within three years. The intervention of World War II, however, forced the Provisional Committee not only to postpone plans for this meeting, but to carry on a large and unforeseen program of activities in connection with the emergencies brought about by the war.[11]

In February of 1946, a meeting of the Provisional Committee for the World Council of Churches was held in Geneva. Its chief business was to lay plans for the first Assembly, which is now scheduled for 1948.

It is, of course, too early to venture any lasting estimate of the significance of the World Council of Churches. It is the most comprehensive of the ecumenical organizations which have been proposed. Its record already, throughout the war years, is impressive. At present writing ninety-three churches have joined it. To it is attached the hopes for a more unified and aggressive non-Roman church throughout the world. It comes as the culmination of a multitude of attempts at co-operative work and at the height of the desire for the unity and the universality of the

[11] For an account of these activities see ch. 3, pt. II.

Church. On the other hand, the problems which it faces, as its leaders well recognize, are immense—for they are the problems before the Christian Church in general in this fateful time. It is a venture of great promise and hope; it must be carried forward with wisdom and care.

One particular problem should be singled out. This is the matter of the relation between the World Council of Churches and the International Missionary Council, the two main ecumenical agencies on the present scene. The complexities of the problem cannot be listed here, but the urgency of it may be noted in the fact that it is from the "younger churches," whose main affiliation is with the International Missionary Council, that the most insistent demands for increasing unity among the churches have come. Such vigorous life must in some way be related to that which is, by the outlines of its structure, the most comprehensive of the two agencies, namely the World Council of Churches. Fully cognizant of the issue, both agencies have appointed a committee which has the matter under study. A meeting of this group in February, 1946, has held large promise for the gradual resolution of the problem, and a number of practical co-operative undertakings were planned at that time.

The original thesis of this chapter is perhaps justified. From the multiplicity of organizations and approaches here mentioned, it is clear that we have been dealing essentially with a *movement*. It is not too much to say that for the past quarter of a century and more the non-Roman churches have both witnessed and been the scene of a spontaneous upsurge of conviction which has led to an increasing unity among Christians. Appearing now here and now there, in this form and that, depending upon not a single but a number of different methods, this movement is, above all, spiritual in nature. Though it of necessity has organizational expressions, it is not at root the projection upon church life of a single organization or plan of organization. Its genius comes, rather, from within, from the working of the Holy Spirit in leading men to realize their true unity in Christ.

Part II. *Ecumenical Fellowship During the War*

Charles W. Iglehart

1. The impact of the war upon the Churches: the United States, Europe, the Far East. 2. The struggle of the churches of North America and Europe and of the younger churches. 3. The increase of world co-operation.

When World War II struck and rocked the earth it found in every land a living Christian community. In some countries the Church is as ancient as the nation itself, and to it every citizen belongs. It is completely interwoven in the culture, the history and the life of the people. In some other countries it lives an uncertain existence as a grudgingly tolerated minority. In still others, as with some of the "younger churches" in Asia, it is so small, so alien and so new amidst the millions in their national history of millenniums that it is scarcely noticed by society at large. Yet in all nations alike the Christians belong to their own people; they are devoted to their community; they are stirred by deep loyalties to their fold; and especially in times of crisis they are eager to share in sacrifice and service. War inevitably hurls them about, grimly sorting them with their people into groupings of ally and enemy, of makers of war and victims of war, and finally of victors and vanquished. In the process there is suffering, separation, privation, destruction, loss and death amidst the crosscurrents of motive and loyalty that tug so desperately at life's moorings.

For all these Christian churches belong, too, to the one, unseen kingdom of God, and they form a world fellowship in a world that is torn apart. Of this fellowship Dr. William Temple in his enthronement sermon as the Archbishop of Canterbury in 1942 said:

> As though in preparation for such a time as this, God has been building up a Christian fellowship which now extends into almost every nation, and binds citizens of them all together in true unity and mutual love. No human agency has planned this. It is the result of the great missionary enterprise of the last hundred and fifty years. Almost incidentally the great world fellowship has arisen from that enterprise. But it has arisen; it is the great new fact of our time. Here is one ground of hope for the coming days.

What then did the war do to the churches of the world? And what did they do in the war experience?

1. THE IMPACT OF THE WAR

The United States

Let us glance, first, at our own country and churches. Superficially viewed, we have been the most fortunate of all in that we have suffered the least of any major participant. Notwithstanding the multitudes who are bearing a private grief in their hearts and homes, we have escaped any major public calamity. Furthermore, to many the years of war have brought wealth, possessions and comforts hitherto unknown. Church finances have been easy, and debts have been cleared.

But at the deeper levels American church life has suffered. The very prosperity of the churches in America pointed to one of two basic difficulties. Free from destruction and its attendant evils, engaged in an immense program of production, America was throughout the war an island of unbounded prosperity in a sea of intense human suffering. The churches reflected this situation. Except for those who, as we have indicated, bore a private grief, American Christians did not walk with their brothers through the valley of the shadow. Personal suffering did not force them back upon the reality of God as fully as was the case in many instances in other lands. Moreover, in a society preoccupied with war the "beloved community" finds itself lifted out of its own world into one strange to its genius, with obligations and tasks that ill-consort with its central function, the expression in society of the holy love of God as known by Christ's redemptive suffering upon the cross. Yet our churches belong to our time and our country, and they cannot blind themselves to its demands. Within our own ranks this dreadful dilemma has been met in varying ways. The World Conference at Jerusalem in 1928 and again at Madras in 1938 registered the deep fissures lying across the Christian conscience at this place. The Committee on the State of the Church of the Federal Council of Churches in North America reported in 1940:

> On the sinfulness of war and the desirability of peace with justice there can be but one mind among Christians. On the steps to secure this end it is inevitable that there should be differences of opinion. It is at this point that we most have need of charity without compromise, conviction without dogmatism.

During the war American Christians suffered the spiritual hazards of breathing an atmosphere filled with passion and hatred. They were subjected to the same massed impact of official information, propaganda and purposed pressures as others. Voluntarily or involuntarily they were a part of the war effort. Few escaped some inner tension. The overseas outreach of the Church was most difficult. With many "mission lands" it was impossible to maintain any direct contact at all. It has been a truncated and a restricted world in which the churches have lived and worked.

Europe

Crossing the Atlantic we come upon a scene of intense suffering from the war. Summing up the battered existence of the people of Great Britain, with the hourly fear of death from the air, and the daily imminence of invasion, a Christian leader recently said:

> England had had a six years break with the decencies and the charities of the pre-war Christendom. Wearied with overwork and poor sleep, not too well nourished, still wearing the clothing of 1939, almost one third of the people have seen their homes destroyed, all have lost near kin. In this gruelling chapter of history fourteen thousand churches and church buildings have been lost or badly damaged. One by one the greatest of Britain's Christian leaders have fallen.

On the Continent the suffering and destruction have been beyond description. Long before Germany launched her attack on her neighbors the people of Germany, and that means the Christians and churches, were paying the heavy price of national ambition and expansion, as were the people of Japan. They, too, had their divisions and reservations regarding the war, their struggles with the state, and their physical privations under the policy of "guns before butter." As the totalitarian net was thrown over the minds and hearts as well as the bodies of all the German people, Christians with the rest were the victims. Then came the actual marching of the troops. Year after year German lads mingled their blood with the youth of other lands all over the Continent. Finally came the holocaust of Allied bombs and the avenging wall of fire and death that dropped the curtain on the last act of Europe's most ghastly tragedy of all history. One by one the horror had swept over the other countries. First Czecho-Slovakia, then Poland, with the neighboring countries of Austria and Hungary, were overwhelmed. Then came in swift succession the invasions of Denmark, Norway, Holland, Belgium and France. Later the desolation spread to

Finland, all the Baltic States, the Balkans and deep into the huge expanses of the Soviet Republics.

The venerable Mother Church of the Russian people had long before the war had to face her Golgotha in the cruel experience of the Revolution. Although the stern requirements of justice had long called for drastic reform, the Revolution saw, not reform, but a near annihilation. Disinherited, stripped of her wealth, her prestige and her power, the Church was an outcaste in her own ancient domain. The systematic "liquidation" of the higher clergy, the expropriation of the monasteries and the prohibition of all training of ministry left her without leadership or a plan. In the early years of the war all this was accentuated under the harsh regimentation of the national life.

Everywhere there was agony; everywhere Christians met the ordeal of fire and death. Tracy Strong draws a poignant picture of the wartime suffering:

> "The Sacred Way which leads to Calvary winds across the world," warns my French colleague. "The day before yesterday in Manchuria, China and Abyssinia; yesterday in Poland, Greece, France and Yugo-Slavia; today the nations one by one become pilgrims on the road." Liquid fire, bursting shells, irresistible tank attacks and bombs from the air destroy persons at the battle front or in the suffocating atmosphere of the bomb cellars . . . the brutality in concentration camps has shocked the world . . . hours of gnawing hunger make children prematurely sensitive to the suffering of others . . . millions of prisoners of war face the stagnant sea of idleness without privacy and without liberty . . . the fear of the secret police has changed the older forms of national hatreds in all the countries to a desire for personal revenge. . . . The fear and horror on the faces of those who have had their passports taken away, is a sight never to be forgotten. . . . Millions have lost their social and moral roots.[13]

[13] Tracy Strong, "Suffering and The People of The Cross," *The Student World*, First Quarter, 1944.

This is the Europe in which the churches had to live and endure. The ordinary canons of moral judgment regarding decisions made under such conditions can scarcely apply. It would be slight wonder if under such strains Christianity were to disappear. Yet Miss Barbara Ward, editor of the *London Economist* writing in the *Christian Newsletter* says:

> Europe is like a country over which a tornado has passed.
> It has torn up all the land marks and institutions, and
> destroyed universities and schools. Practically speaking,
> the only institutions which remain as a continuous link with
> Europe's past are the Christian Churches.

Asia

Across the world, in Asia, another theater of war has pressed upon the Christian movements of the East. In Japan something paralleling the situation in Germany has for years been taking place in the nation, enveloping the little Christian communities in mists and fogs of confusion and bewildered decisions. In a state leaping to empire on the stepping-stones of continuing successful wars all of society gradually becomes abnormal. Every institution is bent toward the unified national effort. If the majority churches of the West were shaken to their foundations by similar conditions, what about the Japanese Christians who number scarcely one half of 1 per cent of the population? Since the turn of the century they have not had time to catch their breath in the headlong career of their people. Particularly since 1931, when the war really began in the East, both public policies and the indefinable atmospheric pressure of the nation changed the course of life for the churches. Increasingly the veneration of the national heroes and of slain soldiers was elaborated as a civic duty. The deep respect and affection for the emperor felt by the people was lifted into a cult permeating all the life of the country through schools, radio, newspapers and every other form of indoctrination.

In 1940 the pressures became so great that in self-defense

the churches stepped free of financial or personal commitments to the churches of the West, and finally in 1941 most of the Protestant denominations joined in the United Church of Christ in Japan. Although the constitution granted by the government was not unduly repressive, and did not deny the freedom of creedal statement, yet it provided for an organization that was thoroughly fascist in structure. The war from 1937 on brought steady privation and hardship to the churches. Ministers, as in Europe, were not exempt from military service. The membership was decimated by war activities and casualties. Continuous malnutrition has led to semistarvation for many. Deaths have been high, especially among the housewives who have prepared the meager rations for others in the home to eat.

Finally the war came back upon Japan as on Germany, and at the same terrible hands of American avengers. City after city was all but destroyed. Some were entirely wiped out. On March 9, 1945, a tempest of incendiary bombs flooded Tokyo, the capital, with fire, leaving in its wake over a hundred thousand dead and a third of the city leveled. Out of a total of 167 churches in the metropolis only six were left intact.

China's ordeal has been long and bitter. Invaded by Japan first economically and then politically through puppet regimes, and finally in full military conflict, her efforts at domestic reconstruction suspended by the life and death struggle for existence, she, too, has been forced into totalitarian patterns by the harsh matrix of war. And with the others the Christian communities everywhere have had their full share of suffering. During the war there were several Chinas. In the north a sort of unwilling equilibrium with the invading forces was achieved. But in central and southern China the sudden flood of armies with their violence, and with the accompanying cruelties and civilian exploitation found the people unprepared. Many fled, and there was the classic trek of scores of millions of people into the hinterland before the storm. In west China, a comparatively undeveloped region overnight found itself the seat of government and the goal of fleeing multitudes. All manner of emergencies had to be faced, and innumerable problems tackled. The Church was not prepared with either institutions or personnel adequate to such a demand. In each of these regions and situations there were particular sacrifices and sufferings to bear, and in all the Christians had their share.

In other parts of Asia, too, the churches had their troubles. In Burma and Malaya the fighting was fierce, and did not spare Christian institutions. So also with Sumatra and Java. Into the Philippines the war was carried, first by Japan, and then by the American forces. Between the two campaigns there was a large loss of property and of life. Over the island world of the south Pacific the war threw its net, enmeshing native Christians and church institutions with all others.

The Christians of Korea have long had to endure political subjection, and with it a too large degree of control over their life and worship. With the acceleration of speed of the Japanese Empire the peninsular satellite was hurled along into situations of new intensity of hardship. The pressure of State Shinto was constant, and the restrictions on church life progressively repressive. Many ministers were imprisoned—all 240 of the Oriental Missionary Society at one time—and of these over fifty are said to have perished in prison. Of 5,000 churches, 1,200 were closed. The affrighted church members dropped to about one third the usual attendance at the one service permitted each week. Christian schools were closed. The Union Theological School in Seoul was forced to reorient its constitution and curriculum toward the Japanese national goals. Korea was spared physical destruction, but the spiritual anguish of the Christian people was very acute.

In fact, everywhere the Japanese invasion went it carried troublous decisions for the Christian movements. Usually there was no frontal attack by the military government. Rather, the Christian churches were courted as possible centers of pacification. But non-co-operation was likely to be met by a swift turn to harsh measures. The result was that within each of the Christian movements of the occupied countries there was a divergence of attitude and reaction. It was impossible to remain neutral; some degree of compliance was required. But the degrees varied, and with that variation there was the seed for mutual dissension, recrimination and misunderstanding.

Everywhere the Japanese authorities desired a unification of the Christian forces. That was natural, since the one thing all military governments hate and fear is diversification or individual initiative. So union churches were promoted, and where that was not accomplished there were strongly federated groupings. This extended to including not only Protestants and Roman Catholics, but also Mohammedans and Buddhists.

Even in countries outside the immediate orbit of Germany or Japan the war deeply affected the Christian churches. India was harnessed to the war effort. Although an army of two million Indian volunteers was raised, the general attitude of the public toward the involuntary inclusion in the war was one of opposition. In many ways that has brought embarrassment to the Christian movement which is historically related to the countries of the West. Life in the Near and Middle East has been badly dislocated by the war, as it has been throughout Africa. Closed lines of travel and communications have cut off the missionary contacts, and the warping of the economy and even the politics of South America has come through with comparatively small disarrangement of life.

2. THE STRUGGLE OF THE CHURCHES

Thus far we have been looking at the war storm that struck the Christian churches of the world. Let us now see how they came through the ordeal.

North America

Throughout the trying war years the churches of North America found a *via media* between the Scylla of war hysteria and the Charybdis of irresponsible detachment Lessons had been learned from World War I both by the churches and by government and public. It was not expected that Christian institutions or spokesmen should identify the Christian gospel with the war effort. Yet Christian people were not slackers in any area of life. Conscientious objectors to war, while not enthusiastically supported by the major denominations, were nevertheless recognized within the fellowship. Victims of the crisis, such as the Americans of Japanese ancestry, found their best friends and staunchest advocates in the churches. Among the forums for discussion of world issues few have been more realistic or openminded than many held by Christian groups and within the churches. Some of the ablest writing and the sanest thinking has been done by Christian leaders. In the organization meeting of the United Nations at San Francisco Christian influence was conspicuous. Right now it is among the churches that the greatest concern is felt about the future of the world's society. Never have the American churches been more gravely weighted with the responsibility that rightly goes with their great numbers and essential spiritual authority.

In all this the churches have found a new solidarity. Going through common experiences they have discovered deeper harmonies than they had realized before. The men in service and especially at the fronts were served by chaplains of various faiths in a team spirit that was more than mere good sportsmanship. And among themselves men of differing creeds found common ground in times of danger and loneliness.

Preoccupation with the war did not prevent the ongoing support of the Christian world mission of the American churches. The work of over one hundred boards has gone on with unbelievable vigor and efficiency. Channeling through the Foreign Missions Conference they do much planning in unison, and year by year are committing more and more of their common interests to joint administration. Representative committees deal with the various countries overseas, while others focus on such matters as education, medical work, literature and literacy, religious liberty, personnel and promotion. The annual report for 1944 shows that during the year, 224 missionaries had departed for their fields. It is safe to say that in some of the countries reached these messengers of the Christian churches were the only civilian tie with America across a war-torn world. The boards, however, were far from satisfied. They reported 976 openings abroad crying out for someone to come.

Great Britain

The churches of Great Britain command our admiration for their courage during the war. By common suffering they have won the right to speak to their own people with a new meaning. Until he died, Archbishop Temple came nearer to being the voice of Britain's conscience than any man in generations. William Paton, too, before he died, saw the achievement of new and larger tasks among the mission boards as well as the formation of the first Council of Churches for Great Britain. In the midst of their distress and danger the churches remembered their needier neighbors on the Continent. They have now committed themselves to a gift of a million pounds for the reconstruction of European church life. Year by year the Christians of Great Britain stood amid the rubble of their ruined churches and prayed and gave for the furtherance of the Christian mission throughout the world.

Europe

On the Continent a brave story has been written, much of it in the blood of Christian ministers and laymen. Wherever the pagan state reached out to claim men's souls there stood some Christian leader blocking the way in the name of God. This was true in Germany, where the Bishop of Mainz as early as 1930 saw the meaning of the Nazi claims and gave a thundering pronouncement, the "Three Tremendous No's" for the direction of Catholics. Standing on the solid encyclical of Pope Pius IX *"Mit Brennender Sorge"* that church held its line through all

the years since 1936. Perhaps the bravest word came from the
bishops when, gathered at Fulda, beside the tomb of the great
Boniface in 1942, they announced:

> We definitely and firmly refuse the demand that we
> should show our loyalty to our country by being faithless
> to Christ and our Church.

The Lutheran churches, too, stood their ground. Not only
Niemöller from the pulpit of Dalhem and Otto Dibelius from
his professional chair, but entire sections of the church gathered
in the Confessional movement gave an unbroken witness during the entire war. Bishop Wurm of Württemberg addressing the
Provincial Church Council said: "Uncompromising war is declared against Christianity," and he accepted the challenge in a
consistent opposition to the state measures.

Outside of Germany some of the Christian movements simply
were crushed, as in Poland. But even there Archbishop Stanisław
Gall of the Catholic Church in Warsaw when confronted with a
proposal for collaboration from the German governor replied:
"I am a disciple of Jesus Christ, I am not a Judas." His fate and
that of other church leaders was sealed, but the Church had kept
its soul. In 1942 Count Tarnowski could write: "In its modern
catacombs all Europe grows tremendous powers of spiritual life.
It will be a cradle of new power."

In Belgium, where the tradition of Cardinal Mercier's heroic
struggle for freedom in the last war still holds, his successor
Cardinal van Roey boldly shielded the Church against en-
croachment. In Holland the struggle took a classic form in continuing resistance on the part of both Roman Catholics and Reformed Church leaders, who issued partly identical pastoral
letters of defiance, read simultaneously. Norway saw the in-
domitable Bishop Berggrav matching his integrity against the
weak Quisling. Behind him stood the seven bishops of the nation, and behind them a thousand ministers who on Easter of
1942 in protest resigned their official posts as clergy of a state

church, but warned the hostile authorities that they surrendered not one whit of their spiritual functions as shepherds of the people.

This story of heroic proportions has been told in A. L. Warnshuis' *The Church's Battle for Europe's Soul*:

> In the occupied countries, France, Holland, Norway, the churches were not directly attacked, but of their own will they took the offensive. When it became plain that the laws of God were being systematically broken in the life of the state and the people, the churches opened the attack. They protested against the treatment of the Jews, against forced deportation of laborers, against the sterilization policies, against the educational system, and finally against the principles and philosophy of National Socialism and the forceful imposition of them upon the people against their will and in opposition to their own beliefs. The churches became the voice of the free spirit of the people. The pulpit and the sermon were the only uncensored forum of the people.
>
> Sometimes it was a struggle to keep silence, as in France, when the foreign office in Berlin sent a special emissary to Paris to obtain from the churches a public protest against the bombardment of Germany's cities. Pastor Boegner, President of the Federation of French Churches, first declined the invitation to dinner saying that he could not eat with this official representative so long as his colleagues were in prison. Then, when the negotiator pressed his request, the answer was given, "The French Huguenot Church never makes a public declaration at the request of a temporal power."
>
> Constructive forces grouped themselves around these protesting churches. Their evangelistic opportunity became very great, for people were interested in discovering the secret of the courage and power of the churches. The churches now have a message, not only for the individual, but also for the community and the state and nation.
>
> The church grows truly and strongly by the development

of its own inner life. So it is important to notice some of the characteristics of the re-awakened church life in Europe. Emphasis is placed upon making the local church what it ought to be. The parish church and minister were the centers of the awakening church.

A dominant aspect of this revival is the central position given to the Bible. As the issues challenging Christian faith were those that the individual confronted in his secular vocation, the Bible broke into the life of the common man.

The young people share in the awakening of the churches. In France, for example, under what is becoming widely known as C.I.M.A.D.E. (*Comite Intermouvement Aupres des Evacues*) the Christian young people have been active in giving assistance to the evacuated people from Alsace-Lorraine, to the miserable men and women in the concentration camps (both before and after liberation day) and in the devastated cities in Normandy and Brittany and soon in Alsace. This service has been both social relief and the leading of Bible classes and evangelistic meetings. Now these young people have organized a Christian Youth Alliance which they insist upon relating closely to the churches.

Another characteristic of this revived church life is the development of cooperation and united work. Even between Protestant and Roman Catholic churches there has been more cooperation than ever before. Both in Holland and in France they have united in issuing sometimes joint and sometimes paralleled statements. In France, all the Protestant churches were already united in a Federation, and there and in Belgium national committees for the united planning of relief and rehabilitation have been organized by representatives of all the Protestant churches. The relationships with churches in other lands have become more precious, and the ecumenical fellowship is acquiring new meaning. Formerly that fellowship may have been thought of as a spiritual luxury and not of the stuff of life, but when it became dangerous to have relationships with brethren across the frontier, they found that it was essential. When they protested against the inhumanity and injustice of the German regime, they took care to speak in the name of those universal truths which are embodied in the Christian Faith, and as ministers, not of national bodies, but of the Church Universal. Now they expect something more from us, not merely big conferences and paper documents, but the reality of Christian fellowship and brotherhood. If any American church overstresses its denominationalism, it will be out-of-step with the churches of Europe.

The basic characteristic of the awakening of these churches is their rediscovery of the church as the body of Christ in the midst of a hostile or indifferent environment. They have realized anew that Christ reigns—not that He will reign. He reigns now. He is today the King of Kings. History is in the hands of their invisible Lord.

Of the part Christians and even Christian pastors played in the underground resistance movements the whole story has not yet been told. In all the history of the Church there are few chapters more arresting than this one in which, under the drive of conscience, men in the name of God descended into the pit with lying, stealing and murder as ghoulish companions, taking their lives in their hands hourly in resistance to tyranny and evil. We could name one minister who played three roles at once. He was a member of the Nazi party, an agent of the Gestapo, and at the same time an active worker in the Underground.

The "younger churches"

In different ways, but with no less heroism, Christians of the "younger churches" maintained a vital life. Missionaries in many parts of the world were either withdrawn by the exigencies of war or else remained at their posts and were interned—German missionaries by the Allies and Allied missionaries by the Japanese. This left the "younger churches" served by them without the accustomed aid of either personnel or finances. If any timid friends of these churches had fears that they could not measure up to the new burdens and strains, those fears have been completely dispelled. In every part of the "mission field" the churches have put their shoulders to the load, their own leadership has stepped to the front, and their laymen and women have met the emergency with intelligence and consecration. No Christian movement in any country has gone under. So far as can be learned, all have gained greatly by the experience of added responsibility, and of sacrifice.

In some countries—China, for instance—the work of the churches has been conspicuous. When the people fled before the invading armies some pastors led their flocks out along the hard, unknown roads to the west. Schoolmasters and schoolmistresses took their institutions on foot, interspersing study with tramping until a haven was found beyond the mountain wall. Others remained to care for the refugees streaming by, or the wounded soldiers being moved to the rear. They set up relief stations under incredible conditions, and became good Samaritans even to needy Japanese. Madame Chiang Kai-shek in a broadcast to the nation called attention to the place of affection and gratitude won by the little Christian movement from a Chinese public that only yesterday was howling them down as foreign agents. Bishop Yu-pin may well say: "never has the future for Christianity in China been so bright as now." But Chinese Christians are not resting on their laurels. Life is still desperately grim, for poverty, inflation, homelessness and violence are still stalking the land. The churches as reported by Dr. Frank Cartwright of the Foreign Missions Conference visiting China, are busy with plans for the future reconstruction not only of their own institutions, but of all Chinese society. The National Christian Council in its last annual meeting voted to send a deputation of good will to Japan as soon as passports could be obtained. This action was matched by that of the Chinese Y.M.C.A. which is now eager to meet Japanese student leaders face to face in forgiveness and mutual fellowship.

The Christians of Japan have had a hard time, both physically and spiritually. For years no adequate word could be received, and they were virtually isolated from the rest of the world. But there was one strong tie that held them. In the spring of 1941, as war became imminent, they sent a deputation of eight men and women to meet with leaders of the American churches in prayers for peace, and as an embassy of thanks for the past help from the West. At Riverside in California the two groups met in a retreat during which spiritual links were forged that even the war could not break. As the war came to an end a broadcast in Japan was monitored on this side of the Pacific. It was the voice of a Christian administrator telling his people about the Riverside retreat and expressing a welcome for an American deputation in case there should be planned a return visit. This was the signal for the Federal Council of Churches and the Foreign Missions Conference to send four nationally known persons to carry the greetings of the American churches as well as of the churches of the world. Amidst the horrors and the ashes of Tokyo they met the friends of the years gone by, and in one of the few still standing churches they knelt together in communion at the Lord's table. The outstanding impression of the members of this deputation is that of the integrity of the Japanese Christians. In an unbelievably difficult situation they seem to have found very deep resources of wisdom and courage, and to have come through to a spiritual renewal. Many of them accept not only defeat but the responsibility for it. They are ready with penitence to begin the slow, long task of rebuilding a shattered nation from the ground up. In their destitution they are showing a sturdy spirit of Christian discernment. When Kagawa was asked about the acceptability of American gifts for rebuilding he said: "Perhaps that will come in time, but not yet. We do not wish our churches built before our neighbors have roofs over their heads. Anyway, it is spiritual reunion that we long for, and this must be achieved before money will do much."

3. THE INCREASE OF CO-OPERATION

Orphaned missions

The account, however, is far from complete without mention of the wartime achievements in world-wide co-operative effort. Of these the first is Orphaned Missions, called "the most significant piece of ecumenical co-operation on record." Anticipating the dislocations of war in 1939, the secretary of the International Missionary Council made plans with the German societies for the protection of their mission property overseas. So when war broke out the lines were safely held. The work of interned German missionaries was taken up by volunteers from their "enemy" countries. Then the other countries of Europe were inundated by invasion, cut off from their missions, and some of them even from any communication with the rest of the world. Into this emergency the free Christian movements stepped, and with whole hearts carried the burdens of their distressed brethren throughout the war years. In all there have been over a hundred and twenty mission agencies operating in over twenty different countries which have been aided. Funds disbursed in the five years of war exceeded four million dollars, and came from twenty-five countries, including some of those of the "younger churches." So far as we know, not a single mission station has had to be closed, and not a single worker withdrawn for lack of financial support. In the meantime, in all of the isolated "home-base" countries, including Germany, funds were regularly collected, missionary rallies steadily held, and personnel recruited for future resumption of missionary service when the ways should open.

Other co-operative ventures, far-reaching in scope, centered in Europe around the newly formed Provisional Committee of the World Council of Churches. Though it had been established only in 1938, and had met only once, it was able through the necessities of the war situation and the vision of its leadership to command resources for a widespread program. As might be expected, this consisted of emergency measures to meet needs brought forth by the war; it developed in four main aspects.

War prisoners

The first referred to prisoners of war. The War Prisoners Aid of the Y.M.C.A. and the International Red Cross were both serving large educational, recreational and material needs of the nearly ten million prisoners. The religious needs were cared for by the neutral chaplains engaged by the Ecumenical Chaplaincy Commission of the World Council of Churches. The strategy of the work called for a program of ceaseless visitation to the prisoner camps on the part of a few chaplains, the discovery in each of men able to act as ministers for their fellow prisoners, and help with the necessary steps of organization and limited supplies which would insure centers of worship. Not only did they maintain this important service to men who showed a deep gratitude for it, but by their very presence in the lands where the prisoners were on both sides of the struggle they were able to keep in contact with the leaders of the Churches. Even in the United States three Swedish Lutheran chaplains served through the latter years of the war in maintaining contact with the numerous camps throughout the country and in providing for religious ministries to the men in them. In addition, collaboration with the American and the British and Foreign Bible Societies provided the chief means for supplying the Bible in great quantities to the men behind barbed wire. Many congregations were organized in the camps and significant study and discussion groups formed. Large numbers of men who were helped by these activities have gone back into the life of the nations with a new conception of the possibilities as well as of the actualities of Christian unity.

Information

A second aspect of this program had to do with the supplying of information. The closed frontiers throughout the world meant a complete shutoff of news of contemporary Christian activities for many churches and individuals. Two means were used, both of them openly in some cases and surreptitiously in others. The first was by persons—neutrals going from the center in Geneva, visiting those in confinement, returning, visiting those who were free, acting as in fact they were, couriers for the Christian movement. The second was by the written word, notably through the International Christian Press and Information Service. An agency now in its twelfth year of service, it was steadily maintained throughout the war, carrying on its wires and pages news of the Christian world. The Christian leader in Shanghai who now reports this news service to have been his only source of information during the Japanese occupation—its relatively regular arrival a source of amazement—is symbolic of the service thus rendered.

Refugees

Undoubtedly one of the most tragic results of the war was the creation of millions of persons without home or country. Refugees moved without end and in increasing numbers across the map of Europe. Here also the churches engaged in co-operative work. Under the World Council, the Ecumenical Refugee Commission sought to help in an almost hopeless situation. At first the victims were Jews and Christians of Jewish ancestry; later, for a host of political and religious reasons, the refugee belonged to all nationalities and races and varieties of religious belief. Blessed by its neutral base, the Commission was able not only to help the thousands who poured into Switzerland, but also to foster the organization of refugee committees in many nations, which could deal at first hand with the omnipresent problems of housing, food, clothing and legal papers.

Reconstruction

As the war developed and destruction increased, problems of reconstruction and relief pushed to claim first attention. The necessity of planning for action at the end of the war became obvious. The fourth phase of ecumenical activity in Geneva centered in the Department of Reconstruction and Inter-church Aid, which includes a Material Aid Department. The objectives are double: to provide as much material relief as may be made possible by contributions from Christians throughout the world, and to provide help in the reconstruction of church life on the Continent. A staff, loaned by churches in different countries, a series of national committees, and the disbursement of funds running into millions have enabled the Commission to make significant progress. Its philosophy is perhaps the most important of all: to help Christians in Europe to surmount the difficulties of their postwar situation, in order that they may make the basic contribution to the reconstruction of their own national life.

As we view the churches of the world we cannot but ask ourselves whether we may not have to revise our terms in thinking of ourselves and them. In relation to the churches of Asia we have called ourselves older, and them younger. But in the presence of such evidence of maturity we wonder whether in their suffering they have not become older in experience than we. Across in Europe are what we have called the old, mother churches, while we are the younger ones. But recent visitors are unanimous in saying that the crushing experiences of the past decades have winnowed out the old, till all that is left is something newer than we in our unbroken society now know. We wonder whether we can bring ourselves into a mood of harmony with the Brandenburg Synod of the Evangelical Church of Germany, which called for a day of penance with the words:

> We Germans have removed the Ten Commandments from our public life, and have acted contrary to the law of God. Now we are reaping the consequences of our deeds. All the innocent bloodshed cries to God against us, all the inhumanities which took place in our midst.

More challenging to reconciliation still is the message that went out from Stuttgart in November, 1945, from the Council of the Evangelical Church of all Germany:

> We with our people know ourselves to be not only in a great company of sorrow, but also in a solidarity of guilt. . . . Now a new beginning is to be made . . . our hope is in the God of Grace and Mercy that he will use our churches as his instruments. . . . We hope in God that through the common service of the churches, the spirit of violence and revenge may be brought under control in the whole world, and the spirit of peace and love may gain the mastery, wherein alone a tortured humanity may find healing. So in an hour in which the whole world needs a new beginning, we pray
> *"Veni, Creator Spiritus."*

In the words of Hachiro Yuasa, "this church, and only this church can be the reconciler among men and the restorer of peace among nations." This is the world Christian fellowship which has come through the war, scarred but unbeaten, ready in God's providence for a truer witness in the world of to-morrow.

4

THE CHRISTIAN COMMUNITY AND WORLD ORDER

O. Frederick Nolde

Introduction. 1. A Christian world outlook: the transcendence of national boundaries and achievement of an international approach. 2. The primacy of the Gospel: the source of principles for world order. 3. An attack upon the root causes of war: war as a symptom of a disease having various causes. 4. Co-operation of all men of good will: the development of a world ethos. 5. An approach to government: the influence of Christian principles of world order upon government. 6. An approach to the people: the participation of citizens in the world order movement. 7. The world Christian fellowship as an example of world community. 8. Conclusions. 9. Significant statements on world order.

The Christian community has entered the arena of the contemporary world. It has not forsaken its heritage of the centuries. It has not lost its vision of eternity. With its resources pointed by a sense of prophetic mission, it has challenged in new fashion the forces which today make for anarchy and chaos on an international scale. It has come to grips with these forces by seeking to lay foundations upon which men may more securely build a world of order and peace. The frequency with

126

which the Christian community has mustered its strength to influence international policies and practices during the last six years and the apparent interrelationship of its activities seem to indicate that a new movement is emerging and taking shape—a Christian movement toward world order.

The significance which may reasonably be attached to these happenings makes an appraisal of them imperative. Is this emerging movement merely the product of a war atmosphere and therefore destined to be short-lived? Does it represent a fundamental Christian concern and must it accordingly find appropriate place in the continuing life of the Christian community? While the perspective of history is indispensable to fair appraisal, decisions must be reached as history is made. The limitation of proximity must be endured in the interest of progress. One question cannot be ignored. Having entered the arena of the contemporary world, in what manner is the Christian community justified in remaining there?

The need to answer this question lends purpose to an analysis of Christian activity to promote world order during the period of the war. The distinguishing marks of the emerging world order movement must be identified and they must be viewed in the light of a growth in ecumenical Christianity over the preceding thirty years. However, the projected survey must be animated by more than a desire merely to describe what has happened. The Christian community stands at a crossroad. It must decide what its future responsibility in the field of world order shall be and, in face of its decision, what lines of action it must pursue. A study of what has happened in the past ought to be undertaken with a view to shedding light on what should be done in the future.

The activities of the churches in relation to international affairs seem to be marked by seven important characteristics: (1) a Christian world outlook; (2) the primacy of the Gospel; (3) an attack upon the root causes of war; (4) attempted co-operation with all men of good will; (5) an approach to government; (6) an approach to the people; (7) an example and a demonstration of world community in Christian fellowship. Each of these will be considered on the background of recent developments in ecumenical Christianity and then more fully described in its actual manifestations. While illustrations will be drawn from the work of the churches in different countries, the emphasis rests on what took place in America. This emphasis seems inevitable and reflects the extent to which the people of America were in a position to devote themselves to the study of peace, partly because they were removed from the scene of actual fighting and destruction. The developments in the Christian movement toward world order, as well as the conclusions which may be drawn therefrom, must be scrutinized in face of the Christian community's continuing responsibility in the world of men and nations.

1. A CHRISTIAN WORLD OUTLOOK

The Christian Movement toward world order transcends national boundaries and seeks to cultivate an international Christian approach to the solution of international problems.

The extended outlook wherein the sense of world Christian fellowship was nurtured throughout the war had found tangible expression in the ecumenical conferences of the last three decades. With sufficient clarity to be revolutionary, the World Missionary Conference at Edinburgh in 1910 had dramatized an awakening recognition of Christian unity in faith and purpose among non-Roman churches.

> . . . One world, waiting, surely, for who shall carry to it and place in its empty hands one Faith—the only thing that can ever truly and fundamentally unite it or deeply and truly satisfy it, bringing its one human race into one Catholic Church through the message of the "One Body and One Spirit, One Lord, One Faith, One Baptism, One God

and Father of all, who is over all, and through all, and in all."[1]

What had been begun at Edinburgh was carried on and strengthened in the Jerusalem and Madras Conferences of the International Missionary Council, in the Conferences on Faith and Order at Lausanne and Edinburgh, in the conferences on Life and Work at Stockholm and Oxford, and in the Christian youth conference at Amsterdam. At Utrecht, the structure of the World Council of Churches was fashioned and provisionally set up to permit further expression of the fellowship of the churches. The ecumenical ideal had been firmly established. While Christian people far and wide had not caught its significance or committed themselves to it, an increasing number of leaders had come to view the problems of the world through an ecumenical lens. When the second World War divided the nations into hostile camps, unity in Christian fellowship survived to direct the action of churches toward a just and lasting peace.

The Conference at Geneva in 1939 stands as a link between the major ecumenical conferences and the activities of the churches during the war. Thirty-five men and women from eleven countries were called together by the Provisional Committee of the World Council of Churches to discuss the points at issue in international tensions and conflicts. With an international Christian outlook, the Conference agreed upon a definite statement of guiding principles for the solution of international problems. Its findings were sent to the churches of the world for their guidance and, in a number of countries, were submitted to high government officials.

Because of the restrictions upon travel and communication imposed by the war, Christian activity directed specifically toward world order was carried on most intensively within separate nations. National church bodies instituted commissions, convened study conferences, issued statements of Christian prin-

[1] W. H. T. Gairdner, *Echoes from Edinburgh, 1910* (New York: Fleming H. Revell Company, 1910) pp. 6, 7.

ciples, contributed to the enlightenment of public opinion and
established contacts with government officials. An approach to
the understanding of this activity can be found in the study
of the pronouncements which came from Christian sources. A
mere recital of the documents by title appears drab. Warmth is
immediately added when the pronouncements are projected on
the background of the purposes and zeal with which they were
drafted and the effectiveness with which they were used. Perhaps one of their most significant marks is that, while they were
prepared in national groups, they consistently pictured the problems of peace and order in a world setting.

The Malvern Conference in England was the first meeting of
its kind to be convened by churches in a nation at war. Christian leaders assembled to consider the requirements of peace
while their land was under almost continuous bombardment
from the air. On December 21, 1940, the London *Times* published an Open Letter signed by the Archbishop of Canterbury,
the Moderator of the Free Church Federal Council and the
Archbishop of York. The Open Letter contained the Ten Peace
Points,[2] five of which had been previously proposed by Pope
Pius XII. *Social Justice and Economic Reconstruction* was issued
by the Commission of the Churches for International Friendship and Social Responsibility, a body consisting of delegates
officially appointed to represent the various Christian communions in Great Britain with the exception of the Roman
Catholics. It was adopted by the Commission and published in
pamphlet form to promote study, discussion and criticism. *The
Christian Church and World Order* was issued under the authority of the same Commission with the purpose of stimulating
the formation of principles by which action could be guided
in postwar situations.

In the United States, the Federal Council of Churches appointed a Commission to Study the Bases of a Just and Durable

[2] For the text of the Ten Peace Points, see "Significant Statements on
World Order" at the close of this Chapter, p. 158.

Peace. Two general statements prepared by the Commission are particularly important because of the wide influence they came to exert. The first of these, a *Statement of Guiding Principles*,[3] sets forth moral and spiritual foundations for a just and lasting peace. It was given general endorsement by the National Study Conference at Delaware, Ohio, in March, 1942. In its final form, it was adopted by the Federal Council of Churches, 1942. The second, a *Statement of Political Propositions* (*Six Pillars of Peace*),[4] embraces certain broad political conclusions which seem to flow from the Guiding Principles. A study of pronouncements by church bodies in different countries and consultation with political, economic and church leaders in the United States preceded its release in March, 1943. The Delaware Conference released its own Message dealing with The Relation of the Church to a Just and Durable Peace, Political Bases, Economic Bases, and Social Bases. The Cleveland Conference, held in January, 1945, also issued a Message to the churches wherein, among other matters, nine specific recommendations were offered for the improvement of the Dumbarton Oaks Proposals.[5]

Activities were not confined to Great Britain and the United States. Church groups were at work in New Zealand and Australia. In Canada, at the recommendation of the executive committee of the General Council for the United Church, the Board of Evangelism and Social Service organized a Commission on the Church, Nation, and World Order; the Commission gave general approval to a Memorandum known as the *Interia Report*. In South Africa, the Fort Hare Conference was held under the

[3] For the text of the *Statement of Guiding Principles*, see "Significant Statements on World Order," at the close of this chapter, p. 160.

[4] For the text of the *Six Pillars of Peace*, see "Significant Statements on World Order," at the close of this chapter, p. 164.

[5] For the text of the Dumbarton Oaks Proposals of the *Cleveland Message to the Churches*, see "Significant Statements on World Order," at the close of this chapter, p. 167.

auspices of the Christian Council and issued an abbreviated statement of its findings with the consent of the Council.

An international concern of the churches was clearly evident in the conferences which were convened by national church bodies and in the pronouncements which were issued to promote study and action. In many instances, documents prepared in one country were widely circulated in other countries. An interchange was consistently effective between Great Britain and the United States. Whenever possible, Christian leaders came from one country to another to cement relations and to confer on problems of world import. One of the most dramatic evidences of world outlook in many countries was the international reception accorded the *Six Pillars of Peace*. The Statement was prepared in the United States. After a critical examination of it by a group of eminent British Christians, an analysis expressing essential agreement was issued over the signatures of fourteen foremost leaders in the British churches. The International Round Table at Princeton, New Jersey, gave substantial endorsement to the *Six Pillars*. The Statement in microfilm was flown to China. It was broadcast by short wave to Germany and the occupied countries, as well as to many English-speaking lands. Through the underground, printed copies were distributed among people in the Axis countries and in countries controlled by the Axis powers. Christians were not only bent upon expressing their convictions. They were eager to evaluate and, where possible, to accept the convictions expressed by Christians in other lands.

Two indications of a world Christian outlook must be added to those which appeared under the auspices of national church groups. The first is a document, *The Church and International Reconstruction*,[6] prepared by W. A. Visser 't Hooft and issued under the auspices of the Geneva Study Department of the

[6] For the text of the eleven points of agreement in *The Church and International Reconstruction*, see "Significant Statements on World Order," at the close of this chapter, p. 165.

World Council of Churches. It analyzes and compares church attitudes throughout the world, with particular reference to international order. It sets forth what may be termed an "ecumenical consensus," or world-wide interchurch agreement. Following each of the eleven points of agreement, there are presented disagreements between the churches or within the churches concerning the theological, ethical and practical implications of the common affirmations.

Another manifestation of the Christian world outlook appeared in the International Round Table of Christian leaders held at Princeton, in the summer of 1943. Sixty-one leaders from twelve countries on five continents participated. The preface of the *Message* states:

> The Round Table gave visible expression to the ecumenical spirit of the Christian Church. The very fact that it was held, with its international representation, testified that the life and concern of the Christian Church transcend national lines even at a time when the greater part of the world is torn by war. While full ecumenical representation was obviously impossible, all deliberations were entered upon with a clear consciousness of the Church's ecumenical character and function.

A Christian world outlook prevailed in the activities of the churches in behalf of world order, whether those activities were carried on by the churches in separate countries or by international Christian co-operation. For the ability of the churches in different countries to transcend national lines in co-operating against the common enemy of world chaos, credit is due the ecumenical movement. Quite possibly, the ecumenical movement may find substantial stimulation in the new understanding and sympathy which co-operation in behalf of a lasting peace has awakened.

2. THE PRIMACY OF THE GOSPEL

The Christian movement toward world order recognizes the primacy of the Gospel and, in its address to the world, derives from the Gospel the ethical principles upon which world order must be built.

From its beginnings, the Christian Church has recognized the proclamation of the Gospel as its primary task. As the Christian community moved more definitely into the contemporary world, many feared that the churches would step out of cast and forsake their essential commission. As a safeguard against this danger, the ecumenical movement established a sound precedent. Two quotations will serve to reveal the conviction that fidelity to the Church's primary purpose is imperative for a sound contribution to a better world. These are not taken from discussions on Christian faith where an emphasis upon the Gospel would naturally fall. They appear as a distinguishing Christian note in the consideration of international issues.

The Oxford Conference report on *The Universal Church and the World of Nations* contains the statement:[7]

> These purposes [of the church] are and must remain to proclaim the gospel of God's love in Jesus Christ to all mankind, to administer the sacraments, to fulfill the Christian ideal of fellowship and to guide the souls of her children in the ways of holiness. No other activity in which she may engage can be a substitute for these. For the church is supremely concerned with persons, and world problems have their roots ultimately in the hearts of persons who "must be born again." She must speak therefore in the name of God to the individual men and women who make up the nations and must announce to them, in language they can understand, the news of the world's Saviour. As

[7] J. H. Oldham, ed., *The Oxford Conference, Official Report* (Chicago: Willett, Clark & Company, 1937), pp. 153, 154.

the greatest need of the world is new men, and the church's chief opponents in our time aspire to change the very structure of human nature in those whom they control, the church of Christ throughout the world should work unceasingly for human renewal and the cure of souls in his name and through his strength "who maketh all things new."

In considering *The Church and the International Order*, the Madras Conference took this position:[8]

> The primary appeal of the Church must ever be through the preachings of the Word and the demonstration of its fellowship. Since the causes of war always impinge upon the moral sphere, the Church must convince men of their sin writ large in conflict and suffering. By life and word it must proclaim the gospel of forgiveness and the transforming power of God's redeeming love in Christ.

Christian leaders sought to face realistically and boldly the situations created by the war and the needs anticipated upon the close of the war. At many points they encountered the danger of posing as political and economic experts. Only in scattered instances did they move beyond their competence. Fidelity to the spirit and methods of the Christian Church predominates in the pronouncements that were forthcoming. As the severity of the war mounted, the need for faith and moral purpose was increasingly stressed. When the discovery of atomic fission was put to destructive use, this emphasis in many quarters took on an apocalyptic impulse. Men can find no safeguard against self-destruction other than in the exercise of those qualities which root in the Gospel.

Evidence of fidelity to the essential message of Christianity is found, first of all, in the fact that practically all the messages from important conferences contain a reaffirmation of Christian faith and an indication of its pertinence to the issues of the day.

[8] *The World Mission of the Church: Findings and Recommendations of the International Missionary Council, Madras, India* (New York: International Missionary Council, 1938), p. 118.

For example, the *Preamble* of the Delaware *Message* sets forth the function of the Church and summons men to commit themselves to Jesus Christ and to the cause of the kingdom of God. The *World Order Message* of the Princeton International Round Table calls upon the Church to lead the world to God through Christ and to win acceptance of His will for human relationships. The *Cleveland Message to the Churches* begins with a strong statement of the Christian faith wherein the purposes of world order are fashioned. Testimony to the primacy of the Gospel is not confined to sections where Christian faith is the sole object of scrutiny. Even where propositions are directed to the solution of concrete political and economic problems, they are in the main derivations from the Gospel or implications of the Gospel for human relations. The *Preamble* of the *Statement of Guiding Principles* reveals the manner in which ethical requirements moved within the orbit of full Christian conviction:

> As members of the Christian Church, we seek to view all problems of world order in the light of the truth concerning God, man and God's purpose for the world made known in Jesus Christ. We believe that the eternal God revealed in Christ is the Ruler of men and of nations and that His purpose in history will be realized. For us He is the source of moral law and the power to make it effective. From this faith Christians derive the ethical principles upon which world order must be based.

The claim that the primacy of the Gospel was recognized must not be misunderstood to mean that the full and complete Gospel was incorporated in every statement. Relevant aspects of it were introduced as required by the situation under consideration and the people addressed. It must constantly be remembered that the pronouncements of the churches were intended for two audiences. The first is composed of those who profess the Christian faith and who have maintained some affiliation with the Christian Church. This group is addressed in two capacities.

As members of the Christian Church, their attention is called to the implication of Christian faith for world order and to the impulse to action which inheres in the Christian faith. As citizens of a commonwealth or nation, their attention is called to the more specific ways in which the implications of Christian faith must find expression in a social order.

The second group is composed of those who do not profess the Christian faith and who have no direct affiliation with the Christian Church. The manner in which this group is addressed as over against the former has been described in these words:[9]

> What then is the difference between these two types of witness? The first we have described. It is the witness to the life in Christ, the life within the community of those who recognize Him as their Lord, the distinctive Christocentric ethics of the Church. The second, however, is concerned with the Will of God for the common life of men in the era in which Church and world remain distinct entities. The difference is not that between supernatural and natural law, but between those ethics which are based on God's purpose for the world "outside." Speaking to its own members and to those whom it would draw into its own life, the Church explains what it is to live as a member of the Body; speaking to the world as a whole, or to the powers and institutions of this world, or again to its own members concerning their life in the secular realm, the Church declares what the provisional purpose of God is for the State, for social life, for the common life of men in general. Church ethics in the full sense of that word are, as we have seen, dominated by the indicative of the new creation. The ethical witness of the Church to the world is in the form of an imperative, that is of a reminder of what it is meant to be.
>
> The Church has then a definite ethical task in relation to the world. It is not only to defend itself against the

[9] W. A. Visser 't Hooft *The Ethical Reality and Function of the Church,* p. 30 (mimeographed).

world, but also to take the initiative to call the world to
order, that is to say, to remind it of its duty before God.
It is to speak positively about God's will for the State, for
society, for international life, and all that goes to make up
the life of the world as a whole. . . .

The proclamation of the Gospel in its fullest sense remains
the primary task of the Church. In the area of world peace, the
distinctive message addressed to Christians has to do with the
implications of Christian faith for international order, and
with the impulse to action which inheres in the Christian faith.
The message to Christians and to non-Christians finds common
ground when attention is called to the more specific ways in
which the implications of Christian faith must find expression
in a social order.

3. AN ATTACK UPON THE ROOT CAUSES OF WAR

*The Christian movement toward world order views war
as a symptom or manifestation of an international disease and
seeks to bring permanent Christian truths to bear upon the root
causes or tension points from which international maladjustments or wars inevitably emerge.*

The traditional attack upon war as an evil in itself came increasingly to be regarded as unrealistic, certainly as ineffective.
At the Conferences in Stockholm and Oxford, the discussions
centered somewhat more upon various causes which give rise
to international conflict. Oxford called insistent attention to the
evils in absolute national sovereignty and in a system of power
relationships. This approach was considerably sharpened in the
deliberations of Christians during the war. The Geneva Conference cited specific and immediate causes of international disorder.[10] A similar approach is found in the report of the Com-

[10] *The Churches and the International Crisis* (Pamphlet). A memorandum prepared by an international conference at Geneva, 1939 (New York:
Federal Council of Churches).

mission on the Churches and the War.[11] In the new method of attack which was being devised, pacifists and non-pacifists found a common ground. War came to be looked upon as the symptom, not as the real disease. Consequently, effort was directed to the identification of the causes of war and to the provision of counter-irritants or preventives. Generalization on the basis of the many statements that appeared from different countries is hazardous. Nevertheless, certain ideas appeared frequently enough to be accepted as indicative of a trend in thinking. A brief summary of these ideas in terms of causes for war and an approach to the eradication of them here follows.

(1) *Violation of moral law.* Underlying many difficulties which give rise to international friction is the disregard of moral law. Operating under a system of national sovereignties, unbridled self-interest has largely governed the policies and practices of nations. Political and economic acts have followed the course of power relations and have, in many instances, ignored the claims of justice and human well-being. The absence of a consistent moral purpose has not only worked hardship on those who lacked power but has bred suspicion and prevented co-operation among those whose strength placed upon them added responsibility for world order.

Christian leaders contend that moral law, no less than physical law, undergirds our world. The moral order, which is fundamental and eternal, is relevant to the corporate life of men in nations and in society as well as to the life of individuals. The sickness and suffering which affect our present society are symptoms and proof of an indifference to, and a direct violation of, the moral law. Guilt for this indifference or violation becomes a relative matter, and no nation upon earth is completely free from a measure of responsibility. Christianity, therefore, proclaims that moral law must become controlling, not only in the lives of men as individuals, but also in their corporate life as nations.

[11] *The Relation of the Church to the War in the Light of the Christian Faith* (New York: Federal Council of Churches, 1944).

(2) *Inadequacy of international government.* The people of the world are victims of an unbalanced growth. Politically, governments are still swayed by the spirit of nationalism. Many areas of life have become considerably internationalized. Tremendous improvements in communication and transportation have knit the peoples of the world closely together in social, economic and cultural intercourse. The problems which inevitably arise from those contacts on a world scale have found no corresponding directive or control in political structure.

In recent decades, Christians have come to recognize a characteristic which inhered in Christianity from its inception. Neither Christianity nor the Christian Church is a national phenomenon. In its truest sense, there is no Christian Church of the United States, or of England, or of Germany. Christianity is ecumenical; it represents a universal or catholic mind. Prompted in part by this growing realization and in part by a recognition of the obstacles to world order in perpetuating a system of competing nations, Christians leaders have taken the position that national states cannot represent the final word in government. Where the life and activities of different nations or peoples meet, some kind of world organization is needed to offer justice and security to separate nations, to direct the diversified activities of the human race, and to make possible the effective accomplishment of the common purposes of mankind. The test of the desired world organization lies not so much in its particular form as in the possibility of its successful functioning. To assure a stable world order, an international structure must provide the political conditions for promoting co-operation among the peoples of the world and for substituting trust and good will for fear, hate and envy.

(3) *Economic maladjustments.* The basic nature of economic issues as a cause for disturbance among nations is obvious. The more apparent problems of tariffs, quotas and currencies run out into endless lines of agriculture, manufacture, commerce, transportation and ultimately touch the life, not only of every

nation, but also of every last individual within each nation. In spite of recognized international repercussions from many of the economic enactments by separate nations, no adequate steps toward international control over economic relationships have been effected. In the realm of economic activity, each nation has gone its independent way with the result that the seeds of international controversy are continuously sown.

Christianity is concerned with the effects of economic provisions upon people, and Christianity is concerned that the people who make the economic provisions shall do so with a regard for the rights and privileges of others. It recognizes that economic injustices work hardship on people as individuals and have an adverse effect upon Christian fellowship. Christian leaders are becoming more determined in their stand that the government of economic relations must be such as to provide opportunity for all men in all countries of the world to meet their basic economic need. In the definition of basic economic need, two criteria operate: (a) the rights and well-being of the individual; (b) the rights and well-being of society or of individuals comprising the social group. The major problem seems to rest in the effort to keep the operation of these two criteria in proper balance; that is, in the effort to establish conditions under which the individual may rightfully seek his own welfare, and, at the same time, not interfere with but actually contribute to the welfare of others. Toward this end, Christian standards must direct the requirements to be met by individuals, by industry, by the national state and by any world organization.

(4) *Denial of human rights.* The difficulties arising in this connection may fall within the confines of a single nation. For example, the people of the United States must recognize more intelligently the problems and responsibilities occasioned for them by the large Negro population in this country. Too frequently efforts to meliorate the situation have been animated by sentimentality or by the desire for political support. The

problem remains and dare not be ignored. The difficulties at
tached to the denial of human rights also take on an interna
tional complexion. When people are denied freedom of speec
or the right of access to information, a government may de
velop policies which lead to international friction without fea
of criticism or opposition by its citizens. Further complication
arise in dealing with national minorities within any country, in
establishing national borders, in immigration and emigration re
strictions, and in the determination of economic and cultural op
portunities. Persecutions and discriminations frequently resul
and international tensions mount.

There is a marked tendency among Christians to regard th
violation of human rights anywhere as the concern of mei
everywhere. Christianity believes in the brotherhood of mai
under the Fatherhood of God. The Christian gospel relates t
all men, regardless of race, language or color. While the race
and peoples of the earth stand at various levels of achievement
there is no Christian basis to support a fancied intrinsic superi
ority of any one race. The advancement of one group beyon
another brings with it not special privilege, but only adde
responsibility. The rights and freedoms of all people in al
lands should be recognized and safeguarded. Freedom of reli
gion and religious worship, of speech, of assembly, of the press
of cultural interchange, of scientific inquiry and teaching ar
fundamental to human development and in keeping with th
moral law. International political co-operation is needed t
create conditions under which these freedoms may become a
reality.

(5) *Colonial possessions.* A variety of conditions fertile t
world disorder exists wherever a somewhat powerful nation re
gards a territory and its inhabitants as personal property. A
colonial people may rebel against some form of exploitation, o
they may merely reach a point where group or racial prid
leads to a declaration of independence. Granted a sufficien
measure of physical and material strength, they will resort t

war. Or, a powerful nation near a colony which is held by a distant nation may feel that its operations are restricted and thus find an excuse for precipitating warlike acts. Even in times of peace, when friendly relations are maintained, colonial possessions are a disturbing factor because of the everlasting threat of war. A colony may be entirely harmless to a nearby nation in normal times and yet become a thorn in its side in the event that war should be declared with the holding country.

The pronouncements of Christian leaders have maintained that no nation is inherently superior to another and that the people governed should have a substantial voice in their government. The resources of a dependent area ought to be exploited neither by a national state nor by corporations whose activities are permitted or endorsed by a national state. Colonies should be granted self-government or independence within a world family of nations as rapidly as their internal stability permits. So long as outside control is needed in any colonial possession, there should be some kind of international supervision to assure the rights of the inhabitants and to promote reasonable progress toward autonomy.

(6) *Armaments.* The condition in which separate nations may develop military machines without restriction leads to a mad race, the end of which no man can conceive. Disarmament treaties have fallen short of their purposes in that they were not sufficiently inclusive, and contracting nations too frequently were reluctant to enter into restricting obligations. No international control ensured compliance with treaty agreements. The growth of armaments contributes to the sway of power politics, and nations with sufficient force at their disposal can, by threat of reprisals, gain almost any desired end. The harnessing of atomic energy for destruction and the development of other implements for mass obliteration have colored this situation with the touch of finality.

A Christian view argues strongly for a constructive outlet to human energies and resources. If there is no control imposed upon the development of national military establishments, the human race may obliterate itself. It surely will have no means available for the loftier pursuits of life. The least to be sought is an immediate international control of certain forms of military equipment, looking to the abolition of all national armaments—with an international agency to see to it that the control is effective. It should be emphatically noted that the development of international law and the removal of political, economic and humanitarian causes for war must go hand in hand with the reduction and regulation of national armaments. This is particularly important in face of the difficulties encountered in arranging foolproof inspection of uses to which atomic fission may be put. Suspicion and hostility must give way to sympathetic understanding and co-operation if nations are to be faithful to agreements on disarmament.

(7) *Attitudes toward defeated powers.* The roots of a future war are frequently to be found in the peace settlements by which a previous war was concluded. The tremendous severity of the second World War and the pressures which it has exerted have tended to awaken hatreds and the desire for revenge on the part of many people.

Should the principle of retaliation become determining in the treaty structure, Christian idealism and the best interests of humanity will be ignored. While disowning a vague sentimentalism which overlooks past crimes and future dangers, Christian leaders have repudiated any attempt to settle the war in the spirit of revenge. Adequate safeguards must be given all peoples against military and economic aggression by others; full opportunities must be provided to all, victors and vanquished alike, to develop their own national and cultural life within the framework of world order. Closely related to these needs is the problem of relief and rehabilitation. Governments, churches, secular agencies and individuals must use their full resources without discrimination to alleviate the suffering of all people.

whose lands have been devastated by the ravages of war. The spirit of helpfulness and impartiality may do much to heal the wounds of war and to bind the world together in a just and lasting peace.

(8) *Relations among victorious powers.* History has demonstrated the danger of dissension in peace among the powers which co-operated to achieve victory in war. The excessive power with which some nations emerge from a period of fighting and the inevitable desire to secure compensation for losses endured or to erect safeguards against future hazards breed suspicion and distrust. In the tensions among victorious powers lies a serious threat to world peace and order.

Christian leaders early emphasized the urgent need to cement relations among the United Nations in the period immediately following the cessation of hostilities. They recognized the difficulties which would arise in drafting commonly acceptable peace terms. They anticipated that some of the settlements would be inadequate and some would be unjust. Aware of the devisive tendencies which would appear in the effort to conclude the war, they urged a new pattern of history. According to this pattern, the procedures for arriving at peace settlements and the procedures for building an organization under which the nations can thereafter co-operate in peace must be separate enterprises. The emerging world organization must not be saddled with the inadequacies and injustices of the peace settlements, although it may later become an instrument for their adjustment. The nations ought to be in a position to address themselves to constructive tasks of their own choosing. In successful performance, they may gain renewed understanding for peace and acquire skill in co-operation. A medium can thus be provided for peaceful change to meet the demands of ever-changing political and economic needs.

In seeking to attack the causes of war, Christian leaders attuned their insights much more definitely to the issues of contemporaneous international life. They set forth the goals which ought to be sought. At the same time, they recognized that progress toward these goals would perforce be slow. They urged that attainable steps in the direction of the standards they had proclaimed should be supported by all Christians. When speaking in behalf of the churches, they emphasized spiritual and moral principles, but also indicated broad political and economic implications which seemed inevitable. They gave every encouragement and aid to Christian citizens, as individuals and as groups, to apply these principles and their implications to the concrete and specific problems of world order.

4. CO-OPERATION WITH ALL MEN OF GOOD WILL

The Christian movement toward world order transcends the lines of separation fixed by traditional faiths, and, in areas of agreement, is enlisting the co-operation of men of good will everywhere.

Christians are a minority in the world. International order can become a reality only when a sufficiently large number of people commit themselves to its achievement. In the prewar discussions of international problems, Christian leaders became increasingly aware of this situation. The Oxford report on *Church and State* holds that it is the duty of the churches "to create within the local community, the nation, and the world such agencies of co-operative action as shall make it possible for them to discharge effectively such tasks as can be done in common."[12] The *Memorandum* issued by the Geneva Conference of 1939 emphatically states:

> The immediate task in this field [of international relations] is *to improve the ethos of inter-state relations*—to bring influence to bear upon what has been left, by a long

[12] J. H. Oldham, ed., *op. cit.*, p. 73.

tradition, in a jungle outside the bounds of law, of morality, of courtesy and decent human feeling.[13]

This earlier development found considerable impetus in the action of the churches throughout the war. In the main, co-operation took form in the drafting of pronouncements which could be commonly subscribed to by people of varying religious conviction. Effort was thus made to give content to a world ethos. In numerous instances, co-operative action to make the commonly accepted pronouncements effective followed.

The ten Peace Points issued in the Open Letter to the London *Times* contained items contributed from both Protestant and Roman Catholic sources. Its signatories were representative of Protestantism and Roman Catholicism in England. Somewhat later, Jewish endorsement was given those parts which did not reflect distinctive Christian doctrine. The Ten Points contain the statement (Number 5, taken from the pronouncement by Pope Pius XII):

> They must . . . be guided by that universal love which is the compendium and most general expression of the Christian ideal, and which therefore may serve as a common ground *also for those who have not the blessing of sharing the same faith with us.*

The *Preamble* of the *Statement of Guiding Principles* makes explicit reference to the broader import of specified parts:

> From this faith Christians derive the ethical principles upon which world order must be based. These principles, however, seem to us to be among those which men of goodwill everywhere may be expected to recognize as part of the moral law. In this we rejoice. For peace will require the co-operation of men of all nations, races and creeds. We have therefore first set out (Points 1 to 9) those guiding principles which, it seems to us, Christians and non-Christians alike can accept.

[13] *The Churches and the International Crisis*, p. 12.

In October, 1945, the Catholic, Jewish and Protestant *Declaration on World Order*[14] was released over the signatures of 144 outstanding religious leaders in the United States. Each group set forth its own preamble to express its distinctive emphasis. There then followed seven statements of agreement on imperative needs for world order. This document was widely distributed and studied in Catholic, Jewish and Protestant circles. It became the basis of considerable discussion in the United States Congress. It was frequently used by religious leaders to convey to government officials the convictions about which the religious groups in this country were in substantial agreement.

When the State Department of the United States invited the people to express their views about the Dumbarton Oaks Proposals, an unofficial group composed of Roman Catholic, Jewish and Protestant representatives prepared an analysis entitled *Goals for San Francisco*. This statement contained ten recommendations for improving the Proposals which the drafters considered to be in conformity with the expressed judgments of their respective constituencies.

In enlisting co-operation of all men of good will, Christians were not denying distinctive and fundamental aspects of their own faith. They continued their effort to bring men into fellowship with God through repentance and faith in Jesus Christ. Beyond this they recognized their responsibility to offer an ethical witness to the world. They were bent upon making a world ethos definitive. They were seeking to win co-operation of all men on a level acceptable to the Christian conscience.

[14] For the text of the *Pattern for Peace: Catholic, Jewish and Protestant Declaration on World Peace*, see "Significant Statements on World Order," at the close of this chapter, p. 166.

5. AN APPROACH TO GOVERNMENT

The Christian movement toward world order seeks to urge upon government leaders the importance of Christian principles in international affairs.

The international nature of the ecumenical conferences made direct representation to governments difficult if not impossible. The meetings of the Universal Christian Conference on Life and Work discussed many aspects of government responsibility for world order. Oxford specified six obligations which the churches and their people ought to meet in relation to government:

> (a) That of praying for the state, its people and its governments; (b) that of loyalty and obedience to the state, disobedience becoming a duty only if obedience would be clearly contrary to the command of God; (c) that of co-operation with the state in promoting the welfare of the citizens and of lending moral support to the state when it upholds the standards of justice set forth in the Word of God; (d) that of criticism of the state when it departs from those standards; (e) that of holding before men in all their legislation and administration those principles which make for the upholding of the dignity of man who is made in the image of God; (f) that of permeating the public life with the spirit of Christ and of training up men and women who as Christians can contribute to this end.[15]

Periodic references to the League of Nations appeared. Procedures to maintain effective contacts with officials of government were urged upon the nationals of separate states. It was understood that each group would have to approach its own government in accordance with the laws of the land and such opportunities as might be immediately available.

During the war, Christian leaders recognized that government

[15] J. H. Oldham, ed., *op cit.*, pp. 70, 71.

officials would determine the provisions of peace treaties and the political and economic structures by which the nations of the world would thereafter work together. Consequently they sought in a variety of ways to establish and maintain effective contacts with leaders of government. Methods of doing this varied in different countries. In fashioning procedures in the United States, the churches sought to preserve inviolate the principle of the separation of Church and State. Substantially, they sought to make their testimony to a group of individuals in whose hands was vested the power to determine relations between the nations of the world. In making this testimony they placed at the disposal of government leaders the benefit of Christian insights and judgments.

Most frequently, the approach of the churches to government was envisioned as Christian pronouncements were being drafted. The British Ten Peace Points conclude with the statement: "We have confidence that the principles which we have enumerated would be accepted by rulers and statesmen throughout the British Commonwealth of Nations and would be regarded as the true basis on which a lasting peace could be established." *Social Justice and Economic Reconstruction* proclaims: "Government should be asked to give assurances that this will be the immediate direction of public policy." The *Statement of Guiding Principles* and the *Six Pillars of Peace* were written in part to provide our government and other governments with the formulation of spiritual bases and their political implications for world order. The section of the *Cleveland Message* dealing with the improvement of the Dumbarton Oaks Proposals was prepared in response to a direct request from the Department of State for reactions of representatives in public-opinion-forming groups.

The documents thus framed were in many cases submitted to government by formal resolution. Both the Delaware and the Cleveland Conferences took action to lay their findings before the President of the United States and other government officials. In addition to the submission of formal pronouncements, many opportunities for informal contact were utilized. The leaders of the churches recurringly conferred with leaders in government in order that the positions taken by the churches might be thoroughly understood and appreciated. In numerous instances, officials of government participated informally in the conferences and deliberations of church commission. The prevailing spirit was one of co-operation rather than coercion. The contacts moved on the assumption that leaders in government wanted to reach the wisest and most equitable conclusions and therefore welcomed the assistance which the churches placed at their disposal.

For a time a selected number of church leaders from the Commission on a Just and Durable Peace met in consultative capacity at fairly frequent intervals with officers in the Department of State. This consultative relationship took on a new form when the Department of State invited forty-two agencies to send consultants to the United States delegation at the San Francisco Conference. A number of church bodies of national scope were included in the agencies thus represented.

In their official statements to government, the churches were careful not to move beyond their competence. They recognized clear limits within which their representations had to fall. In the main, they submitted spiritual and moral principles and cited broad political implications which were derived therefrom. The procedures which were followed and the cordial spirit in which contacts were maintained broke new ground for co-operative relations between the state and the non-Roman churches in the United States, without violating traditional principles of separation.

6. AN APPROACH TO THE PEOPLE

The Christian movement toward world order seeks to enlighten and strengthen the consciences of Christians in all walks of life so that they will assume a responsible part as Christian citizens.

The need for widespread study and action has been pointed out in a quotation from G. K. Chesterton: "If you want to make something live, make it local." One of the tasks undertaken by the Continuation Committees of all the major ecumenical conferences was to make the fruits of their deliberations effective in the life of the parishes. It is a recognized fact that ecumenical consciousness has attained reality mainly in the leadership of the churches, and had not developed very far in the average pastor and parishioner.

A similar problem confronted the churches in the world order movement. The task was somewhat simplified because the need to face the issues of world order was clearly apparent, as men labored under the hardships of war. In the United States, the activities of the Protestant churches centered in the Commission on a Just and Durable Peace. The manner in which it carried on its work was one factor in winning popular attention. The conferences convened under its auspices called together the outstanding Protestant leadership of the country. Advance notices informed people that a meeting of significance was being projected and solicited their co-operation. Newspapers gave the conferences considerable publicity. The Commission published the findings of the conferences for the study of the churches. The social action secretaries of the co-operating communions distributed reports to their constituencies and encouraged study and action. Apart from the findings of conferences, the Commission issued study guides and statements of which copies were distributed by the hundreds of thousands. The Christian Mission on World Order brought teams of Christian leaders to about one hundred key cities for a full day conference on the work of the churches for a lasting peace.

Many denominations established commissions on world order or assigned responsibility for this work to boards of social action. Separately or in co-operation with the Federal Council's Commission, these denominational boards pursued programs of study and action on a national scale.

As a result of the impetus given by national church agencies, many local parishes developed their own programs. They had at

their disposal suggestions for local procedures such as here
follow, and, in varying degree, sought to awaken people to their
responsibility as Christian citizens:

(1) Organize a congregational or community committee on
world order to serve as a clearing house of information and as a
means of directing study and activity.

(2) Arrange study classes, in congregation or community,
dealing specifically with problems of world order.

(3) Provide incidental reference to world order or international friendship in sermons and in Sunday and weekday
church school lessons. In this connection national holidays and
the like ought particularly to be utilized.

(4) Build a library containing pamphlets and books dealing
with the Christian's part in promoting world order. Funds may
be contributed by congregational organizations or by individuals.
Administration may be in the hands of the general committee
or of a separate library committee.

(5) Display appropriate pamphlets or books in the vestibule
of the church or at some other conspicuous place.

(6) Have a current events bulletin board with pictures and
articles from newspapers and magazines.

(7) Encourage financial support of accredited movements that
are seeking to promote world order.

(8) Exemplify peace and order in community life—interdenominational, racial, civic, economic, social and personal.

(9) Take responsible action as a citizen in supporting sound
legislation, in encouraging governmental officials in their sound
policies and, wherever possible, in personally participating as
an official of the government.

(10) Show a constructive influence in all personal contacts—
social and business—to offset provincialisms, hatreds and all
points of view which militate against world order.

Needless to say, the percentage of parishes carrying on a full
program of this kind was exceedingly small. Nevertheless, the
sum total of study and action by people in all walks of life

exceeded previous achievement in any similar venture. Although the program was admittedly inadequate it was sufficient to create an atmosphere which had its healthy effect upon large numbers of people not directly connected with the world order activity of the churches.

7. AN EXAMPLE OF COMMUNITY

The Christian movement toward world order offers the developing world Christian fellowship as an example and a demonstration of world community.

The churches, in different national settings, have sought to approach the problems of international relations with a world outlook. This broadened horizon reflects a development in the internal experiences of the churches. In face of the many differences which exist in language, cultural background, organization, theology and political and economic philosophy, Christian people of the world have been drawn closer together in common interest and action. Part I of Chapter 3 of this book traces the history of the comparatively recent ecumenical movement, and Part II recounts manifestations of an ecumenical consciousness under the divisions and strains of war. The goal of an expressive world Christian fellowship is far from achieved. Notwithstanding, the co-operation of churches in many lands gives tangible evidence of progress already made and justifies the hope of continued advance. In this developing world fellowship, the churches offer to the world of nations an example and a demonstration of world community.

8. CONCLUSIONS

Insufficient time has passed to permit fair appraisal of the effectiveness with which the churches carried on their work in the field of world order. Many who are competent of sound judgment claim that Christian leadership played a significant part in fixing the direction in which the nations should move and in providing impetus for such progress as has been made. The United Nations has become a reality. Related international agencies to deal with education and economic matters have been established. In many respects, these provisions comply with minimum requirements set in the pronouncements of the churches. A framework has been built within which the nations can co-operate if they are so minded.

No organization, no matter how perfect—and the imperfections of the United Nations are widely recognized—can of itself assure world peace and order. Continuing alertness and activity are imperative. What the churches have thus far accomplished will be significant only if the churches continue and, in fact, intensify their efforts. Cast on the background of the ecumenical movement, the Christian movement toward world order holds an indispensable place in the continuing life of the Christian community. The seven characteristics which have been identified may well constitute lines of procedure to be developed and refined in the years that lie ahead.

The Christian community must strengthen its international approach to the solution of international problems. The World Council of Churches, through its provisional structure, is already making its influence felt. When its organization is carried to completion it will offer a strategic center for continuing co-operation. Under its auspices there can be developed facilities for research, for policy forming, for publicity and education, and for contact with its constituent church bodies in countries throughout the world. Through its leadership, national church groups may be stimulated to organize more definitely for activity in the area of world order.

As the churches continue to move in the arena of the contemporary world, they must never forsake the primary task to which they have been called. They must seek to strengthen their own members in the faith to which they are committed. They must proclaim the Gospel to non-Christians in order that men in increasing numbers may be brought into beneficent relations with God through repentance and faith in Jesus Christ. Their primary purpose will always remain to make better people. In this process they will be aided when they remember that the conditions under which people live—political, economic, cultural, social—have a strong bearing upon growth in character and personality. Accordingly the churches will find in their proclamation of the Gospel an appropriate place for an ethical witness to the world.

The Christian community must continue its attack upon the root causes from which international disorder arises. In proceeding with this attack, the competence of the churches will have to be more clearly defined. There are three areas in which concerted Christian action is possible. The first has to do with an announcement of spiritual and moral foundations. The second is concerned with more concrete and immediately pertinent principles of political and economic import. The third involves an address to particular situations in international life by way of criticizing or commending what has been done, or by way of proposing specific solutions. In how far is concerted Christian action in these three areas appropriate? Careful study will be needed to guide the Christian community in its continued attack upon the causes of war.

Co-operation among all men of good will may be initiated by the churches and holds promise of effective results. In stimulating this co-operation and in remaining party to it, the churches must be careful not to ignore or to compromise the distinctive truths and motivations which are their cherished heritage. Preserving that which is fundamental and unique in Christianity, they will see the provisional good that exists in other faiths and will seek cumulatively to achieve an ever higher world ethos.

The churches which, over the war period, have been effective in relations with their governments must profit by their experiences and establish a measure of permanence in their relationships. In many countries where little or no work was possible, new trails will have to be blazed in order that the Christian voice may be raised and heard in responsible political quarters. In addition to contacts with governments in separate states, the evangelical catholic churches through the World Council of Churches and the International Missionary Council will find it necessary to fashion a plan for permanent liaison with the United Nations. This will be required in order that Christian insights and judgments may be communicated to the United Nations and the actions of the United Nations interpreted to the churches.

Of primary importance is the continuing effort to cultivate an informed Christian conscience. The interest of the people during the war was in goodly part the result of the prevailing atmosphere and of the strains imposed by the hardships of war. If the Christian minority throughout the world is to be effective in promoting world order, people in all walks of life must be kept interested and informed. World order issues must find a permanent place in the educational program of the churches. Events of international significance must be utilized from time to time to make convincing the dangers of ignorance or indifference. Christian leaders must continue to open avenues of action for people in the parishes and must keep alive their sense of satisfaction in participation.

The experience of world Christian fellowship must be intensified and extended. A demonstration of world community in the life of the churches is needed in the first instance to justify the call for co-operation among nations through an international political organization. Such a demonstration may also serve a far-reaching purpose. As the churches strengthen Christian fellowship in the countries around the earth, they will cultivate sympathetic understanding and facility in working together. Herein may be found a substantial backlog for the effort to achieve world order at the political level.

How successful the Christian movement toward world order will be, no one can now foretell. The exercise of Christian influence in the life of the world dare not be conditioned upon the promise of success. It is characteristic of Christianity to mount to its highest effectiveness when confronted by most serious opposition. The Christian community must continue to proclaim the Gospel. It must fashion new ways to challenge the forces of evil. Having entered the arena of the contemporary world, it must continue its struggle there for world peace and order.

9. SIGNIFICANT STATEMENTS ON WORLD ORDER

Ten Peace Points

(Open letter to the London *Times*, December 21, 1940)

The present evils in the world are due to the failure of nations and peoples to carry out the laws of God. No permanent peace is possible in Europe unless the principles of the Christian religion are made the foundation of national policy and of all social life. This involves regarding all nations as members of one family under the Fatherhood of God.

We accept the five points of Pope Pius XII as carrying out this principle:

1. The assurance to all nations of their right to life and independence. The will of one nation to live must never mean the sentence of death passed upon another. When this equality of rights has been destroyed, attacked or threatened, order demands that reparation shall be made, and the measure and extent of that reparation is determined, not by the sword nor by the arbitrary decision of self-interest, but by the rules of justice and reciprocal equity.

2. This requires that the nations be delivered from the slavery imposed upon them by the race for armaments and from danger that material force, instead of serving to pro-

tect the right, may become an over-bearing and tyrannical master. The order thus established requires a mutually agreed organic progressive disarmament, spiritual as well as material, and security for the effective implementing of such an agreement.

3. Some juridical institution which shall guarantee the loyal and faithful fulfilment of conditions agreed upon and which shall in case of recognized need revise and correct them.

4. The real needs and just demands of nations and populations and racial minorities to be adjusted as occasion may require, even where no strictly legal rights can be established, and a foundation of mutual confidence to be thus laid, whereby many incentives to violent action will be removed.

5. The development among peoples and their rulers of that sense of deep and keen responsibility which weighs human statutes according to the sacred and inviolable standards of the laws of God. They must hunger and thirst after justice and be guided by that universal love which is the compendium and most general expression of the Christian ideal.

With these basic principles for the ordering of international life we would associate five standards by which economic situations and proposals may be tested:

1. Extreme inequality in wealth and possessions should be abolished;

2. Every child, regardless of race or class, should have equal opportunities of education, suitable for the development of his peculiar capacities;

3. The family as a social unit must be safeguarded;

4. The sense of a Divine vocation must be restored to man's daily work;

5. The resources of the earth should be used as God's gifts to the whole human race, and used with due consideration for the needs of the present generations.

Statement of Guiding Principles

(Adopted by the Federal Council of Churches, December 11, 1942)

Preamble

As members of the Christian Church, we seek to view all problems of world order in the light of the truth concerning God, men and God's purpose for the world made known in Jesus Christ. We believe that the eternal God revealed in Christ is the Ruler of men and of nations and that His purpose in history will be realized. For us He is the source of moral law and the power to make it effective.

From this faith Christians derive the ethical principles upon which world order must be based. These principles, however, seem to us to be among those which men of goodwill everywhere may be expected to recognize as part of the moral law. In this we rejoice. For peace will require the co-operation of men of all nations, races and creeds. We have therefore first set out (Points 1 to 9) those guiding principles which, it seems to us, Christians and non-Christians alike can accept.

We believe that a special responsibility rests upon the people of the United States. We accordingly (Point 10) express our thoughts in that regard.

Above all, we are impressed by the supreme responsibility which rests upon Christians. Moral law may point the way to peace, but Christ, we believe, showed that way with greatest clarity. We therefore, in conclusion (Points 11 and 12) address ourselves to Christians.

Guiding Principles

1. WE BELIEVE that moral law, no less than physical law, under-girds our world. There is a moral order which is fundamental and eternal, and which is relevant to the corporate life of men and the ordering of human society. If mankind is to escape chaos and recurrent war, social

and political institutions must be brought into conformity with this moral order.

2. WE BELIEVE that the sickness and suffering which afflict our present society are proof of indifference to, as well as direct violation of, the moral law. All share in responsibility for the present evils. There is none who does not need forgiveness. A mood of genuine penitence is therefore demanded of us—individuals and nations alike.

3. WE BELIEVE that it is contrary to the moral order that nations in their dealings with one another should be motivated by a spirit of revenge and retaliation. Such attitudes will lead, as they always have led, to renewed conflict.

4. WE BELIEVE that the principle of co-operation and mutual concern, implicit in the moral order and essential to a just and durable peace, calls for a true community of nations. The interdependent life of nations must be ordered by agencies having the duty and the power to promote and safeguard the general welfare of all peoples. Only thus can wrongs be righted and justice and security be achieved. A world of irresponsible, competing and unrestrained national sovereignties whether acting alone or in alliance or in coalition, is a world of international anarchy. It must make place for a higher and more inclusive authority.

5. WE BELIEVE that economic security is no less essential than political security to a just and durable peace. Such security nationally and internationally involves among other things the use of material resources and the tools of production to raise the general standard of living. Nations are not economically self-sufficient, and the natural wealth of the world is not evenly distributed. Accordingly the possession of such natural resources should not be looked upon as an opportunity to promote national advantage or to enhance the prosperity of some at the expense of others. Rather such possession is a trust to be discharged in the general interest. This calls for more than to offer to sell to all on equal terms. Such an offer may be a futile gesture unless those

in need can, through the selling of their own goods and services, acquire the means of buying. The solution of this problem, doubtless involving some international organization, must be accepted as a responsibility by those who possess natural resources needed by others.

6. WE BELIEVE that international machinery is required to facilitate the easing of such economic and political tensions as are inevitably recurrent in a world which is living and therefore changing. Any attempt to freeze an order of society by inflexible treaty specifications is bound, in the long run, to jeopardize the peace of mankind. Nor must it be forgotten that refusal to assent to needed change may be as immoral as the attempt by violent means to force such change.

7. WE BELIEVE that that government which derives its just powers from the consent of the governed is the truest expression of the rights and dignity of men. This requires that we seek autonomy for all subject and colonial peoples. Until that shall be realized, the task of colonial government is no longer one of exclusive national concern. It must be recognized as a common responsibility of mankind, to be carried out in the interests of the colonial peoples by the most appropriate form of organization. This would, in many cases, make colonial government a task of international collaboration for the benefit of colonial peoples who would, themselves, have a voice in their government. As the agencies for the promotion of world-wide political and economic security become effective, the moral, social and material welfare of colonial populations can be more fully realized.

8. WE BELIEVE that military establishments should be internationally controlled and be made subject to law under the community of nations. For one or more nations to be forcibly deprived of their arms while other nations retain the right of maintaining or expanding their military establishments can only produce an uneasy peace for a limited period. Any initial arrangement which falls short of this

must therefore be looked upon as temporary and provisional.

9. WE BELIEVE that the right of all men to pursue work of their own choosing and to enjoy security from want and oppression is not limited by race, color or creed. The rights and liberties of racial and religious minorities in all lands should be recognized and safeguarded. Freedom of religious worship, of speech and assembly, of the press, and of scientific inquiry and teaching are fundamental to human development and in keeping with the moral order.

10. WE BELIEVE that, in bringing international relations into conformity with the moral law, a very heavy responsibility devolves upon the United States. For at least a generation we have held preponderant economic power in the world, and with it the capacity to influence decisively the shaping of world events. It should be a matter of shame and humiliation to us that actually the influences shaping the world have largely been irresponsible forces. Our own positive influence has been impaired because of concentration on self and on our short-range material gains. Many of the major preconditions of a just and durable peace require changes of national policy on the part of the United States. Among such may be mentioned: equal access to natural resources, economic collaboration, equitable treatment of racial minorities, international control of tariffs, limitation of armaments, participation in world government. We must be ready to subordinate immediate and particular national interests to the welfare of all. If the future is to be other than a repetition of the past, the United States must accept the responsibility for constructive action commensurate with its power and opportunity.

11. WE BELIEVE that, as Christian citizens, we must seek to translate our beliefs into practical realities and to create a public opinion which will insure that the United States shall play its full and essential part in the creation of a moral way of international living. We must strive within the life of our own nation for change which will result in the more adequate application here of the principles above

enumerated as the basis for a just and durable world order.

12. WE BELIEVE that a supreme responsibility rests with the Church. The Church, being a creation of God in Jesus Christ, is called to proclaim to all men everywhere the way of life. Moreover, the Church which is now in reality a world community, may be used of God to develop His spirit of righteousness and love in every race and nation and thus to make possible a just and durable peace. For this service Christians must now dedicate themselves, seeking forgiveness for their sins and the constant guidance and help of God, upheld by faith that the kingdoms of this world shall become the kingdom of Christ and that He shall reign forever and ever.

Statement of Political Propositions (Six Pillars of Peace)

(Authorized for publication by the Federal Council's Executive Committee, May, 1943)

1. The peace must provide the political framework for a continuing collaboration of the United Nations and, in due course, of neutral and enemy nations.

2. The peace must make provision for bringing within the scope of international agreement those economic and financial acts of national governments which have widespread international repercussions.

3. The peace must make provision for an organization to adapt the treaty structure of the world to changing underlying conditions.

4. The peace must proclaim the goal of autonomy for subject peoples, and it must establish international organization to assure and to supervise the realization of that end.

5. The peace must establish procedures for controlling military establishments everywhere.

6. The peace must establish in principle, and seek to achieve in practice, the right of individuals everywhere to religious and intellectual liberty.

The Eleven Points

(*The Church and International Reconstruction.* Issued by the Geneva Study Department, World Council of Churches, January, 1943)

The hard lessons churches have had to learn during this war have led to the emerging of what is called an "ecumenical consensus" or world-wide inter-church agreement. This concerns the function and message of the Church in rendering a common witness to the true foundations of world order.

The eleven points of this "Church Charter" are as follows:

1. The Church has a specific task in relation to peacemaking and the creation of an international order. A division on this point, however, arises over the question whether this task consists exclusively in reminding the nations of the Divine Commandments, or should include the interpretation of those Commandments in terms of concrete policy.

2. The Church can perform its task in this realm by itself, constituting a world-wide fellowship under one Lord in which national differences are eliminated.

3. The Church must proclaim to the nations that Jesus Christ is Lord over all men and all powers.

4. The Church must proclaim the Divine Commandments concerning the order that is to reign in the world.

5. The Church will call the nations to repentance for their common guilt and to work for reconciliation.

6. The Church is to proclaim that international relations must be subordinated to divine law.

7. The Church is to proclaim that the State is neither an aim in itself nor a law unto itself, and that its God-given function is to maintain an order based on law that guarantees fundamental human rights.

8. The Church will proclaim that political power must be exercised with a sense of responsibility toward all those who are affected by that power.

9. The Church is to proclaim that society must provide all its members with the opportunity to fulfill a meaningful vocation, and that it should provide conditions of social security for all.

10. The Church is to proclaim that the nations are interdependent, and that they must all have equal access to the resources of the earth.

11. The Church will proclaim that no people can claim the right to rule over another people, and that the dominating purpose of colonial administration must be to prepare colonial peoples for self-government.

Pattern for Peace: Catholic, Jewish and Protestant Declaration on World Peace (October 1943)

1. *The Moral Law Must Govern World Order.* The organization of a just peace depends upon practical recognition of the fact that not only individuals but nations, states and international society are subject to the sovereignty of God and to the moral law which comes from God.

2. *The Rights of the Individual Must Be Assured.* The dignity of the human person as the image of God must be set forth in all its essential implications in an international declaration of rights and be vindicated by the positive action of national governments and international organization. States as well as individuals must repudiate racial, religious or other discrimination in violation of those rights.

3. *The Rights of Oppressed, Weak or Colonial Peoples Must Be Protected.* The rights of all peoples, large and small, subject to the good of the organized world community, must be safeguarded within the framework of collective security. The progress of undeveloped, colonial or oppressed peoples toward political responsibility must be the object of international concern.

4. *The Rights of Minorities Must Be Secured.* National governments and international organization must respect and guarantee the rights of ethnic, religious and cultural minorities to economic livelihood, to equal opportunity for

educational and cultural development, and to political equality.

5. *International Institutions to Maintain Peace with Justice Must Be Organized.* An enduring peace requires the organization of international institutions which will develop a body of international law; guarantee the faithful fulfilment of international obligations, and revise them when necessary; assure collective security by drastic limitation and continuing control of armaments, compulsory arbitration and adjudication of controversies, and the use when necessary of adequate sanctions to enforce the law.

6. *International Economic Co-operation Must Be Enforced.* International economic collaboration to assist all states to provide an adequate standard of living for their citizens must replace the present economic monopoly and exploitation of natural resources by privileged groups and states.

7. *A Just Social Order within Each State Must Be Achieved.* Since the harmony and well-being of the world community are intimately bound up with the internal equilibrium and social order of the individual states, steps must be taken to provide for the security of the family, the collaboration of all groups and classes in the interest of the common good, a standard of living adequate for self-development and family life, decent conditions of work, and participation by labor in decisions affecting its welfare.

The Dumbarton Oaks Proposals

(A Message to the Churches from the National Study Conference on the Churches and a Just and Durable Peace, Cleveland, Ohio, January, 1943)

Part II, Section 1, The Dumbarton Oaks Proposals . . . we recommend that the churches support the Dumbarton Oaks Proposals as an important step in the direction of world co-operation but because we do not approve of them in their entirety as they now stand, we urge the following measures for their improvement:

1. *Preamble.* A Preamble should reaffirm those present

and long range purposes of justice and human welfare which are set forth in the Atlantic Charter and which reflect the aspiration of peoples everywhere.

2. *Development of International Law.* The Charter of the Organization should clearly anticipate its operation under international law and should provide for the development and codification of international law, to the end that there shall be a progressive subordination of force to law.

3. *Voting Power.* A nation, while having the right to discuss its own case, should not be permitted to vote when its case is being judged in accordance with predetermined international law.

4. *Colonial and Dependent Areas.* A special Commission should be established wherein the progress of colonial and dependent peoples to autonomy, and the interim problems related thereto, will become an international responsibility.

5. *Human Rights and Fundamental Freedoms.* A special Commission on Human Rights and Fundamental Freedoms should be established.

6. *Eventual Universal Membership.* The Charter should specify that all nations willing to accept the obligations of membership shall thereupon be made members of the Organization.

7. *Limitations of Armaments.* More specific provision should be made for promptly initiating the limitation and reduction of national armaments.

8. *Smaller Nations.* There should be provisions designed more clearly to protect and defend the smaller nations from possible subjection to the arbitrary power of the great.

9. *Amendment.* In order to permit such changes in the Charter of the Organization as may from time to time become necessary, the provision for amendments should be liberalized so as not to require concurrence by all the permanent members of the Security Council.

5

ECUMENICITY IN AMERICA

H. Paul Douglass

1. The idea of ecumenicity: ecumenicity and the koinonia, *inadequacy of current distinctions, fallacy of institutional mindedness. 2. The American ecumenical movement and current issues: ecumenical foreshadowings, current status in America, major phases of current developments. 3. Interim steps.*

The object of this essay is to note the movement toward ecumenical integration in the Christian Church as unfolded within the American scene, and to try to supply an objective and realistic interpretation of some of its salient aspects.

1. THE IDEA OF ECUMENICITY

Comprehensive theoretical analysis of the idea of ecumenicity belongs to other sections of these volumes. This particular section treats of a series of American phenomena assumed to be ecumenical. However, the reader who may persist in following it to the end will have every right to ask what conception of ecumenicity warranted their selection. Are all of them authentic ecumenical phenomena? Should some have been excluded; should others have been added? Some part of the answer to this last question is to be found in space limitations. With respect to the rest, it is only fair to offer a general answer as to what ecumenicity is understood to mean in the following discussion.

Ecumenicity and the koinonia

Obviously, any exposition of ecumenicity starts with some concept of the Church. In this context it starts with the unity of the Church in its aspect of the Christian *koinonia*. It identifies the koinonia generically with aspects of the organized life of any society which are more fundamental than the institutional.

The church as *ecclesia* corresponds to the institutional phase which is at present characterized by disunity. Nevertheless, unity exists on the level of the *koinonia*. This unity is truly objective, definable and potent, not merely indefinite and subjective nor "a mere ideal and disembodied ghost," to use Professor George Thomas' phrase. It is not merely unity between individual Christians, which is instinctive, given conditions which evoke it. Heart does flow out to heart, but with the unpredictable characteristics of the wind, which "bloweth where it listeth." At the other extreme stands the Church as an ecclesiastical institution with highly defined structure and form and determinate membership.

But is there no stage between? Most discourse about Christian unity proceeds as though there were only these two possible phases of its expression—the personal and spiritual over against the explicit corporate realized as "organic" church union. But this would be to assert that society shows no stage between the bare capacity for society in individuals, not yet historically expressed or developed, and society in its most highly developed form. Social analysis surely contradicts this notion. Between the primary stuff of unity which has not yet become actually united and the full unity of social institutions lies the broad zone of more basic social phenomenon and organization. Historically speaking, there was social organization of a complicated objective sort, as well as numerous particular societies, before any determinate institution had appeared. There was war before armies, teaching before schools, healing before medicine, worship before priests or churches, productive activity before economic specialization, and the arts before any distinction between ordinary craftsmen and artists.

Moreover, the institutionalizing process, however mature it becomes, never exhausts the whole of any social function exercised at the simpler organizational stage. Most teaching still goes on outside the schools, most work outside of factories, and much religion outside of churches, while total war is no longer a matter of armies but of entire peoples. In short, *the greater part of the social processes of civilization is not yet specialized.*

Similarly, between the "spiritual unity" of the Church and ecclesiastical institutions stands the continuous Christian society in its more elementary expression—the *koinonia.* Institutionalism is a third phase of religious development as of social, and not the sole alternative to spiritual unity.

Inadequacy of current distinctions

In this analysis the writer dissents from the current distinction in ecumenical discussion between Christian unity and church union which seems to satisfy some of the most eminent ecumenical leaders. Dr. W. A. Visser 't Hooft, for example, asserts that the current exploration of the possibility of church unity, intimate and devoted acquaintanceship achieved between church leaders, and collaboration in specific tasks, constitute "in no sense or in any degree" the manifestation of the *Una Sancta.*[1] These things, he says constitute "a movement *about* church unity rather than a demonstration *of* that unity." From the writer's standpoint, on the contrary, these things, as manifestations of the *koinonia,* are the very stuff of unity. The better part of the Church is not fully ecclesiasticized. It exists as a habit of cooperation based on the "we-feeling." It has a unity sustained by common symbols. It possesses a recognizable Christian *mores.* It

[1] W. A. Visser 't Hooft in *Christendom*, Vol. II, No. 3, p. 297.

has functional if not legal authority. It creates a variety of agencies on a voluntary basis, for example, the World Council of Churches. All these are objective social phenomena. They manifest the *koinonia*. They constitute an imperfect but still considerable degree of working unity. They are not mere incidents but rather the marks of the Church at its deepest levels.

Institutions are inevitable, but they are inherently superficial. This includes the Church as *ecclesia*. Normally institutions register the results of more basic social processes. The state enacts what society at deeper levels *determines*. The present fashion is for government through propaganda to attempt to create the will to accept its legislative enactments. It does not make laws until it has created the conditions under which laws are effective. But in the use of propaganda the government is not acting directly in its institutional capacity, but is rather appealing to sanctions created at deeper levels. It is attempting to "make the songs of a nation," its slogans and shibboleths. It would be more wholesome if the state would omit its direct propaganda and be patient enough to secure authorization for its enactments from the more authentic and democratic working of social processes. The state, then, should not and in general cannot penetrate to the level of the *koinonia*. The *koinonia*, on the contrary, is the very homeland of the Church which the Church should primarily inhabit and the marks of which it should pre-eminently bear.

Organized social life, then, below the institutional level is a perfectly verifiable objective phase of society. Its ways are definable. They are transmitted by tradition, propagated by habit, made dependable through loyalty and powerful through devotion; but they lack the meticulous self-consciousness, the brittleness, the over-precision of the legal enactment and conceptually developed creed, the prescribed code, the legal incorporation. So likewise the ecumenical Christian society, the Church as *koinonia*, is an objective fact with a discernible organization structure and common ideology, ethical standards, liturgical

ways, and common practical interests. These marks are more
subtle and at the same time freer and stronger than the creed,
the code, the official objectives and the property ties of the
ecclesiastical churches. The Church has united on this deeper
level, in no perfect degree or final form but in true and significant unity.

Fallacy of institutional mindedness

The fallacy of institutional mindedness is that it fails to see
that it is equally possible, and much more important, to devote
effort to the development of social processes profounder than the
institutional ones than it is to seek institutional ends. By the
same token it is possible and indeed of primary importance to
seek and promote church unity at the level of the *koinonia*, to
hold and transmit the common ideology without the imposition
of rigid creeds, to seek common ethical ends without demanding
identical regulations, in short, to live at the profounder level
of unity than the institutional.

Furthermore, maximum motivation for the pursuit of unity
appears only at the level of the *koinonia*. It has been much
debated whether the Church is an end or only the means. The
ecumenical idea may well assert that as *ecclesia* the Church is
only means; it has to be translated back into the terms of
koinonia to become established as the end. *Koinonia* as fellowship of the Body of Christ in the Church is clearly an end, part of
the final good and goal of mankind. God made the Church as
and for fellowship. This is an ultimate.

To this ultimate the ecumenical spirit brings a devotion and
loyalty of a higher order than that which derives from concern
for unity as a device for securing results. It is undoubtedly true
that if the churches do not hang together they are likely to hang
separately. Moreover, not merely self-defensively but for the
sake of their mission, unity is imperative. Every separate aspect
of the Church's concrete functioning in the world—its evangelism, its religious education, the implementation of its social

responsibility and the adjustment of religious life in local communities—would be measurably strengthened by a greater degree of objective unity. The world will not believe until it sees some demonstration of unity at its own level. When all this is said, there are some things about the unity of the Church which the world cannot be expected to apprehend but which, to the Christian, should glow with the light of the central sun. The *koinonia* is a direct expression of the indwelling of the spirit of God in the Church. Unity of this sort is "grand in itself."

What follows in this chapter is the discussion of a series of specific phenomena of church integration in America, all of which are believed to fall within the ecumenical movement as *koinonia*. This is not to say that they are all of equal rank or that some of them may not superficially clash with and measurably contradict one another. They are, however, the actual expression of growing unity in the Church as *koinonia* which have to be regarded when one surveys the contemporary American scene.

2. THE AMERICAN ECUMENICAL MOVEMENT AND CURRENT ISSUES

Ecumenical foreshadowings

Despite the characteristic American tendency toward religious differentiation and division a contrary unitive trend has long been established and has continued. Current progress in unity is based on this long-term trend.

Let us begin with the briefest glance into history. Since the earliest years of the nineteenth century, interdenominational cooperation had been going on on no small scale—in the publishing and circulation of the Scriptures and of tracts, in the promotion of frontier Sunday schools, in church extension and in foreign missions. A more homespun and indigenous unifying influence was the frontier revival, which impressed upon pioneer churches "a common pattern of religious life and common religious symbolism. A camp meeting was an early form of denominational co-operation, in which Presbyterian, Methodist and Baptist preachers united. The conversions which took place, whether in response to Calvinist preaching or Arminian appeals, were of the same type. The hymns . . . the prayers, the symbols of heaven and hell . . . were not those of any special group."[2] These experiences, in spite of their sectarian deviations, wrought a common religious tendency in the churches dominated by the distinctive American temper. The plea for organic unity as inherent in the idea of the Church, voiced very early in the century by the Disciples of Christ, was the theological version of these frontier experiences.

In 1838 the Society for the Promotion of Christian Union was founded in New York, the first comprehensive movement of its sort in our national history. The immediate occasion of the organization of the Society was the publication in the previous year by Dr. Samuel Schmucker, professor in the Lutheran Theological Seminary in Gettysburg, Pennsylvania, of an appeal "affectionately addressed to the American churches of every denomination," attached to which was a Plan of Union—in many respects more basic and substantial than any which has been promulgated since.

Schmucker proposed that the respective denominations retain their existing identity, organization and customs, but offered a common creed called "An Apostolic Protestant Confession" made up of "a selection of those articles from the existing creeds of the prominent Protestant churches in which all can agree," plus the Apostles' Creed. This composite document was believed to represent a real theological consensus. There was to be free sacramental, ministerial and ecclesiastical communion among the "Confederated Churches" symbolized in any community by annual joint communion services. "The principle of co-operation

[2] William Warren Sweet, *The Baptists,* Vol. I, "Religion on the American Frontier" (Chicago: University of Chicago Press, 1931), p. 64.

regardless of sect" was to be adopted in all matters pertaining to "the common cause of Christianity"; and not relating to the peculiarities of the several denominations. Specifically, printing and circulation of the Bible and religious tracts, and educational work and church extensions should be undertaken interdenominationally. Missionaries going to foreign lands would "use and profess no other creed than the Bible and the annexed Apostolic Protestant Confession," connected with whatever church government and form of worship they preferred. "For the sake of our bleeding Saviour our sectarian divisions ought not to be transplanted to heathen lands."

Schmucker anticipated that the present denominations would come to be described as the Baptist Branch, Lutheran Branch, etc. of the Confederated Churches, but no formal governing body or regular meetings in their corporate capacity were provided for, Schmucker saying that these were not a necessary part of Christian union. What Schmucker called "highly respectable and influential brethren," in all parts of the country, expressed adherence to the scheme, and local auxiliaries for the promotion of Christian union began to be formed in numerous communities. Perhaps the most realistic welcome to the plan came from the frontier as voiced by Asa Turner, the famous Iowa missionary pioneer, who declared:

> [It] would be like the waters of salvation to the little villages and sparse populations of the West [if] all evangelical denominations agree to send no more ministers to one spot than the wants of the people demand. In little villages of from one to two thousand inhabitants, it is not uncommon to see from four to six ministers! These find a meagre support from hearers, and must fan the sectarian flame much of the time to retain their footing. You know what would be the natural fruit of such a course of procedure; of course many other places lie desolate because ministers cannot be had. Your plan would add one-third to our efficient laborers.

Later with the upsurge of the sectarian spirit, the current on which the founders of this Society relied ran more feebly, but it never ceased to flow. From 1846 forward the Evangelical Alliance was the chief world-wide movement designed to "exhibit the essential unity of the Church of Christ." Men active in the American branch of the Evangelical Alliance in its later years were also leaders in movements which were the direct fore-runners of the establishment of the Federal Council of the Churches of Christ in America. In brief, the ascendant and growing practice of unity in our own land shows an unbroken tactual succession of the most literal sort which spans a century and a half.

Recent ecumenical progress in the United States is thus profoundly based on long-term tendencies which have never left the consciousness and aspiration of the nation without a witness to the conviction that the Church is and must be one.

Current status of the ecumenical movement in America

The present status of the ecumenical movement in America is the result of the accelerated pace and the gathering power of the ecumenical movement throughout the world reinforcing the long-existing American urge, converging its major streams and spreading over all levels of the Church's life and organization. The outstanding facts are widely recognized and need only brief comment.

(1) The continued secular assimilation of American people to a common type in spite of the strongly diverse original elements which have gone into the making of the nation, has proceeded without diminution to such an extent that competent foreign observers began to complain of the "sameness" of America. Parallel forces working in the Church have brought out a dominant Protestant temper taking an essentially unified pattern both of private and of social religious life, so much so that, to strangers, most of our divided denominations seem very much alike. A common tone pervades most widely read religious

books and publications. The books to be found on the shelves of a Mormon and a Methodist theological seminary would be more largely the same books than different ones. Within such a setting the most keenly felt differences tend to be overborne by the present community of thought.

(2) The unifying effects of secular assimilation are particularly potent where the original disunity of the Church had cultural, social or economic origins without profound divergences in the realm of Christian faith or church polity. Someone has counted forty-two "imported" denominations in America during the Colonial period. Successive waves of immigration from European countries which had state churches imposed the ecclesiastical map of Europe upon the United States. This is most conspicuous in the case of Lutheran and Eastern Orthodox bodies, but is equally true of others.

Three-way schisms which later appear in many of the churches of the same general family and outlook—between the more conservative, the middle-of-the-road, and the radical positions— often reflected nothing more than three different periods of immigration by people of the same stock. The later comers to these shores found their fellow believers who came a few decades sooner subtly changed; and tended to set up new churches reflecting their sense of separation. Progressive elements in the older immigrant groups, on the other hand, went on faster than the main body of their people, more quickly abandoning the foreign tongue and more rapidly taking on American ways. Churches representing these more liberal tendencies frequently separated from the original imported denominations. But as immigration was checked or virtually stopped and cultural advantage was gradually equalized, the slower tended to catch up with the more advanced. Religious divisions of this sort then ceased to be meaningful, and large-scale reintegrations began.

Other divisions in the Church, originating largely with underprivileged people, living in isolation especially on the frontier, were also primarily social in significance. Their faith was essentially a conservative version of the common faith with certain emotional excrescences which should never be allowed to disguise the basic common element. Whenever these movements have removed from their original isolated habitations and become exposed to the common influence of national life, they have manifested a very rapid cooling-off process in which their peculiarities are minimized and their separatist tendencies reduced. This process has been greatly accentuated during the war period, as the separatist sects have been spread into new territory by wartime immigration. The consolidating process has been exceedingly rapid. This is particularly manifest on the Pacific Coast. On the whole, the integrative tendency greatly outweighs any significance to be found in the numerical multiplication of these sects. They are exceptions which prove the rule.

Meanwhile religious divisions based on sectionalism have also been largely modified or removed as the cultural status of the American sections has become more nearly equal. All along the line distinctions based on the older social and cultural inequalities have worn down and will continue to do so except as new injustices and discriminations may perpetuate social class struggles out of which new disunited churches may arise.

(3) The pragmatic background for specific unity movements, particularly in America, is further found in the virtually interchangeable use of the churches in connection with the amazing mobility of our increasingly assimilated population. Particularly as incident to urban growth, millions of Christians have transferred back and forth across denominational lines. Thousands of ministers have similarly gone back and forth, thus proving in actual experience the essential common Christianity to which the great bulk of the denominations belong. In 1920 the Congregational churches ordained ninety-six men but accepted ninety-two more ordained by other denominations. In 1926 the General Council of the Presbyterian Church, U. S. A. reported that 38

per cent of all its accessions to the ministry during the past five years had infiltrated from other denominations.

(4) Animosity and prejudice between churches have demonstrably declined and are now at an exceedingly low ebb. The felt barriers to union have largely dissolved away. This can be verified by the memory of almost any person beyond middle age. "Religious distance" tests conducted on a large scale reveal a great central core of the church membership of the major denominations who recognize very little of the sense of barrier or sundering prejudice or conviction between themselves on some of the most sensitive points of religion.

(5) The structure of a world confederation of non-Roman churches is now nearing completion, at least in skeleton. This structure—more extensive and complete in the United States than anywhere else—consists of local councils and federations of churches in most of the larger and many smaller communities and in a majority of states; and of national federations like the Federal Council of Churches. These are paralleled by similar organizations in numerous European countries and by fifteen or more National Christian Councils in foreign mission lands, the whole now in process of being rounded out by the establishment of the World Council of Churches.

(6) The reality of essential agreement in Christian faith and outlook has been repeatedly reaffirmed over the last two decades by world gatherings of the delegates of churches from all continents and virtually all non-Roman communions—at Lausanne in 1927, at Jerusalem in 1928, at Edinburgh in 1937, and, last, at Madras, India in December, 1938. In all these America prominently participated.

Opinions differ rather sharply as to the genuineness and comprehensiveness of the agreements announced in these declarations.[3] The weighty deliberations of theological study commissions which have reported during the war years have expressed

[3] See W. A. Visser 't Hooft, in *Christendom*, Vol. II, No. 3, p. 298, compared with Henry P. Van Dusen in the same issue, pp. 328-9.

limited agreement, but no decisive advance on issues on which there was previous disagreement; and it is probably safe to say that little or no part of the declared agreements has been embodied in the formal theological confessions of any denominations. From the standpoint of the *koinonia*, however, the fact that differences have been steadily faced together, plus the enormous amount of personal contact and confidence achieved, constitute truly significant advances. Theological thought-processes that flourished in isolation have been thoroughly broken up, and it is believed by many that a new group of younger theologians has arisen whose basic thinking is more genuinely ecumenical than any which has existed before.

(7) The World Council of Churches in process of formation is simply an extension in principle—and the structural culmination—of the trends expressed in the United States on lower levels by these well-established and long-term factors. "A certain rhythm," writes Professor Roland H. Bainton, "is observable between divisive and unifying periods. The genius of our time is distinctly ecumenical."[4] For the moment at least, the age of division has given way to an age of integration. Unitive movements—though by no means unchallenged—are ascendant in our times.

The convergence of such forces undoubtedly puts ecumenicity in a stronger position in America than ever before in our history.

Major phases of current developments

In order to arrive at a more critical appraisal of the American ecumenical situation, certain of its salient aspects require more precise and discriminating consideration.

(1) *Development of a comprehensive system of interchurch councils.* The number of interchurch councils on numerous levels has greatly multiplied and has rapidly developed in a recognized system of co-operative organization. What do these

[4] Roland H. Bainton in *Christendom*, Vol. II, No. 3, p. 387.

expanding lists of councils mean? They mean that a definite ecclesiastical structure is being evolved parallel and supplementary to the denominational system. This co-operative structure has substantially the same sanction as the denominations themselves, namely the formal action of representative church bodies perpetuated by established habit.

The latest directories show thirty-five states maintaining the inclusive type of interdenominational organization, that is to say, one that attempts to combine all-co-operative interests under one grouping. In contrast with this only seven states still maintain separate and limited forms of co-operative organization, such as councils of religious education, Sunday school associations and home missions councils. Counting both the comprehensive and the more limited type of councils, only one state is left without any form of state-wide co-operative organization. Some eighty-five city, county and district councils covering virtually all of the major communities outside of the Southern States, have been created, generally and increasingly of the comprehensive type, under paid leadership. A very much larger number of communities maintain councils on a volunteer leadership basis. All told 535 councils are currently catalogued.

Perhaps equally significant is the partial assumption of the role and functions of councils of churches by great numbers of local interdenominational ministerial associations. Instead of remaining professional clubs, hundreds of these associations, without specific authorization, have begun to do the things which the council of churches would do, and to exercise representative co-operative functions in the religious life of their communities.

The evolution of the councils has been marked by a steady broadening of their spheres of action under the axiom of doing together what is better done together than separately. All the time more things are discovered which can best be done in common. Meanwhile standards have noticeably lifted. While formerly very few of the departments of social work in city councils were staffed by trained professionals in social work, recent studies indicate that full professional standing on the part of the members of such staffs is now the general rule.

Other significant changes include the widening circle of participating denominations, which are coming to include bodies which in the past have generally been regarded as somewhat erratic and marginal. This inclusiveness has been greatly stimulated by joint war emergency projects. All told, it has become fairly characteristic for American communities to expand the co-operative unity of their Protestant churches through formal organization. The constitutions of the more recently established councils tend to be expressed in more definitely ecumenical terms, and the most recent general interpretations of the movement as a whole explicitly identify it with local ecumenicity.

(2) *Mergers of churches*. Meanwhile, actual unions of American denominations have reduced twenty-eight to twelve since 1900. The union of the three major Methodist bodies into one great church of more than eight million members is the most conspicuous example. Generally, though by no means always, the uniting churches have belonged to the same general denominational family or type. Some of these piecemeal unions are in the making. Current formal negotiations for union between the Evangelical and United Brethren; the Congregational-Christian and Evangelical Reformed Churches; the Reformed in America and United Presbyterian churches, are in various stages of development that give promise of being consummated. Perennial formal discussions of union keep going on between branches of the Presbyterian Church, and important negotiations between the Presbyterian Church, U. S. A. and the Protestant Episcopal Church are under way.

What general significance have these partial unions? They invariably base themselves on the affirmation of the inherent spiritual unity of the Church, and work out some of the objective advantages of unity. They create an atmosphere. They are a challenge to bodies not directly involved. To a considerable extent such mergers have accomplished relief to communities from rivalry and duplication of local churches, thus partially obviating the weakness of division. The effect of these examples is thus both theological and practical.

Furthermore, such partial unions constitute extremely useful laboratory experiments applicable to more comprehensive efforts. They are working out on a small scale features which are basically essential to any inclusive scheme of American church unity and which hitherto have had no large-scale demonstration.

The idea of union between churches of the same denominational families is almost universally accepted in theory and is significantly progressing in accomplishment. It would appear that numerous additional American churches not sundered by profound differences of belief might well come together speedily. Perhaps this is the most characteristic contribution that America can make to the cause of general reunion and the one which will most effectively contribute to its immediate momentum.

(3) *Community churches.* Some twenty-five hundred American communities have transcended denominationalism in whole or in part by the establishment of united local churches of various types. If all were combined into one separate denomination—which God forbid—they would constitute one of the major American groups. A minor fraction of the community churches are strictly nondenominational and independent of all ecclesiastical connections. Probably twice as many are federations of congregations of two or more denominations. They maintain unimpaired their legal connection with the parent groups, but combine locally under a common ministry and for worship and parish life and work. Numerous denominational churches have arrogated to themselves the name "community," but, strictly speaking, the community church is one which has been recognized by other denominations as serving its community in a comprehensive spirit in behalf of the total Christian body. This recognition has often been connected with an agreement guaranteeing the church an exclusive field so far as the co-operating denominations are concerned.

A smaller but growing number of multi-denominational churches has recently come into existence. These are recognized and listed by two or more denominations at the same time, and their ministers are usually in complete and good standing in two or more denominations at once.

During the early years of the church federation movement one could not have said with confidence how it would turn out. The impression was somewhat widely held that they would prove ephemeral and disastrous to the denominational standing of the separate units. Intensive studies conducted in 1934, however, seem to indicate clearly that (1) once federated, churches do not tend to fall apart; (2) nor is the weaker partner likely to be absorbed into the denominational church of the stronger partner; (3) nor are the practical denominational ties usually broken with the passage of years. This finding, as concerns federated Baptist churches, was confirmed in 1944 by a study conducted by Mark Rich and John Halko, which revealed that the Baptist units of federated churches generally remain Baptist, that their growth and prosperity were not in general inferior to that of similar Baptist churches, and that in certain areas the level of the success of the federated Baptist units was greater than that of the other Baptist churches in the same territory.

All told, then, it seems established as a fairly permanent situation that denominationalism does not generally lose out in federated churches but remains as an integral feature of permanent church structure. In the exceptional case, when the process of local integration does eventuate in the obliteration of the separate denominational segment, the alternative of multi-connection may preserve the denominations from any numerical *loss* as the result of such a process.

Here, then, in the various types of community churches, is a group of processes which more or less have achieved immediate limited local church unity in some thousands of American communities.

As to the significance and ecumenical quality of these processes, opinion is somewhat sharply divided. The general climate of American religious opinion is favorable to all sorts of practical experiments in small over-churched communities. The actual assimilation of different denominations to a common religious type and the lack on the part of laymen of a nice sense of theological distinctions make the community church seem only natural in multitudes of situations. People of the community are bound together by intimate property and social ties, including the intermarriage of Christian families. They desire to escape from the burden of divisiveness and the competition of sectarian churches in the community, accompanied as they often are by an envious and unchristian spirit. These are strong sanctions for the establishment of local community churches.

On the other hand, it is a distinct inconvenience to the denominational system to make and administer the exceptions required by such churches. And the movement is feared because in certain expressions it has been definitely and militantly anti-denominational. Thus the community churches have remained in a somewhat equivocal position with respect to the ecumenical movement. Formal action by a considerable number of state and local church federations has legitimized the community church under proper sponsorship. Thus the Chicago, Cleveland, Cincinnati and other strong councils have agreed that when local circumstances and the majority demand of the people of the neighborhood indicate the desirability of an interdenominational church not exclusively related to any denomination, the council itself would recognize and administer such a church. Recent action of the Southern California Council of Churches, for example, proposes the establishment of a Commission on Interdenominational Projects which may administer such projects "as may be required." In all such cases it is implied that the moral and ordinarily desired method of churching a community is through the properly related denominational churches, but that in exceptional cases properly sponsored community churches are legitimate and desirable. Such sponsorship saves them from being orphans, provides fellowship, help and guidance in crises, and aids in the securing of proper ministers.

(4) *A closer and more effective federal union.* Meanwhile, the demand for a closer and more effective federal union of national scope has been repeatedly voiced in responsible quarters since the first World War and is now a genuinely live issue.

This demand was officially marked by such action as the vote of the Federal Council of Churches in 1936 directing the Executive Committee to proceed when possible "to work out a plan whereby the unity of the churches of Christ in America may be more fully realized"; also by a formal overture from the Presbyterian, U.S.A. Church requesting the Council to study anew the possibility on the part of its constituent churches of achieving "a fuller unity in Christian service . . . and, particularly, means by which the churches may do their work at home and abroad in greater unity through the Federal Council or other organizations." On February 2, 1939, one thousand ministers participating in the Ohio Pastors' Convention voted their conviction that existing federated movements are not and cannot be adequate and that "there should be an immediate effort to achieve the organic union of many, if not all, of the Protestant denominations. . . . There are insufficient differences in essential belief to keep us apart. The compelling needs of our world outweigh all other considerations."

This aspiration to unite, at an early date, a large group of American denominations has taken form in a notable series of essentially kindred plans offered to the American churches since the first World War. All of these plans have exhibited a common central idea and purpose. The purpose is to secure quickly the advantages of such union as the churches are already prepared for.

The basic idea, on which the entire group of plans has agreed, has been to secure the adoption by the uniting of denominations of a common name—The United Church of the United States, or some similar title—and of a central organization with responsibility going beyond that committed to any existing federations but still with narrowly limited powers, leaving the present denominational structure in all other respects essentially as it is now. Such federal union was the essence of the plan of union proposed by the Conference on Organic Union attended by representatives of nineteen denominations in 1918 and 1920; of suggestions for union derived from a canvass of opinion in preparation for the twentieth anniversary of the Federal Council in 1928, and of subsequent resolutions of similar import by several denominations.

This type of proposal has remained continuously in the arena of popular discussion since 1936-7, when Dr. Stanley Jones of India began to advocate it on several occasions in a telling address entitled "The Next Great Step—Unite." The popular response of Dr. Jones's proposal was unexpectedly great; and the strong family resemblance characterizing all the main versions of this oft-repeated proposal would seem to indicate that here is a very authentic expression of contemporary American hopes and purposes on behalf of the unity of a large section of the American church.

In advocating union by the adoption of a common name, moreover, these recent proposals put themselves in line with the original watchword of the Disciples of Christ. A common name and the assumption of branch relationships by the existing denominations within a united church was also something which Samuel Schmucker in 1839 thought would come along in due course. It is strongly argued that such a step is imperative to give the Church an organ of effective unity in its dealings with the world; but also that such union would further improve the inner attitudes of the branch churches, increase the spiritual unity which now informs them, and, in turn, make for the adoption of broadening spheres of common effort and service.

In brief, the specific terms of the proposals under discussion are believed to provide only a basis and a beginning. They anticipate the strong probability of growth of a more powerful

central organization for the united church with enlarged functions—just as the federal government of the United States has
grown in authority and scope.

The elaborated Stanley Jones plan is currently being promoted under a national committee. Is this not, then, clearly the
next step for the American church? An adequate immediate
sanction for closer union has been evidenced in the facts just
reviewed, both in terms of objective tendencies and in subjective
feelings. Why not, then, all unite behind some acceptable version of the typical American proposal?

(5) *The issue of a universally recognized common ministry
and sacramental intercommunion.* One answer to the question
just posed is that in spite of the frequency with which it has
arisen and its wide acceptability, any proposal on the plane of
those just discussed appears superficial to considerable groups
of American Christians. A radically different approach challenges the adequacy of the grounds upon which such unity is
anticipated and proposes to hinge the whole matter on the issue
of a properly authenticated common ministry and sacramental
intercommunion.

While historically this aspect is much less characteristic of
the American ecumenical movement, yet seen in the perspective
of world insights and convictions it may appear to have a crucial significance in the American context. Moreover, it must
be recalled that the most general official formulation of this
point of view on the part of the Anglican churches through the
world—the Lambeth Quadrilateral—actually originated in resolutions of the Protestant Episcopal General Convention in Chicago in 1886. The Quadrilateral proposes unity on the basis
of the Scriptures, the Nicene Creed, the sacraments of baptism
and the Lord's Supper, and the historic episcopacy. This last involves the issue of a commonly recognized ministry and, by implication, sacramental intercommunion.

As developed in discussion this formula focuses upon what
the Edinburgh World Conference on Faith and Order identi-

fied as the chief issue of union—namely, the circumstance that a great proportion of the Church regards some particular form of order or sacramental worship as part of the faith.

> Behind all particular statements of the problem of corporate union [says the Report] lie deeply divergent conceptions of the church. . . . We have, on the one hand, an insistence upon a divine givenness in the Scriptures, in orders, in creeds, in worship; we have, on the other hand, an equally strong insistence upon the individual experience of divine grace as the ruling principle of the "gathered church, in which freedom is both enjoyed as a religious right and enjoined as a religious duty. . . ."

On this analysis the issue lies between two major types of Christianity. The necessity of adjustment of differences, at least in principle, on this issue, is widely believed to underlie the problems of a common ministry and unlimited communion between Christian churches.

For America the issue has been concretely formulated in current negotiations for union between the Presbyterian, U.S.A. and Protestant Episcopal churches. The specific terms of these negotiations in their first phase were embodied in a proposed Concordat aiming at the establishment of sacramental intercommunion and ministerial interchangeability between the two churches. The Concordat proposed that in order to make possible the union of members between the two churches into one worshiping congregation in any local community sharing the common sacraments and life of the church under common ministry, the Episcopal and Presbyterian ministers—in addition to their present authorizations—might each receive "an extended commission" from the other church empowering them to administer the local united church and its sacraments.

The crux of the situation is found in the fact that an Episcopal minister may become a Presbyterian and receive authority to minister in a Presbyterian church without ordination. His status as a minister is not in question; he only needs expanded jurisdiction. But a Presbyterian similarly going into the Episcopal Church, according to the latter's canons, would have to be ordained, or, from the Presbyterian standpoint, reordained. Something may be lacking in the authentication of his ministry which would thus be conveyed. He needs something more than an expanded jurisdiction.

The question arises whether the extended commission, though carried out in identical form, would have a different meaning in the case of the Presbyterian Church from that which it would have in the case of the Episcopal. Many commentators agree that the Concordat is equivocal at this point. Each church, it is clear, intends to add to the ministry of the other whatever sanction it has to convey. But if deeply discrepant conceptions of the Church lie behind the transaction, can they really be overcome by a merely extended commission such as proposed? (The more recent course of Presbyterian-Episcopal negotiations seems to have strayed from the main point and to have become increasingly indecisive.)

Five phenomena have now been described as significant elements of the American ecumenical movement, acquaintance with which is basic for an understanding. They are:

(1) The system of councils of churches;
(2) Unions of numerous denominations;
(3) The community church;
(4) The trend toward a stronger federal union;
(5) The approach via the issues of the ministeries and intercommunion.

How these elements are put together will determine the course of our ecumenicity in the near future. Will they reinforce one another or will some oppose or neutralize others? What relative value and what priority will be given to each? On these questions hang decisions which will determine whether the ecumenical movement is accelerated or further deflected or divided.

3. INTERIM STEPS

Meanwhile, what next? Considering the American temper and the strong demand for closer union, together with the increasing momentum of the total ecumenical movement in the world, it is unthinkable that our churches should do nothing while we wait on the solution of unresolved issues. The Edinburgh World Conference on Faith and Order had to accept currently insurmountable differences, but it nevertheless went on to rough out a considerable series of interim measures. The subsequent ecumenical movement has been in large measure a following out of the steps indicated in the faith that in time this procedure would clarify the ultimate goal. Is there a particular American series of interim steps growing out of our special orientation and the stage of our development? Seven possible measures are suggested in the following paragraphs.

(1) *The unification of the unifying agencies.* The well-established interchurch organs which seek to unify the American church in co-operative action are not themselves united. Eight such agencies are commonly recognized of which the Federal Council of the Churches of Christ in America, the Foreign Missions Conference of North America, the Home Missions Council and the International Council of Religious Education are the most conspicuous. A definite movement toward merging some or all of these agencies was formally launched in 1932 in resolutions of the Federal Council proposing "more effective integration with the co-operative agencies in the field of religious education and missions." Since that time the proposal for merger has taken definite form and is now pursuing a rather deliberate course. A draft of a plan has been approved in principle by the major agencies and is now before the constituent churches and boards. The infrequency of the meeting of the plenary bodies of some of the denominations will delay final decision for some years yet, but a strong majority of those

which have acted, including very important ones, have been
favorable, and the ultimate merger of the interchurch agencies
operating primarily in American territory seems highly prob-
able.

This would involve no essentially new principle since the
agencies are now undertaking increasing blocks of jointly administered work through numerous inter-council committees
and through a joint field department. But their actual merger
would tremendously increase their strength and the harmony of
their functions.

(2) *The drawing of a larger number of denominations into
the existing federated structure of the American church.* A second ecumenical process of outstanding importance is the extension of the range of denominational commitment to federated action through the council system. When all the important larger organizations mentioned above are considered,
but few important denominations of any group remain that do
not belong to at least one of them. Most of the significant denominations belong to at least two or three. However, certain
important denominations have remained aloof from or in some
opposition to the Federal Council as an agency of general federal
union. One great value of a merger of the interchurch agencies
would be to break the continuity of this particular phase of
prejudice by removing its object. Nearly all churches are feeling the force of the ecumenical current and many unwilling to
join the Federal Council are finding place within the emerging
World Council of Churches. This would seem to create the obligation to make good within American relationships the general
and ideal principles which the World Council incarnates.

It is also most important to secure the backing and co-operation of hitherto marginal churches as well as a considerable number of smaller denominations. A fortunate by-product of the
urgent challenge of the war emergency has been that churches
both of the emotional sects and of the more conservative theological tradition have been drawn into numerous local co-

operative enterprises. In the Portland-Vancouver area, for example, several Lutheran branches, unaccustomed to close cooperation with others, on the one hand, and such sectarian groups as the Assemblies of God and the "Jesus Only" cult, on the other, have become associated with a wide range of "regular" denominations and the Salvation Army in united Christian ministries. These precedents should be expanded on the national scale. They are already being duplicated in a widening association of churches in European relief and reconstruction.

(3) *Extension of quantity and range of co-operative undertakings.* Another important line of effort should bring more and more significant types of Christian activities and ministries under inter-church co-operative control.

In 1937 the Federal Council instructed its Commission for the Study of Christian Unity to explore the possibility of "a larger measure of unified administration; the possibility of delegating substantial responsibilities and functions to central agencies like the Federal Council and Home Missions Council; the exploration of specific functions now fulfilled by denominational agencies which might be committed to interdenominational bodies." The Council later received a request from the Presbyterian Church, U.S.A. that the Commission "particularly consider means by which the churches may do their mission work at home and abroad in greater unity through the Federal Council or other organization."

If one adds up the administrative work of the Federal Council, such as supervising union churches in the Canal Zone, securing chaplains for the Army and Navy and for state and federal penal institutions, plus the immense amounts of relief and emergency work in which it shares often as a partner with other agencies, together with forms of activity directly administered by the Home Missions Council, such as ministries in connection with Indian schools, to migrant groups and in emergency and industrial areas; if one also takes into account the broad educational processes, including the promotional and curriculum-

making work of the International Council of Religious Education, one gets an impressive body of already united services
which, if pooled, would furnish a highly significant core of
activities for a united Church.

The most frequently suggested additional field for co-operative administration is that of service to exceptional populations,
such as missions in Alaska or to American Indians, immigrant
or racial groups, migrant workers and others under special
economic stress. This block of work might very well become a
united responsibility of the churches through a merged co-
operative agency. Increasingly the special inadvisability is felt
of extending American denominational divisions to populations
in which such barriers are historically alien and where they add
a divisive feature to a situation in which integration is a compelling need on patriotic, cultural and religious grounds alike.

(4) *The setting up of regional experiments in actual church
union.* The suggestion has repeatedly emerged that some area
within the territory of the United States might well be selected
for an experiment in full administrative union of the churches
and other interests of the co-operative denominations. For
working purposes there would be a single church in this area.
It would be multi-related, having formal recognition by all the
denominations participating in the joint effort. It would respect
and preserve the variety of traditions and conscientious Christian usages contributed by the uniting elements. In short, it
would do on a larger scale what was repeatedly done temporarily during the war emergency in particular local areas.

Such a proposal assumes a fairly simple situation where the
need for unity is great and the resources of the individual denominations rather small; perhaps where there is need of
maximum aid from the outside and of course where the internal
conditions for achieving unity are favorable. Alaska and Puerto
Rico have been mentioned as areas fulfilling such specifications,
also the Intermountain Area, where a council of leading denominations requested "a study of the advisability of a simple over-

organization such as might be called the United Church of the Intermountain Area" to be composed of such communions as would unite, and evangelize the area "without discrepancies of social and denominational services and objectives." Similarly, a state like Vermont has been suggested, where there are relatively few denominations, where many federated or otherwise united churches already exist and where there is a possible inclination to make such an experiment. All that would be necessary to effect a regional union along these lines would be for the respective denominations to give permissive authorization to their local churches to enter into a united church, as has often been done on the foreign field.

(5) *Co-operative planning for the re-churching of America.* A long next step would be the extension and implementation of efforts to avoid competition in the regular church work of the co-operating denominations, especially in the smaller American communities. For nearly a decade a group of the major home mission boards have periodically reviewed case by case grants in aid from national missionary funds to rural communities in which any two or more of them are represented. The Federal Council and Home Missions Council both have recently approved the report of the Joint Committee urging the extension of this process and agreement "equally to self-supporting and mission-aided churches." Their report went on to say:

> [This] would mean the listing of all churches, community by community, county by county, and state by state; the identification of all churches that seem duplicatory according to recognized standards; and a concerted effort through interchurch consultation and action to adjust the situation so as to make the best possible religious provision for all American people. However far the process might go, a nation-wide pattern would have been established toward which to work; and experience justifies the expectation that very large numbers of adjustments might be expected promptly.

As to the merits of this proposal, the late Professor Arthur Holt of Chicago Theological Seminary, said:

> I see no way out except that those of us who have been leaders of churches should go to the over-churched communities and make this honest confession, "We acknowledge that we led you into this mess and now we would like to lead you out."

(6) *Closer interchurch co-operation and greater union in foreign mission work.* Still another important and imperative next step is the further development through American agencies of the integrative movement now in process on the foreign field and the recognition and facilitation of union movements on the part of the "younger churches." The recommendation of the Laymen's Foreign Missions Inquiry of 1930 on this point reiterated a very long series of affirmations of the crucial seriousness of this point. It was especially emphasized by the Madras Conference of 1938 that there "has come in many fields a deep and growing conviction that the Spirit of God is guiding the various branches of His church to seek for a realization of a visible and organic union." This conviction was especially voiced in the supplementary declaration of representatives of the "younger churches":

> We, therefore, appeal with all the fervor we possess to the Missionary Societies and Boards and the responsible authorities of the Older Churches, to take this matter seriously to heart, to labor with the churches in the mission field to achieve this union, to support and encourage us in all our efforts to put an end to the scandalous effects of our divisions, and to lead us in the path of union—the union for which our Lord prayed, through which the world would indeed believe in the Divine Mission of the Son, our Lord Jesus Christ.

Recent action by the American foreign mission boards providing that, in future relations with the Japanese churches, missionaries should be jointly commissioned rather than sent by separate boards should give a fresh impetus to measures applicable in principle to all the major fields of foreign mission activity.

(7) *The integration of the United States in the total ecumenical movement with the World Council of Churches.* It seems imperative that a truly representative agency of all streams of the ecumenical movement in America should be developed parallel to the World Council of Churches and that it should be empowered to function as the American section of that Council in relationship with the whole of Christendom. A merged, augmented and freshly authorized National Council of Churches would seem to present a practical agency for this purpose. The British Council of Churches, as is well known, directly constitutes the British branch of the World Council. There is at least an apparent infelicity in not having as at present a single track agency as the organ of the World Council in the United States when we are in the process of creating an all-round agency representing the full range of Christian interests involved in the ecumenical movement.

First, then, to merge our Councils, second to interpret unmistakably all phases of the American ecumenical movement as parts of one whole, then to recognize the agency which expresses this totality in its relation to the World Council would seem to be the obvious requirement of the situation. Such a course of action would constitute for the United States a true expression and effective organ of ecumenicity.

(8) *Affirmation of ecumenical meaning and sanctions.* Last of all, but imperatively important at every stage, is the interpretation of all aspects of the integration movement in the light of their ecumenical meaning and sanction. Whatever measures are taken along any of the lines outlined in this discussion, they should be taken in the underlying consciousness that they fall within the ecumenical context and are oriented toward the ecumenical goal. A quite incidental recommendation of the Edinburgh Conference on Faith and Order illustrates this necessity

and may well prove a major guide to progress. "When the Holy Communion is celebrated, the officiating minister should say words in prayer or in preaching which will help worshippers to identify themselves with the whole Christian fellowship in the act of communion." On the untold millions of occasions in which local ministers and congregations do any of the representative acts of the Church, however variously these acts are explained, let it universally be made plain that it is their intent to act within and for the whole body of the Church. This would go further than all of our theologizing or external measures in behalf of unity. It would make manifest what is now implicit —but only implicit—in the life of our multitudinous denominations and congregations. The unity thus affirmed would be seen as a unity of the spirit showing forth a mystical reality, but it would also be a unity of the objective *koinonia*, a present Christian society, an actual, active fellowship and historical movement which thus widely affirmed, would immediately begin to take on greater substance, solidity and impressiveness.

Thus might the Church convincingly confess the one Lord in the midst of the seven candlesticks—their single light being kindled by the one Spirit.

6

STEPS AHEAD

Part I. *Achieving the Ecumenical Ideal*

W. Stanley Rycroft

Introduction. 1. The obstacles to the achievement of the ecumenical ideal: sociological factors, theological factors. 2. Resources for achieving the ecumenical ideal. 3. Areas in which progress can be made: unity, universality. 4. Principles governing progress toward the ecumenical ideal. 5. Conclusion.

To a distraught and suffering world which so lately has passed through the valley of the shadow of death, a consideration of the ecumenical ideal of the Church may seem irrelevant at this time, and far removed from reality. And yet it is of most vital and far-reaching importance for our contemporary world. In this atomic age it is "one world or none" as the scientists tell us with great earnestness and insistence. In a sense one world already exists, that is, if we mean "one" in terms of a physical drawing together into a whole or an integrated unit. But if we mean by "one world" a world of harmony, agreement, co-operation and mutuality, then we have anything but one world at the present time. On the contrary, the physical unity of mankind has aggravated the friction and enlarged the area of strife and conflict. We have what Raymond Fosdick calls "a frightening propinquity." The scientists have not only helped make the world one, physically, with tragic consequences for us all, but have multiplied the means of civilization's autodestruction; and some of these scientists are looking to the Christian Church to help create the spirit of universal community with all the elements of "togetherness" and good will as the only means of salvation. There is an increasing recognition that a world community cannot be created by a fiat of government or a constitutional formula. Rather a growing sense of community and mutuality and an increasing spirit of oneness among the nations of the world will make a world government a necessity.

The way in which true, effective co-operation must come from within rather than from the outside was brought out in an article by Admiral William V. Pratt of the United States Navy. Referring to co-operation during World War II he says:

> Cooperation, because of its dual character, is a very elusive factor. When the need is urgent enough it can be forced from the outside, but let the necessity pass and pressure be removed, and it bursts apart like a bomb, because of the disruptive elements in it. Some cooperation comes from within. It is a matter of the spirit dependent upon similarity of ideals and purposes. . . . Try to apply force to internal cooperation and the very purpose of its existence is defeated, for true cooperation is as free as the air.[1]

An ecumenical Church will be the most potent and universal factor in the creation of a world community because it alone can create that spirit of co-operation, harmony and good will among men. Should it become dynamic and purposeful, and were it really implemented throughout Christendom, this concept would not only enable the Church to speak with one voice at this supreme crisis in the history of mankind but provide the moral and spiritual equivalent of atomic energy. It would restore the moral power that would be equal to the task of con-

[1] *Newsweek*, November 5, 1945.

trolling technological progress for the good of mankind rather than for its destruction.

The ecumenical ideal must not be understood as meaning a secular world order or community, though it is not unrelated to this for, indeed, the Christian faith is the only hopeful source of the ultimate approximation to the unity of mankind. Rather it is derived from the very nature of the Church, not as it is at present, but as it should be. It is not, as some believe, the sum total of ecumenical or interdenominational organizations; rather it is the spirit or the principles which brought them into being. Again, the ecumenical ideal must not be equated with some form of church union, for as Dr. Bennett has pointed out in Chapter 2, Part II, it might even be a threat to the realization of the ecumenical ideal. Ecumenicity implies Christian unity of such a kind, however, that could lead to union if that were organizationally desirable.

According to Professor Latourette,[2] the Protestant church appears to be moving toward a kind of unity in which there is great diversity rather than toward the union of existing ecclesiastical bodies. This process of diversification may, of course, be even more accentuated as the "younger churches" develop their own forms and characterizations. But we must not overlook the fact that while these centrifugal forces are operative so are also the centripetal forces making for spiritual unity.

There are, of course, two commonly held views of the Church; one, that it is the *koinonia*, a fellowship, and the other that it is the *ecclesia* or an institution. Those who hold that it is a fellowship tend to stress the importance of the spirit of unity as basic in the ecumenical Church, and it is true that in the early church as described in the New Testament, unity is spiritual rather than organizational. On the other hand, those who view

[2] Kenneth Scott Latourette, "The Church and Christian Society Today in the Perspective of History," in *The Gospel, The Church and The World*, Kenneth Scott Latourette, ed., Vol. III of "The Interseminary Series" (New York: Harper & Brothers, 1946).

the Church as an institution can point to the fact that the ideal of "One Lord, one faith, one baptism" has never been lost down through the ages. The ecumenical ideal embraces both these concepts, a fellowship and an institution or organization. The task of the institution is to make the fellowship world-wide or universal.

Professor Latourette maintains[3] that "the Catholic Church of the first four centuries was an introvert. It was chiefly concerned with its own life." The ecumenical movement of today, he says, is an extrovert. By that he means that it looks away from itself and devotes its attention to meeting the needs of the world. This brings out an important aspect of the ecumenical movement. If the Church would save its life it must lose it.

A united Church, a universal Church operating in a world context, not so much concerned with its own existence and power as with the overwhelming needs of a sinful, broken world, would be an ecumenical Church. Like a great arch it would tower over the political, social and economic issues of the world, but like the leaven it would permeate all the life of the world. It would transcend denominational narrowness, sectarianism, provincial-mindedness, racial pride and national frontiers. It would be essentially the Church according to the mind of Christ, a divine-human fellowship.

There are evidences throughout this volume of the growing spirit of ecumenicity in the Christian Church and of the existence of an ecumenical movement which has come into being for such a time as that in which we are now living. Great progress has been made but there is still a long way to go. There are many obstacles in the way of achieving the ecumenical ideal and the first step toward overcoming these is to recognize them and face them. What are the obstacles or difficulties which cause misunderstandings and division and which limit fellowship?

[3] *Op. cit.*

1. THE OBSTACLES TO THE ACHIEVE-MENT OF THE ECUMENICAL IDEAL

Sociological factors

(1) *Group consciousness.* In the Christian Church we have failed to give due importance to a study of psychology as a means of interpreting or explaining individual and group behavior. We have not recognized the fact that Christians both as individuals and as groups are subject to the laws of psychology just the same as any other human beings. Group consciousness with its exclusive loyalties is an obstacle to understanding and co-operation among groups whether large or small.

From earliest times man has made a distinction between his own group and the outsider. In modern times groups are less closed and more interrelated, but we still find them differentiating between themselves as chosen people or superior beings and other or alien groups as inferior. The different is often inferior. The traditional division of the peoples of the world into believers and heathen has produced a form of group consciousness which has given rise to a feeling of superiority on the part of many Christian people as compared with non-Christians.

(a) *Denominational groupings.* How does this group consciousness manifest itself in the Christian Church? First of all, we find it in denominational groupings. Individual Christians who belong to a denomination tend to acquire certain thought forms and behavior patterns common to the group. One might go so far as to say there is a Lutheran mind, a Methodist reaction, a Presbyterian or Baptist behavior and so on rather than a Christian or ecumenical mind or conscience.

Professor Salvador de Madariaga, one of the outstanding Spaniards of today, while in England observed that in spite of the differences of opinion which separate the sects, these same sects "think of nothing but unity" and that the religious activity grouped in the various sects corresponds to what in other countries would be isolated individualism.[4] That may be true of Great Britain, though not as much as Madariaga thinks, and it is only true with regard to the United States in a limited sense. As Paul Douglass has pointed out in Chapter 5, there is an observable "sameness" about the Protestant denominations in America, a certain unified pattern of social and religious life and even a common tone pervading their publications. Many individuals move with a certain ease from one denomination to another.

But the tragedy of denominationalism is that it has belied, and prevented the full development of, the ecumenical spirit which is basic in the Gospel. Denominationalism springs primarily from the principle of freedom of choice and the right of private interpretation, inherent in the Protestant Reformation. Systems based on freedom of choice and interpretation, whether political or religious, always tend to be more chaotic and less efficient than authoritarian systems. This new-found freedom to dissent, and to separate from the main body however large or small whenever differences arose, tended to overshadow the principle of unity in diversity and the interdependence of members of one body, inherent and implicit in the Christian gospel. Paul's teaching at this point was very clear:

> For just as the body is one and has many members, and all the members of the body, though many, are one body, so it is with Christ. For by one Spirit we were all baptized into one body—Jews or Greeks, slaves or free— and all were made to drink of one Spirit. For the body does not consist of one member but of many. If the foot should say, "Because I am not a hand, I do not belong to the body" that would not make it any less a part of the body". . . . And if the ear should say, "Because I am not an eye, I do not belong to the body," that would

[4] S. de Madariaga, *Englishmen, Frenchmen and Spaniards* (London: Oxford University Press, 1931), p. 238.

not make it any less a part of the body. If the whole body were an eye, where would be the hearing?[5]

The result of this fissiparous tendency in the name of freedom and the neglect of the Pauline principle of ecumenicity has been doubly unfortunate. First, it has given the impression to the world that Protestants are a group of irresponsible and rebellious critics of the Roman Catholic Church. Secondly, it has given rise to a denominational rather than an ecumenical conscience. We now have "churches" rather than a Church. The new freedom which the Reformation brought to the religious world atomized the Christian witness and divided Christians in many groups. These groups are like circles around a core of doctrine, a form of worship or an ecclesiastical structure, some special insight; but the circles always overlap one another. And yet one of the great achievements of our time is the way in which these denominations have been coming together and cooperating to such a degree that the hope of some day achieving the ecumenical ideal has been really kindled. There is now general agreement that the denominationally-minded person who cannot see beyond his own group and always thinks in terms of his own denomination is less Christian than the person who, while loyal to his own denomination, can work harmoniously with and appreciate fully those of other denominations.

A serious weakness, however, exists at what we may call the "grass-roots" level. While at the top the denominations have achieved a certain amount of interdenominational co-operation yet the church is still one of the most divisive agencies in the local community. It is there, especially in the more rural areas, where we need to achieve more unity of action. "Protestantism is weak at its base, namely, its local church," says Charles Clayton Morrison.[6] This is the weakness of "localism," a state

[5] I Cor. 12:12-16. From the Revised Standard Version of the New Testament (copyrighted 1946 by the International Council of Religious Education).

[6] "Protestant Localism," in *The Christian Century*, May 29, 1946.

of mind in which the local church tends to think of itself as an end in itself, a self-contained unit, rather than an expression of the ecumenical Church. This localism exists, Dr. Morrison maintains, because the significance of denominations is decaying, and there is no ecumenical Church to which the loyalty of the group may be transferred. Here we see the tragic results of the neglect of the Pauline principle of being members in a body. Many people, faithful members of a local church, think of the Church as an aggregate of independent entities rather than as an organic whole, a body. The local congregation is jealous of its own rights and prerogatives. Referring to this problem, William Adams Brown says:[7]

> Even in those denominations like the Presbyterian, where the title to the property of a local congregation is subject to denominational control, the trustees who are responsible for the management of the property are often surprised when they are reminded of this fact. Under all ordinary circumstances they feel their responsibility to the local congregation alone.

Owing to the decay of denominationalism the local church is left orphaned, bereft of the spiritual care and sustenance that are necessary for its spiritual growth. It is like a fallen branch, receiving moisture as it blows off the leaves of the tree, instead of the sap which alone can give it life. Dr. Morrison says:

> The denomination formerly served this purpose, but, having lost so much of its theological, ecclesiastical and spiritual significance, it has been reduced, virtually, to a mere pragmatic agency through which its local churches clear their missionary and benevolent activities.[8]

In spite of a certain amount of interdenominational co-operation, it is more and more evident that denominational sover-

[7] *The New Order in the Church* (New York: Abingdon-Cokesbury Press, 1943), p. 20.

[8] Charles Clayton Morrison, *op. cit.*

eignty is obsolete. Denominational or ecclesiastical sovereignty prevents the realization of the ecumenical ideal of one Church, just as national sovereignty stands in the way of achieving one world. Among the nations as among the denominations, treaty arrangements are no longer valid as methods of co-operation. Wendell Willkie truly said that "sovereignty is something to be used, not hoarded." It is imperative that we realize that it is not a matter of surrendering sovereignty, either nationally or denominationally; but rather that, because the world is the kind of world it is, sovereignty is being taken away from nations and denominations, and superseded by something larger and more inclusive.

In an address called "A Challenge to Co-operation" given at the Annual Meeting of the Home Missions Council in January, 1946, Ross W. Sanderson said:

> Comity is another word made obsolete by the march of events. It is imperative that we cease to use it, that we find a better one. It is time we moved out of the kindergarten stage of well-mannered courtesy into the vigor of mature co-operative enterprises.

We have agreed to certain comity arrangements, certain divisions of territory both at home and abroad with the best of intentions. Now we must move on and plan a more comprehensive strategy; we must consolidate our forces in the United States and across the world, in the interests of the King's business rather than the spread of our denominations.

Some denominations do not even observe the comity arrangements or practice a minimal co-operation on the mission field. They ride rough shod over everyone, believing that they possess a larger portion of light than anyone else and that it is their duty to let it shine. These, we believe, are in the minority but we should be unrealistic if we overlooked the fact that they do exist. A skeptical, pagan world has almost ceased to pay attention to the Church because it has been more impressed by our differences and by the fact that we are custodians of our denominational traditions than by our challenging Gospel.

(b) *Group consciousness within the denomination.* Group consciousness is also manifest in social groupings within the Church. Racial, linguistic and other cultural factors have played a large part in producing divisions and separatism. In some denominations little attempt is made to bridge the chasm which often separates the wealthy and more privileged from the poorer classes. Location in poor sections of a town or in a select wealthy neighborhood seems to determine social isolation or grouping in local churches easily distinguishable as of one class or another.

There is also another aspect of the problem of divisions in the Church because of the inequality in the economic status of different units within the Church. There is still, in spite of progress made, a large difference in salaries of ministers in city churches and those in the rural areas. There seems to be a belief among some people that a minister or religious worker because of the very nature of his calling is motivated by unselfishness and that, therefore, the question of whether or not he has a living wage should never be raised. If the Church could face this problem of economic maladjustment in the matter of all its servants it would have a greater influence on the outside world where similar problems arise constantly.

Another aspect of the sociological factor is the racial groupings within the Church. While there is more serious concern in the Church over the race problem and attempts are being made to solve it in a Christian way, yet it is still true that the race issue is a divisive factor in the Church itself. The Church could make a contribution to the problem as a whole by demonstrating in its life and worship that there is no discrimination on the basis of race. While each denomination must seek to solve its own particular race problem efforts should be made to secure agreement of different denominations on this issue with a view to united action.

(c) *Group consciousness on the national level.* There is also a group consciousness on the national level which is inimical to the ecumenical ideal of the Church. Nationalism, in other words, is a danger within the Church as well as in the outside world. It is perhaps only natural that there should be an American church, a British church, a Chinese church, because each partakes of the culture and environment in which it has developed, but such a characteristic can be a real hindrance to the growth of ecumenicity. Even the desirable trend toward making the Church indigenous on the mission field sometimes has strong elements of nationalism in it which need a corrective.

This grouping on a national basis can sometimes be seen in the division between "home" and "foreign" missions giving rise to a rivalry or competition of interests within the Church. Fortunately this mood is passing and there is increasing recognition that "in Christ there is no home or foreign."

Theological factors

The differences in theological outlook and viewpoint as well as in doctrinal standards constitute some of the most obstinate difficulties in the way of achieving the ecumenical ideal.

(1) There are, first of all, the differences which cut across denominational lines. The fundamentalist-modernist controversy divides denominations or churches into two camps and often the only nexus between them is an inherited tradition. In his book *Cooperation and the World Mission* Dr. John R. Mott quotes a Canadian Mission board executive as saying, "We have not yet discovered any harness by which the fundamentalist and modernist can be yoked together. Instead of plowing they fight it out in the furrows." In one denomination the high church-low church controversy produces division while in others it is the neo-orthodox as opposed to the liberal theological position.

(2) Theological differences have also become embodied in denominations. Broadly speaking, these differences fall into two groups, the liberal and the conservative, with variations and

accentuations in each. The extreme ends of both groups have
failed to vindicate the true nature of an ecumenical Christian
faith in the face of secular culture. On the one hand, liberalism
has endeavored to come to terms with and to appease modern
culture while, on the other, conservatism, totally unaware of
the nature of modern culture, has withdrawn into a cultural
isolationism. But happily there is a growing tendency in the
Church to recognize that it must be not only the critic of culture and all forms of humanism but also that it must dare to
be itself and to reveal and proclaim the supreme truth as it is
in Christ, the truth by which culture itself shall be weighed
and measured.

Nothing is more incongruous to the person outside the Christian Church than the fact that it is divided by theology and doctrines while at the same time professing to follow Christ, the one
who spoke of love toward God and man as of supreme importance.

The truth must be recognized that no church, no denomination, no group has the whole truth or monopoly on the truth.
Christians who differ theologically would be more ready and
eager to unite and to work together if they could but realize
that they only have part of the truth about God and His universe
and that in a number of respects they can conceivably be wrong
or only partially right in their theological viewpoint or doctrines. Theological differences, given their rightful place and
emphasis, should not constitute insurmountable obstacles in the
road towards ecumenicity.

In an article entitled "The Ecumenical Issue in the United
States" Reinhold Niebuhr[9] maintains that "sectarian theology
is particularly inclined to be critical of the theological traditions
of the ages and to imagine that an ecumenical theology could
be developed if only everyone understood the Scripture as
simply as it does." This brings out another aspect of the problem which is peculiar to American Protestantism, namely, the

[9] *Theology Today*, January, 1946.

deprecation of theology as an essential part of the life of the Church. Reinhold Niebuhr calls theology the "skeleton" of the faith of the Church and polity the skeleton of its common life. The flesh on these bones is nourished by "the more immediate transmission of religious vitality." On the one hand, then, we may have the bones of theology protruding so as to prevent the true nourishing of the body which is the Church, or we may have no bones, or at least, a softness of bones and weakness and ineffective functioning of the body. "All one body we" is only true when we transcend our theological differences or transmute them into a higher loyalty.

(3) *Faith and order*. Again we find that there are serious difficulties in the way of translating the ecumenical ideal into reality in the realm of faith and order, or in such matters as sacraments, creeds and ecclesiastical organization. These have divided Christians down through the ages and it is quite understandable that in attempting to further or promote the ecumenical movement Christians tend to be motivated more by common action, that is, in the realm of life and work.

At the same time we must recognize that so often Christians have given primary, or at least undue, emphasis to matters of secondary importance, especially in the realm of faith and order. They have exaggerated out of proportion those things which separate one denomination from another. They have failed to evaluate and to treasure their likenesses while they have clung too much to their differences in interdenominational thinking. Nothing which can separate Christians in matters of faith and order is half so important as the things that unite them.

On the fundamental doctrines of God, Christ and man there is a large area of agreement among the Protestant churches. The differences that do exist are not important enough to keep them apart.

The Edinburgh Conference on Faith and Order in 1937 said:

> In regard to the relation of God's grace and man's free-
> dom, we all agree simply upon the basis of Holy Scripture

and Christian experience that the sovereignty of God is supreme. By the sovereignty of God we mean His all-controlling, all-embracing will and purpose revealed in Jesus Christ for each man and for all mankind. . . . Many theologians have made attempts on philosophical lines to reconcile the apparent antithesis of God's sovereignty and man's responsibility, but such theories are not part of the Christian faith. . . .

We are glad to report that in this difficult matter we have been able to speak with a united voice, so that we have found that here there ought to be no ground for maintaining any division between churches.[10]

The report went on further to say:

We agree that the Church is the Body of Christ and the blessed company of all faithful people. . . . We agree that the Word and the Sacraments are gifts of God to the Church through Jesus Christ for the salvation of mankind. . . . Among or within the churches represented by us there is a certain difference of emphasis placed upon the Word and the Sacraments, but we agree that such a difference need not be a barrier to union.[11]

There are differences among the churches as to what is meant by the term "church." For some it is both the visible, redeemed community and the invisible company of the redeemed, the saints who have passed on. For others the church would exclude reference to the invisible company known only to God. Furthermore, there are differences as to the relationship of the Church to the kingdom, and as to the degree to which the kingdom is made known and realized here on earth. But these are not such serious and deep-seated obstacles to ecumenicity as are varying concepts of the sacraments, particularly the Eucharist, Baptism and ordination of ministers. Of these the ordination of the ministry presents the most serious difficulty.

[10] Leonard Hodgson, ed., *The Second World Conference on Faith and Order*, (New York: The Macmillan Company, 1933), 225.
[11] *Ibid.*, p. 226-7.

(4) *Spiritual obstacles*. Besides the obstacles in the realm of theology and in faith and order there are spiritual obstacles in the way of an ecumenical Church of a rather subtle nature. These are denominational pride and prejudice, with selfishness or egotism and fear on the reverse side. There is a point beyond which the individual's loyalty to his own church or denomination becomes inordinate pride which is closely akin to prejudice. There is a legitimate place for pride in achievement, but even this may create a sense of superiority and an inability to appreciate the worth and the values of other groups. The leaders of the churches or denominations, especially those who are brought into contact and fellowship with representatives of other churches through interdenominational, co-operative experience, learn to appreciate the fine qualities and values of other denominational groups. This experience, however, is not always available to the members of the local church and it is here that pride and prejudice prevent harmony and Christian brotherhood.

2. RESOURCES FOR ACHIEVING THE ECUMENICAL IDEAL

In face of all the difficulties to be surmounted and obstacles to be overcome, ecumenically-minded Christians may take encouragement from reminding themselves of the resources that are not only available but are being used in the strengthening and widening of the ecumenical movement.

Spiritual resources

First of all are spiritual resources. These are the longings in the hearts of many Christians for closer fellowship with others and unity around the centrality of Christ, as well as the desire to widen the boundaries and responsibilities of Christian discipleship. There are the many prayers of individuals and groups in different parts of the world for a oneness of Church and of Christ and for a widening of the vision of the Christian community for a time like this. The desire for unity of the Christian Church may be still inchoate but it is nevertheless growing.

There is hope for a Church which recognizes frankly its weakness and its dependence on God to lead it out into a larger faith and a greater witness. In the words of the great affirmation adopted by the Conference on Faith and Order in 1937:

> Our unity is of heart and spirit. We are divided in the outward forms of our life in Christ, because we understand differently His will for His Church. We believe, however, that a deeper understanding will lead us toward a united apprehension of the truth as it is in Jesus.
>
> We humbly acknowledge that our divisions are contrary to the will of Christ, and we pray God in His mercy to shorten the days of separation and to guide us by His spirit into the fulness of unity.

Here are great spiritual resources coming from God Himself and mediated to those who catch the vision in humility and faith.

Leadership

The second resource is in the able leadership in the ecumenical movement. The names of men like Mott, Temple, Paton, Brent, Van Dusen, Schmucker, Boeger, Visser 't Hooft, Leiper, Soderblom and many others occur over and over throughout this volume. Some have passed on but their influence and inspiration still live on. There are hundreds of others who believe passionately in the ecumenical Church of Christ and are willing to serve as well as lead.

Freedom

Then there is in the Protestant churches as a whole a freedom to seek the truth which is inherent in the principle of mutual recognition. One of the basic principles of the Protestant faith is individual freedom and the right of private interpretation. In spite of the force of denominational tradition and practice individuals and groups enjoy a certain freedom to explore new forms of co-operation. This is seen particularly in four forms of mutual recognition, namely, interchange of membership, interchange of ministries, intercommunion and comity in missions.[12]

Growing ecumenicity

Perhaps the greatest resources are to be found in the rising tide of the ecumenical movement itself. No one can read the history of the development of the Protestant church during the last five decades without a profound sense of the working of the spirit of God not only in the geographical expansion of the Church but in the drawing together of men of different shades of belief and from many lands.

As Professor Latourette has pointed out,[13] Christianity is more widely and more evenly distributed than ever before. The nineteenth century ushered in a movement of great expansive vigor. Not only have churches been planted among non-European peoples, but there has emerged an indigenous leadership and in many cases, self-supporting churches, independent of Western control. Fort the first time Christianity is becoming a world faith. There is every expectation that these "younger churches" will continue to grow in vigor and influence. The International Missionary Council which grew out of the Edinburgh Conference of 1910 is the ecumenical organization which has given a great impulse to this aspect of the churches' life.

Besides this expansion and growth of Christianity into a world-wide movement there is the development of inter-confessional movements. The way in which these movements have come into existence during the last thirty or forty years has already been described.[14] We may note, however, that it is a rising tide, developing along many different lines; or, to change the figure of

[12] For further discussion of these see ch. 2, pt. II.

[13] Kenneth Scott Latourette, *op. cit.*

[14] See ch. 3, pt. I.

speech, there are many streams and rivulets all of which feed into the great flowing river of the ecumenical Church of Christ. There are, as we have seen, the Faith and Order and the Life and Work Movements with their emphasis on those important aspects of the Church's witness; there is the International Missionary Council composed of such national councils as the Foreign Missions Conference of North America, the British Conference of Missionary Societies and the National Christian Councils around the world which promote the expansion of the Church throughout the world and help weave an ecumenical pattern; there are youth movements and student movements which are preparing the leaders of tomorrow to take their place in the ecumenical Church; there are women's movements such as the United Council of Church Women; there are such bodies as the World's Sunday School Association and the International Council of Religious Education which draw many church groups together on important problems in religious education across the world. On the national level there is the Federal Council of the Churches of Christ in America which focuses the united attention of many denominations on a host of problems confronting mankind, among them the race question, peace and international good will, social questions, home and family life. The Home Missions Council also has succeeded in promoting the ecumenical Church with a united approach to the outstanding problems of social and religious life in America. On the local church level there are 535 councils of churches covering the majority of the states in America, promoting co-operation and understanding and common action. This rising tide is one of our greatest resources.

3. AREAS IN WHICH PROGRESS CAN BE MADE

The areas in which progress can be made toward the goal of ecumenicity are broadly speaking around the concepts of the unity and universality of the Church.

Unity

We must progress toward a unified message. Primacy should be given to the full-orbed Gospel of Christ, not as a philosophical theory or theological system or even a program for social or human betterment, but as the gift of God to a sinful world. The Church needs to explore the unfathomed depths of meaning and relevancy of the Gospel as a source of power for social regeneration, for the overthrow of false gods and for the overcoming of hatred, prejudice and ill will. The Church needs fully to comprehend, and then to make known everywhere, the Christ as founder and head of a new society, One who has knit together the whole family in heaven and on earth. We must seek a unifying faith in Christ. The dynamic of the ecumenical movement is in its faith. The ecumenical conferences of Lausanne, Jerusalem and Edinburgh gave central place to the person of Jesus Christ as the great unifying power. "Our message is Jesus Christ," said the Jerusalem Conference. It is not a message *about* Jesus Christ. He *is* in a very real sense the message, the Christian gospel.

We must, secondly, continue to direct our thoughts and activities to the urgent need for unity among Protestant denominations. At the Madras Conference in 1938 the representatives of the "younger churches" gave expression to the passionate longing not only for unity but for visible union. Said the Conference report:

> Instances were cited by the representatives of the younger churches of disgraceful competition, wasteful overlapping, and of groups and individuals turned away from the Church because of the divisions within. We confess with shame that we ourselves have often been the cause of thus bringing dishonor to the religion of our Master.

There was a recognition of the growing spiritual unity and increasing co-operation and understanding among the denominations, but they said, "Visible and organic union must be our goal." Through loyalty to the mother churches, the younger churches are sometimes prevented from consummating union on the mission field unless it should receive the blessing and support from the sending country.

Here, great progress could be made in the preparation for, and interpretation of, church membership in a wider setting, a world context. Prospective church members could be instructed in the meaning of membership in the Church universal to such a degree that a person joining a Presbyterian, a Methodist or a Baptist church would be equally conscious of becoming a member of the wider fellowship. Churches could do a much more thorough job in educating all their members both through presentation of the Gospel message and also by encouraging reading and discussion of the ecumenical aspect of the Christian Church.

The task of uniting the Church will not be completed suddenly. Achieving the ecumenical ideal is one of the greatest and most difficult tasks before the Church of Christ. It will necessarily be a gradual process. There must, however, be a blueprint or a map. We must know, and not only know, but use, the roads which ultimately will lead to the King's highway. Churches must endeavor to understand the beliefs of other groups which differ from their own and, while agreeing to differ and remaining loyal to their own sincerely-held doctrines and polities, seek to unite in common action one with another.

The third area in which progress can be made is in greater emphasis on the Church, its nature and meaning for our day. As Dr. Bennett has pointed out[15] the Christian Church is a distinctive community living in a hostile world. This Church is now showing signs of increased vitality and vigor. The discovery of the existence of the world-wide beloved community whose boundaries no one can yet define, is one of the encour-

[15] Ch. 2, pt. II.

aging signs of a trend toward the ecumenical ideal. There is need for fresh thinking on the nature of the Church, the divine human community of believers. We get glimpses of this community at times of great ecumenical gatherings where there is a sense of oneness especially in worship. The writer remembers the thrilling experience at the Madras Conference in 1938 where on one occasion over 471 delegates, speaking 101 languages, repeated the Lord's Prayer, each in his own language. Men and women, of different race, language, creed, color and customs could gather round a common Lord and say "Our Father."

The fourth area is in what Dr. Bennett calls unofficial organizations and fellowships that have a specific purpose. We have already mentioned some of these; the World's Student Christian Federation, the International Council of Religious Education, the World Alliance for International Friendship through the Churches, the Foreign Missions Conference and the International Missionary Council, the United Council of Church Women. Each of these deals with and "promotes" some important phase or phases of the ecumenical Church.

We need in the Church today "areas of ecumenical living" and these unofficial organizations provide such experiences. As an example we cite the Student Christian Movement. The Church owes a great deal to this movement which has brought together students of different denominational backgrounds into a common Christian fellowship and helped them maintain their Christian witness. Much more could be done, however, to give the Movement a genuinely ecumenical character. Students on the campuses should be confronted with the theology of the Church and its basic implication of ecumenicity, so that, rather than thinking along traditional, denominational or sectarian lines, they become conscious of a united fellowship in a world task, with the denominational emphasis receding into the background.

The fifth area is that of mutual recognition in interchange of membership, and of ministers, intercommunion and comity in missions. Progress is already being made in some of these matters. For instance, it is quite common for Protestants in America to change with ease from one denomination to another. However, if there were a more extensive mutual recognition there would be less overlapping in local areas and less unnecessary competition.

Universality

Reference has been made to the great expansion of the Christian movement out across the world. The expansion of Christian missions in the last hundred years is one of the epics of the Church. But it is true to say that Christianity as practiced in the Western world is still largely self-centered. A vastly greater proportion of wealth is spent on building costly churches and paying high salaries to ministers than is spent on the most important aspect of Christianity, namely, its missionary expansion. As Walter W. Van Kirk has stated it:[16]

> To introduce Jesus Christ to the hundreds of millions of people who live in Asia, Africa, the Near East and Latin America, each Protestant Christian in the United States contributes each year a sum equivalent to the cost of a bottle of hair tonic.

The Church constituency as a whole has not been made conscious of its great responsibility and its compelling task. There is as yet no real understanding on the part of many Protestant church members of what the nature of the missionary task is. The mandate from Our Lord to take the Gospel to every creature has not yet penetrated deep into the mind and heart of Christian people.

The task of making the Church truly universal involves not only geographical expansion but also a penetration into the many aspects and problems of human living, and the influenc-

[16] Walter W. Van Kirk, *A Christian Global Strategy* (Chicago: Willett, Clark & Company, 1945) p. 41.

ing of whole cultures. Viewed thus in its totality one is forced to the conclusion that the Church is just at the beginning of its missionary task. Strategic and statesmanlike planning is called for in order to avoid unwarranted or unnecessary overlapping and competition on the mission field. Mission boards must have vision and daring to explore new paths and blaze new trails, if possible, together. The days of pioneering both geographical and functional are not over.

4. PRINCIPLES GOVERNING PROGRESS TOWARD THE ECUMENICAL IDEAL

The principles governing progress toward the ecumenical ideal are derived from the two basic aspects of the ecumenical movement, namely, unity and universality, and from the nature of the Christian gospel itself.

(1) The first of these principles is that the Church must function ecumenically at all levels. Beginning with the individual Christian himself, up through the local church, the local areas (presbyteries, conferences, etc.), state units (conferences, synods, etc.), national bodies (assemblies, conferences, conventions), individual members and groups, small and large, should be aware of, and ought to be loyal to, the commitments made by the entire denomination in interdenominational relationships and in organizations such as the Federal Council, the Home Missions Council, the Foreign Missions Conference and the World Council of Churches.

(2) The second principle is that new fields or areas of activity should be explored energetically at different levels of the Church's life with a view to further advance and progress being made in Christian unity.

(3) The third principle is that the Christian Church must be universal in its vision and field of activities, not only in a geographical sense, but also sociologically, making an impact on the heights and depths of society throughout all the nations.

(4) The fourth principle is that the individual Christian and the local church should be exposed to a community-wide ministry and a world-wide, comprehensive, missionary program rather than be circumscribed by a segmented, parish program or a purely denominational outlook.

(5) The fifth principle is that all activities and programs of the Church be subject to, or based upon, a recognition of the Lordship of Jesus Christ in every aspect of the Church's life and the supremacy of his spirit of love and unity among all God's children.

5. CONCLUSION

The supreme task of the Church of Christ in the present hour is to bend all its efforts toward achieving the ecumenical goal and to make the Gospel of Christ relevant in all human relationships. This will mean wider horizons and enlarged vision, more inclusive loyalties and greater sacrifice; it will require vivid imagination, thoughtful planning and far-sightedness on the part of individual Christians and groups and churches. It will involve greater devotion to the kingdom interests and a willingness to serve a lost world. The Church of Christ is faced with great rival faiths and many false gods.

In the last analysis the ecumenical Church will depend on the individual Christian. Will there be a large enough company of men and women with the necessary quality of faith and life and witness to carry forward this great work already nobly begun? The appeal of Christ, "Go ye into all the world," making His Church universal, and His high priestly prayer "that they all may be one," thus bringing about the unity of His Church, come to us down through the centuries with all the freshness of springtime. The Church must seek to bring its message of healing, love and unifying power to a broken, disunited world, a world sundered by hate and suspicion and fear. For such a time as this was the ecumenical movement brought into being, by the Grace of God and through His Spirit.

Part II. *Implementing the Ecumenical Ideal at the Parish Level*

by Elmore M. McKee

~~~~~~

William Temple has said that the ecumenical movement is "the great new religious fact of our times." Horizon-wise that is certainly true. Locally I am not so sure. And unless it become so locally, then even the horizon will fade as the horizon-painters become discouraged.

Ecumenical headquarters needs "grass-roots" encouragement. Without the latter G.H.Q. will find itself in the unhappy predicament of being generals without an army. The local parish on the other hand needs headquarters to dramatize in vivid ways the fact of the campaign and of its stirring goals.

I shall write of "grass-roots" ways in which to implement the ecumenical ideal.

"Accentuate the positive"

First, by accentuating the positive between Communions. There are areas of agreement. Very well, stress them. There are practical tasks of indisputable moment. Very good, tackle them. A 1945 popular song, describing, interestingly enough, a preacher's tale of how to fight sin, ran like this:

> Ac-cent-tchu-ate the positive
> Eliminate the negative
> Don't mess with Mister In-between.[17]

[17] From the song *Ac-cent-tchu-ate the Positive* by Johnny Mercer and Harold Arlen. Used by permission of the copyright owners, Edwin H. Morris & Company, Inc., New York.

That a song-hit should hit the spiritual nail on the head should not deter us from accepting its additional weight of authority. Doubtless sin rather than truth is a major cause of church disunion. Therefore that breach in relationships which is sin will stand more chance of being overcome by stressing positively areas of agreement and facing tasks of clear common concern than by lingering negatively among the briar patches of controversy. As our mutual interchange in matters of agreement and practical responsibility make us know one another better and discover the common pulls of a common task, we shall come to care more deeply for one another, and caring, to find a theological and an ecclesiastical way to organic partnership. Fellowship will banish sin, and then release order.

Four illustrations. In 1942 I was one of a team of four men, two ministers and two Y.M.C.A. leaders, who visited Johnstown, Greensburg, Lancaster, Reading and Philadelphia, as part of the coast-to-coast World Order Mission of the Federal Council of Churches. In addition to the rare fellowship built among the four team-members, a Baptist, a Congregationalist, a Methodist and an Episcopalian, by common response to the common task of doing our bit to prevent World War III by stimulating interest in world order, there was the sense of growing unity developed among the pastors and people among whom we spoke. I recall especially a meeting in Reading where certain Lutherans with a deep theological emphasis that made them cautious toward the practical activities of the Federal Council, and certain Methodists of a predominantly ethical concern, found themselves deeply one in the task of preventing war. *It was response to a common task which made their common life, too often hidden, apparent.*

In 1926 to 1930 I served as chaplain of Yale University. Yale is Congregational in early background; and the Yale Church of Christ still gathers monthly following the preaching service, for the celebration of the Lord's Supper in traditional Congregational style. As an Episcopalian minister it was agreed by the Yale authorities and the Bishop of the Diocese that I should be permitted to celebrate the Holy Communion according to the Book of Common Prayer form at an altar in the Yale Chapel at nine each Sunday morning. This was done, making of the Holy Table an altar with candles, kneeling cushions, etc. The celebrant wore Episcopal vestments. But it was assumed that I, the chaplain, would also celebrate, or assist the visiting preacher in celebrating, the service of the Lord's Supper according to the Congregational form at twelve noon, once a month. Bishop Brewster of Connecticut gave me permission to do so, then under pressure retracted it. Bishop Acheson, succeeding him, said to me: "McKee, don't you know a priest may often do what a Bishop cannot give him permission to do?" Father Sill, O.H.C., Headmaster of the Kent School, said: "I do not see how you can, in the name of your Master, refuse to conduct the service which has been held at the heart of Yale for over two hundred years."

Now here was a practical need, the kind of need an army or navy chaplain faces even more than a university chaplain, the need to minister to men (and women) under special circumstances. I am convinced it would have been sin against the Holy Ghost to refuse to administer the Communion in both the Prayer Book and the Congregational manner. *When Church laws and customs do not sanction such action, it must nevertheless be taken, if it be clear that a pressing need has arisen to serve the souls of men.*

On the Lower East Side of New York we have organized the East Side Ministers Fellowship. In our membership we include men of Congregational, Methodist, Episcopalian, Presbyterian, Lutheran, Baptist, Reformed and Quaker affiliations. Some of our members conduct foreign language services in Italian, Spanish, Russian, Swedish or German. We hold our Ash Wednesday night service all together. Last year over eleven hundred persons gathered in Grace Church to hear Bishop Nicholai of Okrida, Yugoslavia. Twenty ministers made up the choir. Our monthly meetings are more apt to be built around a particular member's somewhat biographical insights into his own personal problems, convictions and aspirations and the needs of his job and parish. I have never belonged to a group of ministers who felt more closely knit. *This is because we started by being friends, by really knowing one another. It is also because we have been celebrating areas of agreement and tasks of common concern,* namely (1) we live in the same neighborhood town and plow the same furrows; (2) we share the same loneliness and frustrations in a great, rapidly changing impersonal city (an Italian minister said to me: "Do you mean to tell me you ministers of 'big' churches want to know us who don't count much?"); (3) we face the same tasks; juvenile delinquency, shifting population, spiritual illiteracy in the public schools, etc., not to mention the building of five great new housing projects requiring a united front at our several doorsteps.

Which leads me to the fourth and last illustration. A few weeks before writing this chapter, I visited Father O'Connell, pastor of the neighboring Roman Catholic Church of the Epiphany. I said to him: "Five housing projects are about to open up in our neighborhood presenting a great new opportunity to all churches. We live in a democracy with team work as essential to its success. Can we not work entirely together in making calls upon our new neighbors?" "Certainly we can," said Father O'Connell, "and we will. We will divide up the new buildings into sections and make periodic reports to each other. And why can't we do also a better job at the Post Graduate Hospital, making it standard procedure that the Jewish, Catholic and Protestant chaplains are notified daily of the arrival of patients of their faith so that spiritual ministrations may begin at once? Why can't we have a sign in the admitting office stating who the chaplains are and what are the nearest churches or synagogues open for the use of relatives of patients?" All three of these plans are now in process of being worked out. *It is well for us to seek areas of agreement and of practical co-*

operation where they exist, not neglecting the possibility of greater ultimate Protestant-Roman ecumenical accord, fed from the grass-roots.

Accentuate the positive; this will subordinate the negative; must there not then a way appear?

"One world" in the parish

Second, the ecumenical ideal will be implemented in the local setting by making each parish a *one world microcosm*.

How?

(1) *By building the Church where the people are, and staying there.* Too often churches seek beautiful locations by rivers, with their backs to water not people, in smart avenues where mink coats glisten but the poor are not. Granting that there have to be some one-class churches, drawing largely from the top-rental families in select urban or suburban spots, surely most churches must be "people's" churches, located in spots that suggest the democratic way and near where the population is densest. Stay there where the poor are and let others make the effort to come and let all gain the great reward of feeling a part of something greater than their kind.

(2) *By having all seats free and unassigned.* There must be no distinctions in the house of ecumenical worship. (When William S. Rainsford came to St. George's from Toronto in 1883, one of the three conditions he made was that of free pews at once. This single fact helped mightily to save a parish that was almost extinct.)

(3) *By welcoming all nationalities, all races and all backgrounds,* not simply to worship but to activities and facilities and to leadership in common tasks. (We desire many more Negroes as members. Though 10 per cent of our choir is now Negro and a dozen Negro families are in our parish, this is only, we hope, a beginning. We have a number of Nisei members, including the present chaplain of our camps; also a number of Christian Jews.)

(4) *By distributing responsibility on all committees*, in organizations, and on the governing board, in a truly representative fashion. The Christian parish is a significant opportunity to make democracy, which is the political expression of the Christian feeling for life, work. (Two hundred fifty of us serve on rotating committees, under a Parish Council, created by Charter from the Vestry. Over twelve hundred pay the bills. More people give $12.50 a year than any other specific amount. Our endowment meets less than a third of our needs.)

(5) *By standing within the parish for world horizons.* Pastor, staff (if there be any) and social relations committee must be ready to think, study, write, publicize and speak out, as need arises. Church school teaching and adult religious education must be characterized by and shot through with ideals of ecumenical and world order. (We protested to the Metropolitan Life Insurance Company regarding its policy of discrimination against Negroes in Stuyvesant Town; we assigned an associate minister to serve as arbitrator in an Eagle Pencil Company strike; we held seminars on Russia and Germany; also seminars on labor-management relations; and held meetings on behalf of World Order and the United Nations. During the war our three conscientious objectors were treated in the same manner as three hundred members of the armed forces, in prayer, monthly letters, parish rosters, etc.) Every parish needs a social action or World Christianity committee to be alert to social frontiers about which it must make the parish student body sensitive.

We learn more by situations than by books and talk. Parishes are places where skills in relationships are learned. One has no right to thump the pulpit for social justice or world order unless the life and structure of the parish validates internally one's pronouncements to the world. For example, it is certainly morally invalid for us to preach industrial peace if we are not still more concerned about the social security and salaries we provide our own janitors.

A parish which proves in the microcosm that one world is more than a dream, and which proves in its relations to other parishes and communions that one Church is an increasing reality, will become a self-encouraging and outreaching force, first for church unity and then for world unity. Grass-roots are meant to succor and keep alive the treetops of the ecumenical movement as they reach to the north, the south, the east and the west.

7

APPENDIX

The following documents are appended because in a real sense they are "ecumenical landmarks." The Message of the Lausanne Conference has come to be recognized as a classic, as has the Madras Message on the Faith. The messages from the two meetings in February, 1946, although not framed by as representative groups nor with as great care as the foregoing, are important as the first messages to be issued by groups officially representing the World Council of Churches Provisional Committee and the International Missionary Council after World War II. Both constitutions are included in order to provide first-hand information as to the character of their respective bodies and as examples of the principles of representative ecumenical organization.

THE CHURCH'S MESSAGE TO THE WORLD—THE GOSPEL

The Message of the Lausanne Conference

The message of the Church to the world is and must always remain the Gospel of Jesus Christ.

The Gospel is the joyful message of redemption, both here and hereafter, the gift of God to sinful man in Jesus Christ.

The world was prepared for the coming of Christ through the activities of God's Spirit in all humanity, but especially in His revelation as given in the Old Testament; and in the fulness of time the eternal Word of God became incarnate, and was made man, Jesus Christ, the Son of God and the Son of Man full of grace and truth.

Through His life and teaching, His call to repentance, His proclamation of the coming of the Kingdom of God and of judgment, His suffering and death, His resurrection and exaltation to the right hand of the Father, and by the mission of the Holy Spirit, He has brought to us forgiveness of sins, and has revealed the fulness of the living God, and His boundless love toward us. By the appeal of that love, shown in its completeness on the Cross, He summons us to the new life of faith, self-sacrifice, and devotion to His service and the service of men.

Jesus Christ, as the crucified and the living One, as Saviour and Lord, is also the centre of the world-wide Gospel of the Apostles and the Church. Because He Himself is the Gospel, the Gospel is the message of the Church to the world. It is more than a philosophical theory; more than a theological system; more than a programme for material betterment. The Gospel is rather the gift of a new world from God to this old world of sin and death, the revelation of eternal life in Him who has knit together the whole family in heaven and on earth in the communion of saints, united in the fellowship of service, of prayer, and of praise.

The Gospel is the prophetic call to sinful man to turn to God, the joyful tidings of justification and of sanctification to those who believe in Christ. It is the comfort of those who suffer; to those who are bound, it is the assurance of the glorious liberty of the sons of God. The Gospel brings peace and joy to the heart, and produces in men self-denial, readiness for brotherly service, and compassionate love. It offers the supreme goal for the aspirations of youth, strength to the toiler, rest to the weary, and the crown of life to the martyr.

The Gospel is the sure source of power for social regeneration. It proclaims the only way by which humanity can escape from those class and race hatreds which devastate society at present into the enjoyment of national well-being and international friendship and peace. It is also a gracious invitation to the non-Christian world, East and West, to enter into the joy of the living Lord.

Sympathising with the anguish of our generation, with its longing for intellectual sincerity, social justice and spiritual inspiration, the Church in the eternal Gospel meets the needs and fulfils the God-given aspirations of the modern world. Consequently, as in the past so also in the present, the Gospel is the only way of salvation. Thus, through His Church, the living Christ still says to men "Come unto me! . . . He that followeth me shall not walk in darkness, but shall have the light of life."

The Faith By Which the Church Lives

The Message of the Madras Conference

1. The Need of the World

The Christian Church to-day is called to live, and to give life in a world shaken to its foundations.

When the International Missionary Council met at Jerusalem ten years ago, the faith was strong that a new and better world had been born amidst the destruction of the Great War, and that the Church might lead in building it up. To-day that faith is shattered. Everywhere there is war or rumor of war. The beast in man has broken forth in unbelievable brutality and tyranny. Conflict and chaos are on every hand, and there is little hope that statesmanship can do more than check temporarily their alarming spread.

The outward confusion of man's life reflects, and is reflected in, the confusion of men's hearts and minds.

Many have lost all faith. Not only their faith in the gods of their fathers; but faith in all they had believed most certain and important—in reason and in truth, in honor and in decency, in the possibility of peace and the power of right. They are overwhelmed by a sense of utter impotence and despair.

In others there is a resurgence of faith, often faith in new gods. For whole peoples, faith in their nation or class serves as religion and wins absolute devotion. These faiths come as rebukes and challenges to an easy and hesitant Christianity. But, rooted in false or inadequate ideas of man and the world, they tend to aggravate the world's disorder; their issue is war, persecution and cruelty of men to one another.

Others, though bitterly disillusioned, still seek to rest their confidence in science and man's power to redeem himself, yet secretly they feel that confidence is vain. They long for a faith that can bring a surer hope to their own lives and to their civilization.

Meantime want, ignorance, superstition, fear still hold their sway over the lives of countless millions. The cry of the multitudes for deliverance still goes up. They know not where to turn, or whom to trust.

Mankind's great need is for a true and living faith.

2. *The Heart of the Gospel*

It is in and to this world that the Church must conduct its mission, seeking to repossess and proclaim its God-given message in all its truth and power.

But first we must come in penitence to the feet of God. In the presence of these disasters and forebodings, we see the judgment of God's righteousness upon our society; but we see also His judgment upon our churches—so enmeshed in the world that they dare not speak God's full word of truth unafraid, so divided that they cannot speak that word with full power, so sullied by pettiness and worldliness that the face of Christ cannot be clearly discerned in them, or His power go forth through them for redemption. We must come too in deep humility, knowing that no merely human deed or word of ours will suffice to meet humanity's need. God's words and deeds alone are the healing of its sickness. Yet it is still His will to utter and accomplish them through His Church. His promise is still that His strength shall be made manifest in our weakness.

What then is the Church's faith, not in its whole range and depth, but in its special meaning for our time?

We live by faith in God, the Father of our Lord Jesus Christ.

Above all and in all and through all is the Holy Will, the Creative Purpose, of the Most High. The world is His and He made it. The confusions of history are in the grasp of his manifold Wisdom. He overrules and works through the purposes of men, bringing to nought their stubborn and rebellious lust for power but building their fidelity into the structure of His Reign upon earth.

Man is the child of God, made in His image. God has designed him for life in fellowship with Himself, and with his brothers in the family of God on earth. Yet in the mystery of the freedom which God has given him, man chooses to walk other paths, to seek other ends. He defies his Father's will. He seeks to be a law unto himself. This is the deepest cause of the evil and misery of his life. Alienated from God he seeks his salvation where it cannot be found. Impotent to save himself, he stands ever in need of conversion, of forgiveness, of regeneration.

Who then shall save? God saves, through Jesus Christ our Lord. "God so loved the world that He gave His only begotten Son that whosoever believeth on Him should not perish but have everlasting life." This is the heart of the Christian Gospel, the Gospel which we proclaim.

God in His infinite love has acted for men's salvation. He has come among them in Jesus of Nazareth, His Word made flesh. In Him, He has conquered the power of sin and death. Jesus Christ in His teachings and life of perfect love recalls men to that which God would have them be, and brings them to shame for their betrayal of His expectation. Through His faith and perfect obedience they come to trust the only true God. His suffering and death on Calvary bring them to see the exceeding sinfulness of sin and assure them of God's pardon. His resurrection is the victory of holiness and love over death and corruption. Through His risen and living presence, men who dedicate their wills to Him become with Him partakers of eternal life. In the strength and joy of forgiveness, daily renewed at the foot of the Cross, they are made more than conquerors over every evil.

For Christ, the Kingdom of God was central. He called His followers to seek first God's Kingdom and His right-eousness. Through acceptance of His call to suffering love and through trust in divine help, men are summoned to be co-workers with Him for the increase of justice, truth and brotherhood upon earth. His Kingdom is both within and beyond this world. It will be consummated in the final establishment of His glorious reign of Love and Righteous-ness, when there shall be a new heaven and a new earth where death and sin shall be no more.

To the gift of Christ, God has added the gift of His Holy Spirit in the Church. Christ's true Church is the fellowship of those whom God has called out of darkness into His mar-vellous light. The guidance and power of the Spirit are given to this Church that it may continue Christ's saving work in the world. It seeks to build up its own members in the knowledge of Christ, challenging them anew with the message of His redeeming love, comforting them with the assurance of God's forgiveness in Him, teaching them the way of love through service for their brethren in Christ.

For those that are without Christ the true Church yearns with the love of its Master and Lord. It goes forth to them with the evangel of His grace. It practices His ministry of compassion and healing. It bears witness against every in-iquity and injustice in their common life. It bears their sorrows and heartache on its prayers. To it is given the solemn privilege of entering into the fellowship of the suf-ferings of Christ.

In spite of all the weakness and shortcomings of our

churches, Christ's true Church is within them; and our hope for the redemption of mankind centers in His Work through them. Through the nurture and discipline of the Church, Christian life comes to completion; in glad service within the fellowship of the Church, Christian devotion is perfected.

If the Church is to repossess this its faith in all its uniqueness and adequacy and power, one indispensable thing demanding special emphasis to-day is the continuous nourishing of its life upon the Bible. We are bold therefore to summon all Christians to a deeper and more consistent study of the Bible, instructor and sustainer of the Christian faith through the ages. Only as, in its light, they seek together in prayer and meditation the guidance of the Holy Spirit, will they be able to fulfill their calling amidst the confusion and unbelief of this age.

3. *The Call of the Church*

This faith the Church seeks to declare by word and by deed. For Christianity comes to the world both as a Message and as a Movement.

In this time when brute force stalks the earth, the Church is summoned to bear courageous and unflinching witness to the nations that the base purposes of men, whether of individuals or of groups, cannot prevail against the will of the Holy and Compassionate God. It is commissioned to warn mankind of the judgment which shall assuredly overtake a civilization which will not turn and repent. It is under obligation to speak fearlessly against aggression, brutality, persecution and all wanton destruction of human life and torturing of human souls.

Recognizing that Christ came to open to all the way to life abundant but that the way for millions is blocked by poverty, war, racial hatred, exploitation and cruel injustice, the Church is called to attack social evils at their roots. It must seek to open the eyes of its members to their implication in unchristian practices. Those who suffer from bitter wrong, it is constrained to succor and console, while it strives courageously and persistently for the creation of a more just society.

Above all it is called to declare the Gospel of the compassion and pardon of God that men may see the Light which is in Christ and surrender themselves to His service. And all this it must do at any cost, in fidelity and gratitude to Him who at so great cost wrought its salvation.

But the further summons to the Church is to become in itself the actualization among men of its own message. No one so fully knows the failings, the pettiness, the faithlessness which infect the Church's life as we who are its members. Yet, in all humility and penitence, we are constrained to declare to a baffled and needy world that the Christian Church, under God, is its greatest hope. The decade since last we met has witnessed the progressive rending of the fabric of humanity; it has witnessed an increasing unification of the body of Christ. As we meet here, from over sixty nations out of every continent, we have discovered afresh that that unity is not merely an aspiration but also a fact; our meeting is its concrete manifestation. We are one in faith; we are one in our task and commission as the body of Christ; we are resolved to become more fully one in our life and work. Our nations are at war with one another; but we know ourselves brethren in the community of Christ's Church. Our peoples increase in suspicion and fear of one another; but we are learning to trust each other more deeply through common devotion to the one Lord of us all. Our Governments build instruments of mutual destruction; we join in united action for the reconciliation of humanity. Thus in broken and imperfect fashion, the Church is even now fulfilling its calling to be within itself a foretaste of the redeemed family of God which He has purposed humanity to be. The Church itself must stand ever under the ideal of the Kingdom of God which alone can guard it against becoming an end in itself and hold it true to God's purpose for it. By faith, but in deep assurance, we declare that this body which God has fashioned through Christ cannot be destroyed.

Meanwhile in countless obscure places in the world where through the centuries disease and darkness, poverty and fear have reigned, the Christian Church to-day is bringing effective healing, enlightenment, alleviation and a true and living faith.

To all who care for the peace and health of mankind we issue a call to lend their aid to the Church which stands undaunted amidst the shattered fragments of humanity and works tirelessly for the healing of the nations. And those who already share in its life, and especially its leaders, we summon to redouble their exertions in its great tasks, to press forward the evangel among all peoples, to strengthen the younger Churches, to speed practical co-operation and unity, to bear in concrete ways the burdens of fellow-Christians who suffer, and above all to take firm hold again of the faith which gives victory over sin, discouragement and death. Look to Christ, to His Cross, to His triumphant work among men, and take heart. Christ, lifted up, draws all men unto Him.

This day calls to no easy optimism, but to penitence, to unwavering confidence in the wisdom, love and power of God, to patient and unwearied service in the name, the spirit, and the power of the Risen Redeemer. The outcome of man's present distresses we cannot foretell. But this we know—in Christ's death and His risen Presence with His Church, God has shown us that the final outcome is with Him. His Kingdom is an eternal Kingdom. To those who share Christ's faith and devotion, He offers even now participation in its triumph, in time and in eternity.

Thanks be to God for His unspeakable gift!

MESSAGE FROM THE PROVISIONAL COMMITTEE OF THE WORLD COUNCIL OF CHURCHES
GENEVA, SWITZERLAND, FEBRUARY, 1946

The Provisional Committee of the World Council of Churches assembled at Geneva for its first meeting after the World War, sends forth the following message:

The world today stands between life and death. Men's hopes of a better world have not been fulfilled. Millions are enduring intolerable suffering. The nations seem impotent to deal with the crucial problems of international order. A heavy burden weighs upon all mankind.

We face this crisis as Christians, whose own consciences are gravely disturbed. Yet God in His mercy has committed to us the ministry of His Word, and that Word we are bound to declare. Men are going the way of death because they disobey God's Will. All renewal depends upon repentance, upon turning from our own way to God's way. He is calling men to a supreme decision. "I have set before you life and death: therefore choose life."

War is the result of human self-will and of men's tragic inability to find the true solution of their conflicts. We pray God that the United Nations will choose the way of life and save future generations from the scourge of war. But the time is short. Man's triumph in the release of atomic energy threatens his destruction. Unless men's whole outlook is changed, our civilization will perish.

An illusory peace is little better than war. No peace can be lasting unless it is built on true spiritual foundations. We appeal to all men of good will and all who believe in spiritual values and forces to work together for an order of justice and humanity.

All nations are under the judgment of God. Those that have been defeated are suffering a fearful retribution. But the springs of their recovery are within; and if they turn to God and heed the voices of those among them who, even in the darkest days, withstood the forces of evil, they can yet take their proper place in a world community. The victorious nations have also suffered greatly, but their victory brings with it a new responsibility to God. They should combine justice with mercy. To seek vengeance against their former enemies by depriving them of the necessities of life, or by mass expulsion of their populations, or in any other manner, can only bring fresh disaster.

There must be a new beginning in the relationships of all nations. The nation has its own place in God's purpose for mankind, but national egotism is a sin against the Creator of all peoples, great and small alike. No nation can fulfill God's purpose for itself which fails to answer His call for full co-operation and fellowship with other nations as members of one family. There is a mutual inter-dependence between social order and international order.

We therefore appeal especially to the Government of the Five Great Powers to rise to their responsibilities to the world. It was by the union of their forces that they won victory in the war. We ask them to unite their whole strength in a common purpose now for the establishment of justice, for the relief of hunger, and for the development of a world community of free peoples. Unless they turn from their old ways of reliance upon mere might and own their subjection to God's law of righteousness and love, they pursue the way of disaster and death. "I have set before you life and death: therefore choose life."

A special duty is laid upon the Churches to help the nations to choose the way of life. Christians are called to be the salt of the earth and the light of the world. To them is given the ministry of reconciliation. It is their responsibility to bear witness by word and deed that the law of God finds its fulfillment in the love of Christ. We call upon all followers of Christ to do whatever they can to help those who are enduring the terrible need and suffering of the present day, and to strive after a better order in which the rights of man will be fully recognized and protected. We trust that those Churches which are stronger will continue to aid the Churches in the liberated and suffering countries, and that all will increasingly support the world mission of the Church. We earnestly urge that all will pray without ceasing for forgiveness, for unity, and for real human brotherhood.

We ourselves give thanks to God for our ecumenical fellowship in Christ. Through the years of war that fellowship has been broadened and deepened, and by God's grace we have discovered anew that He strengthens us in the universal fellowship of His Holy Church. We rejoice that we have been able to come together again after the trials of these years, and have found our hearts knit together in Christian love. We testify that in this first meeting after the war we have met and worked together as one brotherhood in a spiritual unity in Christ which has transcended our differences. For this experience our hearts are glad and thankful, and in it we see a sign of hope for all mankind. In this God hath made known to us the mystery of His will, that in the dispensation of the fulness of times He might gather together in one all things in Christ. He is our peace. In Him is the life of mankind.

"I have set before you life and death: therefore choose life."

Message of the Ad Interim Committee of the International Missionary Council, Geneva, Switzerland, February, 1946

Our first word must be to place on record our thankfulness to Almighty God who has brought us together after long years of war and separation. It is of His Grace that our personal contacts have now been renewed and our Christian fellowship restored. We rejoice that we have been able to see each other face to face and unitedly to praise the God and Father of our Lord Jesus Christ.

Since last we met the second world war has fallen upon the nations and has dealt such swift and staggering blows to the missionary movement that it might well have been brought to a standstill; in addition loved and trusted leaders like William Paton and William Temple, V. S. Azariah and Elizabeth van Boetzelaer van Dubbledam have been taken from us; but we record with thankfulness that the work of the International Missionary Council has been carried forward with vigor and with vision. We remembered with gratitude that the Council will this year complete its twenty-fifth year of service, and it was a special satisfaction to us that continuity with our foundation days was embodied in the person of our dear friend and honorary chairman, Dr. John R. Mott.

In our conference together few things have moved us more than what we have heard of God's dealings with those missions that were cut off, for shorter or longer periods, from their parent societies and churches during the war. We have rejoiced to learn that by the generous help gladly given by churches and societies in many parts of the world, the work of the Orphaned Missions was so effectively maintained that scarcely an area was entirely abandoned nor a single missionary left without assistance whose need was known and who could be reached. This is not only one of the great achievements of Christian history but the outstanding proof in our time of the reality of our fellowship in the family of Christ. It has prompted many to affirm that "the spirit of Tambaram still lives" and it has led all to determine that the new relationship shall not be allowed to die.

We have also heard with deep thanksgiving of the faithfulness of our fellow Christians under pressure and persecution. None present will ever forget the statements to which we listened of the experiences of the churches in Scandinavia and in Holland, in Germany and in France, in China and in Japan, in Korea and in Indonesia, in Burma, Thailand, and in the Philippines. From them all have come stories of suffering and of heroism which have not often been equalled in the history of our faith. Rarely, if ever, has there been so widespread or so determined an attack upon the Christian cause, yet the Church not only lives but shows increasing proof of God's power in the midst. Evidence of this is to be found, especially in the warstricken lands, in the discovery of the relevance of the biblical message, in the closer interrelation of missionary societies and churches, in the growing concern for missionary work, in the generous giving for its support, and in the large number of candidates offering for service overseas.

Our second word is that there has been laid upon us the conviction that God is calling us in this new epoch to a fuller share in His redemptive purpose.

During the war years Christian men everywhere have discovered that the universal Church is, in the phrase of Archbishop Temple, "the great new fact of our time." While the nations have been fighting one another, God has been continuing to fashion and to perfect this His chosen instrument for the winning of the world. During those same years He has put into men's hearts a growing concern for evangelism in its widest terms, including both the building of a world wherein dwelleth righteousness and the setting forth of the Gospel to men in such a fashion as to command their attention and win their response. In these and other ways God has been making the crooked straight and the rough places plain so that in due time the glory of the Lord shall be revealed and all flesh shall see it together.

"Believing that God is calling us today to attempt a great new evangelistic advance in His name and power, we call upon the constituent conferences and councils of the International Missionary Council to join with us in joyously dedicating ourselves, our souls and bodies, to this task which is our reasonable service. We rejoice in the vigorous growth of the World Council of Churches, and we set ourselves to discover what relationship between the International Missionary Council and the World Council of Churches will contribute most to the speedy bringing of the whole world to the feet of Christ. We learn with deep interest of the increasingly close integration of the missionary cause into the life of the churches in many lands, and we pledge ourselves to do all in our power to quicken the mission-consciousness of the churches and the church-consciousness of missions. We gratefully acknowledge the precious fruits of cooperation in planning and in action, and we are resolved to give the clearest possible proof of our essential unity and of our common eagerness to carry out the Great Commission of our Lord by developing yet further this method of discovering and carrying out the gracious will of God. We draw particular attention to the need for study and research by the International Missionary Council and the World Council of Churches acting jointly, to the necessity for their joint consideration of far-reaching international issues such as religious liberty, to the close cooperation of the two bodies in the planning of world conferences, the distribution of ecumenical news. Attention should also be drawn to such ventures as the opening of the way for a wider participation of women in the cooperative work of the Christian enterprise, the winning of the ardor and vision of youth for the service of the world church, the putting of Christian literature in a central place in the life of all lands, the selection and training of missionaries for the new day in the light of the expressed desire of the Younger Churches for men and women with special graces and qualifications, and the provision of an adequate ministry for the Younger Churches.

A great chapter in the history of the International Missionary Council has come to an end and a new chapter begins. We and those we represent can do no other than give humble and hearty thanks for God's leading hitherto, especially during the war years, and we joyously respond to the revealing of His purpose which has been granted to us during the memorable days of prayer and consultation.

CONSTITUTION FOR THE PROPOSED WORLD COUNCIL OF CHURCHES

I. *Basis*

The World Council of Churches is a fellowship of Churches which accept our Lord Jesus Christ as God and Saviour. It is constituted for the discharge of the functions set out below.

II. *Membership*

All Churches shall be eligible for membership in the World Council which express their agreement with the basis upon which the Council is founded.

After the Council has been organized the application of Churches to become members shall be considered by the Assembly or its Central Committee as it may be advised by national or confessional associations of Churches.

Note: Under the word "Churches" are included such denominations as are composed of local autonomous Churches.

III. *Functions*

The functions of the World Council shall be:—

(1) To carry on the work of the two world movements, for Faith and Order and for Life and Work.

(2) To facilitate common action by the Churches.

(3) To promote cooperation in study.

(4) To promote the growth of ecumenical consciousness in the members of all Churches.

(5) To establish relations with denominational federations of world-wide scope and with other ecumenical movements.

(6) To call world conferences on specific subjects as occasion may require, such conferences being empowered to publish their own findings.

Note: In matters of common interest to all the Churches and pertaining to Faith and Order, the Council shall always proceed in accordance with the basis on which the Lausanne (1927) and Edinburgh (1937) Conferences were called and conducted.

IV. *Authority*

The World Council shall offer counsel and provide opportunity of united action in matters of common interest.

It may take action on behalf of constituent Churches in such matters as one or more of them may commit to it.

It shall have authority to call regional and world conferences on specific subjects as occasion may require.

The World Council shall not legislate for the Churches; nor

shall it act for them in any manner except as indicated above or as may hereafter be specified by the constituent Churches.

V. *Organization*

The World Council shall discharge its functions through the following bodies:—

(1) An *Assembly* which shall be the principal authority in the Council, and shall ordinarily meet every five years. The Assembly shall be composed of official representatives of the Churches or groups of Churches adhering to it, and directly appointed by them. It shall consist of not more than 450 members who shall be apportioned as provided hereafter. They shall serve for five years, their term of service beginning in the year before the Assembly meets.

The membership shall be allocated provisionally as follows:

85, representing the Orthodox Churches throughout the world, allocated in such manner as they may decide;

110, representing the Churches of the Continent of Europe, allocated in such manner as they may decide;

60, representing the Churches of Great Britain and Eire, allocated in such manner as they may decide;

90, representing the Churches of the United States of America and Canada, allocated in such manner as they may decide;

50, representing the Churches of Asia, Africa, Latin America, and the Pacific Islands, to be appointed by them as they may decide;

25, representing the Churches of South Africa, Australasia, and areas not otherwise represented, to be appointed by them, such places to be allocated by the Central Committee;

and, not more than 30 members representing minority Churches, which in the judgment of the Central Committee are not granted adequate representation by the above provisions of this section, such Churches to be designated by the world confessional organizations.

The Assembly shall have power to appoint officers of the World Council and of the Assembly at its discretion.

(2) A *Central Committee* which shall consist of not more than 90 members designated by the Churches, or groups of Churches, from among persons whom these Churches have elected as members of the Assembly. They shall serve from the beginning of the Assembly meeting until the next Assembly, unless the Assembly otherwise determine. Any vacancy occurring in the membership of the Central Committee shall be filled by the Church or group of Churches concerned. This Committee shall be a Committee of the Assembly. The Assembly shall have authority to modify the allocation of members of the Central Committee as herein provided, both as to the manner and as to the ratio of the allocation.

The membership shall be allocated provisionally as follows:

17, of whom at least 3 shall be lay persons, representing the Orthodox Churches throughout the world, allocated in such manner as they may decide;

22, of whom at least 5 shall be lay persons, representing the Churches of the continent of Europe, allocated in such manner as they may decide;

12, of whom at least 4 shall be lay persons, representing the Churches of Great Britain and Eire, allocated in such manner as they may decide;

18, of whom at least 5 shall be lay persons, representing Churches of the United States of America and Canada, allocated in such manner as they may decide;

10, of whom at least 2 shall be lay persons, representing the Churches of Asia, Africa, Latin America and the Pacific Islands, to be appointed by them as they may decide;

5, of whom at least 2 shall be lay persons, representing the Churches of South Africa, Australasia and areas not otherwise represented, to be appointed by them, such places to be allocated by the Central Committee;

and, not more than 6 members representing minority Churches, which in the judgment of the Central Committee are not granted adequate representation by the above provisions of this section, such Churches to be designated by the world confessional organizations.

The Central Committee shall have the following powers:

(a) It shall, between meetings of the Assembly, carry out the Assembly's instructions and exercise its functions, except that of amending the Constitution, or modifying the allocation of its own members.

(b) It shall be the finance committee of the Assembly, formulating its budget and securing its financial support.

(c) It shall name and elect its own officers from among its members and appoint its own secretarial staff.

(d) The Central Committee shall meet normally once every calendar year, and shall have power to appoint its own Executive Committee.

Quorum: No business except what is required for carrying forward the current activities of the Council, shall be transacted in either the Assembly or the Central Committee, unless one half of the total membership is present.

VI. *Appointment of Commissions*

The World Council shall discharge part of its functions by the appointment of Commissions. These shall be established under the authority of the Assembly, whether they be actually nominated by the Assembly or by the Central Committee acting under its instructions. The Commissions shall, between meetings of the Assembly, report annually to the Central Committee which shall exercise general supervision over them. The Commissions may add to their membership clerical and lay persons approved for the purpose by the Central Committee.

In particular, the Assembly shall make provision by means of appropriate Commissions for carrying on the activities of "Faith and Order" and of "Life and Work." There shall be a

Faith and Order Commission which shall conform to the requirements of the Second World Conference on Faith and Order, held at Edinburgh in 1937 (see below).

VII. *Other Ecumenical Christian Organizations*

World confessional associations and such Ecumenical Organizations as may be designated by the Central Committee may be invited to send representatives to the sessions of the Assembly and of the Central Committee in a consultative capacity, in such numbers as the Central Committee shall determine.

VIII. *Amendments*

The Constitution may be amended by a two-thirds majority vote of the Assembly, provided that the proposed amendment shall have been reviewed by the Central Committee, and notice of it sent to the constituent Churches not less than six months before the meeting of the Assembly. The Central Committee itself, as well as the individual Churches, shall have the right to propose such amendment.

The requirements of the Second World Conference on Faith and Order, held at Edinburgh in 1937, referred to above, are the following:

(a) That the World Council's Commission on Faith and Order shall, in the first instance, be the Continuation Committee appointed by this Conference.

(b) In any further appointments made by the Council to membership of the Commission on Faith and Order, the persons appointed shall always be members of the Churches which fall within the terms of the Faith and Order invitation as addressed to "all Christian bodies throughout the world which accept our Lord Jesus Christ as God and Saviour."

(c) The work of the Commission on Faith and Order shall

be carried on under the general care of a Theological Secretariat appointed by the Commission, in consultation with the Council and acting in close cooperation with other secretariats of the Council. The Council shall make adequate financial provision for the work of the Commission after consultation with the Commission.

(d) In matters of common interest to all the Churches and pertaining to Faith and Order, the Council shall always proceed in accordance with the basis on which this Conference on Faith and Order was called and is being conducted.

(e) The World Council shall consist of *official* representatives of the Churches participating.

(f) Any Council formed before the first meeting of the General Assembly shall be called Provisional, and the Assembly, representing all the Churches, shall have complete freedom to determine the constitution of the Central Council.

CONSTITUTION OF THE INTERNATIONAL MISSIONARY COUNCIL

I. *Preamble*

The Council is established on the basis that the only bodies entitled to determine missionary policy are the churches and the missionary societies and boards, representing the churches.

It is recognized that the successful working of the International Missionary Council is entirely dependent on the gift from God of the spirit of fellowship, mutual understanding, and desire to cooperate.

II. *Membership and Meetings*

The Council is composed of the following national missionary organizations[1] and Christian councils:

[1] The term "missionary" is used in this constitution to describe the work of presenting the Gospel to non-Christian peoples, whether carried on by the younger or by the older churches.

National Missionary Council of Australia.

Société Belge de Missions Protestantes au Congo.

National Christian Council of China.

Conseil Protestant du Congo.

Dansk Missionsraad.

Deutscher Evangelischer Missionstag.

Société des Missions Evangéliques de Paris.

Conference of Missionary Societies in Great Britain and Ireland.

National Christian Council of India, Burma and Ceylon.

National Christian Council of Japan.

Committee on Cooperation in Latin America.

Concilio Nacional de Iglesias Evangelicas do Mexico.

Confederação Evangélica do Brasil.

Nederlandsche Zendings-Raad.

Netherlands India.

National Missionary Council of New Zealand.

Norsk Misjonsråd.

Foreign Missions Conference of North America (United States and Canada).

Philippine Federation of Evangelical Churches.

Christian Council of South Africa.

Suomen Lähetysneuvosto.

Svenska Missionsrådet.

National Missionary Council of Switzerland.

Near East Christian Council.

National Christian Council of Thailand.

Confederación de Iglesias del Rio de la Plata (Argentina, Paraguay and Uruguay).

National missionary organizations or Christian councils in other countries or areas may be added to those named above by the affirmative vote of the Committee of the Council, provided for later; and the Committee of the Council shall have full power to determine what qualifications shall be required of a missionary organization or a Christian Council for membership in the Council. Among these qualifications the Committee would take into consideration the thoroughly representative character of the organization, its elements of stability, and the extent and nature of the area that it covers.

The meetings of the Council shall be of two kinds: namely, (a) general Council Meetings, and (b) special meetings for the consideration of particular subjects. The call for these general or special meetings shall be issued by the Committee of the Council. In the case of general Council meetings, the call shall be issued only after the proposal to hold such a meeting has been approved by two-thirds of the national bodies constituting the Council. Special meetings of the Council may be called by the Committee after the proposal to hold such a meeting has been approved by two-thirds of the national bodies which will be expected to send representatives to the meeting.

The number of representatives which each national missionary organization and Christian council will be entitled to appoint for each meeting of the Council shall be as stated by the Committee in its proposal to call a meeting and as ratified by national bodies in their approval of the proposal. In arranging for the membership of any Council meeting, the Committee shall provide, in so far as it is deemed desirable, for representation from countries in which there is no national missionary organization or Christian council and shall determine the method of choosing such representatives. The Committee shall also have the right to propose in regard to any particular meeting, whenever desirable, that a limited number of persons with special knowledge of the subjects contained in the programme of the proposed meeting may be invited to attend that meeting of the Council.

III. *Functions*

The functions of the Council shall be the following:

1. To stimulate thinking and investigation on questions related to the mission and expansion of Christianity in all the world, to

enlist in the solution of these questions the best knowledge and experience to be found in all countries, and to make the results available for all who share in the missionary work of the churches.

2. To help to co-ordinate the activities of the national missionary organizations and Christian councils of the different countries, and to bring about united action where necessary in missionary matters.

3. Through common consultation to help to unite Christian public opinion in support of freedom of conscience and religion and of missionary liberty.

4. To help to unite the Christian forces of the world in seeking justice in international and inter-racial relations.

5. To be responsible for the publication of *The International Review of Missions* and such other publications as in the judgment of the Council may contribute to the study of missionary questions.

6. To call a world missionary conference if and when this should be deemed desirable.

IV. *The Committee of the Council*

The Committee of the Council shall have the power to act for the Council in the intervals between its general Council meetings.

The membership of the Committee shall be elected by the national missionary organizations and Christian councils, and the number of representatives, except as may be determined otherwise by subsequent action, shall be as follows:

National Missionary Council of Australia............ 1

Société Belge de Missions Protestantes au Congo...... 1

Confederação Evangelica do Brasil.................. 1

National Christian Council of China................ 2

Conseil Protestant du Congo........................ 1

Dansk Missionsraad................................. 1

Deutscher Evangelischer Missionstag................ 2

For each meeting the Committee may elect other members, not exceeding three in all, to be nominated by the officers, from countries not otherwise represented, who shall for each meeting have the same rights and privileges as other members. In addition to the above, the Committee may elect other members, not exceeding five in all, to be nominated by the officers, in order to supply special knowledge or experience, who shall be consultants without voting powers.

The Committee of the Council shall have the power to provide representation in the Committee of the Council for national organizations that may in the future be admitted to membership in the Council.

Each regularly established department of the Council may be represented in the Committee of the Council by its Chairman or other representative of the Committee directing the department's work. Such a representative shall have for each meeting the same rights and privileges as the other delegates.

Members of the Committee shall hold office until their successors are appointed, the length of term of office and the method of appointment to be determined in each country or area by the national missionary organization or Christian council.

The officers of the Council shall be members, *ex-officio*, of the Committee and shall serve as the officers of the Committee of the Council.

The Committee of the Council shall, as occasion may require, consult with the constituent organizations in regard to the work of the Committee.

The Committee of the Council shall meet at the call of the officers of the Council, or upon request of a majority of the members of the Committee (sent to the chairman or secretaries in writing), or upon the request of three or more of the constituent organizations. Ten members of the Committee other than the officers shall constitute a quorum, provided, however, that these represent national missionary organizations or Christian councils, members of the Council, in three different continents

V. *Officers*

The officers of the Council shall be a Chairman, not more than six Vice-Chairmen, of whom two shall be women, a Treasurer, and two or more Secretaries. These officers shall be elected by the Committee of the Council. Their terms of office, their respective duties, and their remuneration shall be determined by the Committee. They shall be members, *ex-officio*, of the

Committee. The countries from which they come shall be allowed their full representation in addition to such officials.

VI. *Expenses*

The Committee of the Council shall prepare annual budgets two years in advance, which shall be submitted to the constituent organizations for approval and toward which they will be invited to contribute in a proportion to be recommended by resolution of the Committee. Since in a period of two years unforeseen developments may occur requiring additional expenditure, it is understood that such emergencies may be met by special funds which the Committee of the Council may be able to secure from private sources. If the objects to be sought involve permanent or recurring expense, the approval of the constituent organizations shall be secured before such work is undertaken, even if special funds are available for its support.

VII. *Procedure*

It is understood that the Council and the Committee of the Council will function internationally, and that the members of the Committee of the Council in any one country will not take action as a national group, though they may be called together by the officers of the International Missionary Council for purposes of consultation if this should seem necessary.

VIII. *Amendments*

This constitution may be amended at any future meeting of the Committee of the Council subject to the approval of the constituent organizations.

February 1946

Printed by permission of the International Missionary Council.

FURTHER READING

BAILLE, JOHN and Others. *Revelation.* New York: The Macmillan Company, 1937.

BASS, A. B. *Protestantism in the United States.* New York: Thomas Y. Crowell Company, 1929.

BATE, H. N. *et al. Faith and Order.* New York: Doubleday, Doran & Company, Inc., 1928 (Lausanne Conference Report).

BELL, G. K. A. *The Stockholm Conference on Life and Work. Official Report.* 1926.

BROWN, WILLIAM ADAMS. *The Church, Catholic and Protestant.* New York: Charles Scribner's Sons, 1935.

———. *The New Order in the Church.* New York: Abingdon-Cokesbury Press, 1943.

———. *Church and State in Contemporary America.* New York: Charles Scribner's Sons, 1936.

———. *Toward a United Church.* New York: Charles Scribner's Sons, 1946.

DOUGLASS, H. PAUL. *Church Unity Movements in the United States.* New York: Institute of Social and Religious Research, 1934.

———. *A Decade of Objective Progress in Church Unity.* New York: Harper & Brothers, 1937.

DUN, ANGUS. *Studies in Christian Unity.* New York: Joint Executive Committee of the Life and Work and Faith and Order Movements in the United States, 1938.

Edinburgh Conference (1910) Volumes. 9 Vols. New York: Fleming H. Revell Company, 1910.

HODGSON, LEONARD, ed. *Faith and Order.* New York: The Macmillan Company, 1938 (Edinburgh Conference Report).

Jerusalem Conference (1928) Volumes. 8 Vols. New York: International Missionary Council, 1928.

KELLER, ADOLPH. *Church and State on the European Continent.* London: Edworth Press, 1936.

————. *Christian Europe Today*. New York: Harper & Brothers, 1942.

KRAEMER, HENDRICK. *The Christian Message in a Non-Christian World*. New York: Harper & Brothers, 1937.

LATOURETTE, KENNETH SCOTT. "A History of the Expansion of Christianity" Series. 7 Vols. New York: Harper & Brothers, 1937-45.

LEIPER, HENRY SMITH. *World Chaos or World Christianity*. Chicago: Willett, Clark & Company, 1937.

————. *Christ's Way and the World's*. New York: Abingdon-Cokesbury Press, 1936.

MACFARLAND, CHARLES S. *Steps Toward the World Council of Churches*. New York: Fleming H. Revell Company, 1938.

McNEILL, JOHN T. *Unitive Protestantism*. New York: Abingdon-Cokesbury Press, 1930.

Madras Conference (1938) Volumes. 8 Vols. New York: International Missionary Council, 1939.

The Nature of the Church. Chicago: Willett, Clark & Company, 1945 (Report of the American Theological Committee).

NIEBUHR, H. RICHARD. *The Social Sources of Denominationalism*. New York: Henry Holt and Company, Inc., 1929.

The Official Oxford Conference Books. 7 Vols. Chicago: Willett, Clark & Company, 1938.

OLDHAM, J. H., Ed. *The Oxford Conference, Official Report*. Chicago: Willett, Clark & Company, 1938.

PATON, WILLIAM. *Christianity in the Eastern Conflicts*. Chicago: Willett, Clark & Company, 1937.

SLOSSER, GAIUS JACKSON. *Christian Unity*. New York: E. P. Dutton & Company, Inc., 1939.

SPERRY, WILLARD L. *The Non-Theological Factors in the Making and Unmaking of Church Union*. New York: Harper & Brothers, 1937.

————. *Religion in America*. New York: The Macmillan Company, 1946.

Van Dusen, Henry P. *Church and State in the Modern World.* New York: Harper & Brothers, 1937.

————. *For the Healing of the Nations.* New York: Friendship Press, 1940.

————. *What Is the Church Doing?* New York: Charles Scribner's Sons, 1943.

Wedel, Theodore. *The Coming Great Church.* New York: The Macmillan Company, 1945.

White, Hugh Vernon. *A Theology for Christian Missions.* Chicago: Willett, Clark & Company, 1937.

SUBJECTS AND MEMBERSHIP OF THE COMMISSIONS

COMMISSION I-A

VOLUME I. *The Challenge of Our Culture*

CLARENCE T. CRAIG: *Chairman*

JAMES LUTHER ADAMS
ELMER J. F. ARNDT
JOHN K. BENTON
CONRAD BERGENDOFF
BUELL G. GALLAGHER
H. C. GOERNER
GEORGIA HARKNESS
JOSEPH HAROUTUNIAN

WALTER M. HORTON
JAMES H. NICHOLS
VICTOR OBENHAUS
WILHELM PAUCK
ROLLAND W. SCHLOERB
EDMUND D. SOPER
ERNEST F. TITTLE
AMOS N. WILDER
DANIEL D. WILLIAMS

COMMISSION I-B

VOLUME II. *The Church and Organized Movements*

The Pacific Coast Theological Group:

RANDOLPH CRUMP MILLER: *Chairman*

JAMES C. BAKER
EUGENE BLAKE
KARL MORGAN BLOCK
JOHN WICK BOWMAN
ELLIOTT VAN N. DILLER

GALEN FISHER
ROBERT M. FITCH
BUELL G. GALLAGHER
CYRIL GLOYN
GEORGE HEDLEY

261

JOHN KRUMM
MORGAN ODELL
PIERSON PARKER
CLARENCE REIDENBACH
JOHN SKOGLUND
DWIGHT SMITH
FREDERIC SPIEGELBERG

EVERETT THOMSON
ELTON TRUEBLOOD
AARON UNGERSMA
HUGH VERNON WHITE
LYNN T. WHITE
GEORGE WILLIAMS

Guests of the Theological Group:

JOHN H. BALLARD
THEODORE H. GREENE
EDWARD OHRENSTEIN
EDWARD L. PARSONS

HOWARD THURMAN
STACY WARBURTON
FREDERICK WEST

COMMISSION II

VOLUME III. *The Gospel, The Church and The World*

KENNETH SCOTT LATOURETTE: *Chairman*

EARL BALLOU
JOHN C. BENNETT
NELS F. S. FERRÉ
JOSEPH FLETCHER
HERBERT GEZORK
EDWARD R. HARDY, JR.
ELMER HOMRIGHAUSEN
STANLEY HOPPER
JOHN KNOX
BENJAMIN MAYS

WILLIAM STUART NELSON
RICHARD NIEBUHR
JUSTIN NIXON
NORMAN PITTENGER
JAMES McD. RICHARDS
LUMAN J. SHAFER
PAUL SCHERER
WYATT A. SMART
GEORGE F. THOMAS
FRANK WILSON

COMMISSION III

VOLUME IV. *Toward World-Wide Christianity*

O. FREDERICK NOLDE: *Chairman*
EDWIN R. AUBREY

ROSWELL P. BARNES
JOHN C. BENNETT

ARLO A. BROWN

E. FAY CAMPBELL

J. W. DECKER

H. PAUL DOUGLASS

CHARLES IGLEHART

F. ERNEST JOHNSON

CHARLES T. LEBER

HENRY SMITH LEIPER

JOHN A. MACKAY

ELMORE N. MCKEE

LAWRENCE ROSE

STANLEY RYCROFT

MATTHEW SPINKA

A. L. WARNSHUIS

A. R. WENTZ

ALEXANDER C. ZABRISKIE

VOLUME V. *What Must the Church Do?*

HENRY P. VAN DUSEN